Writing for Real

Practical Essay Strategies for Canadian Students

• **Scott Sneddon** •

• **Lawrence Hopperton** •

• **Lewis Fried** •

Seneca College

Nelson Canada

I(T)P An International Thomson Publishing Company

Toronto • Albany • Bonn • Boston • Cincinnati • Detroit • London • Madrid • Melbourne
Mexico City • New York • Pacific Grove • Paris • San Francisco • Singapore • Tokyo • Washington

I⊤P™
International Thomson Publishing
The ITP logo is a trademark under licence

© Nelson Canada
A division of Thomson Canada Limited, 1996

Published in 1996 by
Nelson Canada
A division of Thomson Canada Limited
1120 Birchmount Road, Scarborough, Ontario M1K 5G4

Canadian Cataloguing in Publication Data

Fried, Lewis L. R., 1961–
  Writing for real

Includes index.
ISBN 0-17-604933-9

1. English language — Rhetoric. 2. Essay — Authorship.
I. Hopperton, Lawrence, 1957– . II. Sneddon,
Scott, 1966– . III. Title

LB2369.F75 1996 808'.042 C95-933070-4

Team Leader and Publisher	Michael Young
Acquisitions Editor	Andrew Livingston
Production Editor	Tracy Bordian
Project Editor	Joanne Scattolon
Production Coordinator	Brad Horning
Editorial and Market Assistant	Evan Turner
Art Director	Liz Harasymczuk
Interior Design	Carole Giguere
Composition Analyst	Linda Mackey

Printed and bound in Canada

  3 4 (WC) 99 98

*This book is dedicated with love to
the life of George Sneddon, a rare
composition that needed no revision.*

C O N T E N T S

Preface

In our experience as teachers of writing, we have often heard our students question the importance of the writing process and the content of writing courses. After all, in the 1990s, hands-on, practical education is of paramount importance; and effective writing skills and strategies can sometimes seem less than relevant to some programs. Instructors, of course, have a litany of excuses for our subject: "Writing helps you to think clearly." "Communication is essential for success." "Good essays will help you get better marks in your other subjects." Some even cite the 1992 *Employability Skills Profile* report from The Conference Board of Canada, a consulting group made up of some of the largest employers in Canada. This report lists critical thinking and written communications as the key skills for success in business and industry. Most often, however, students don't buy this. English is seen as an esoteric and abstract barrier to their post-secondary progress. "Where," students ask, "is the connection between what I am learning in English class and what I am learning in my 'real courses'?"

Writing for Real addresses this. As the title implies, this book is about using the essay-writing process in the real world—the world in which you will live and work. We present a practical, hands-on strategy for developing effective, extended essays within your own disciplines—disciplines ranging from Agriculture to Early Childhood Education to Nursing to Water Resources Engineering. As each essential mode of essay writing is covered, you are repeatedly asked to consider the applicability of the mode to your chosen profession. After all, learning, thinking, and writing are easier if you can envision a practical and tangible product at the end of the process. We will not tell you what that product should be; instead, by bringing your "real courses" into the English classroom, you will be a partner in this.

While your instructor may choose to teach an anthology of readings along with this text, readings are already included with each module. These have been selected from a broad range of practical sources as diverse as newspapers, nursing and business journals, technology discussions, and travel and tourism magazines. If they seem eclectic and unusual, this is so because reality is eclectic and unusual. We wanted real-life, interesting, practical, but challenging examples to represent the issues and the writing styles with which you are faced during your formal education and afterwards. We also made every effort to draw upon illustrations from your fields of study and those of your friends.

Writing for Real is based upon a simple and sensible six-step strategy for developing and producing effective essays. These six steps are previewed generally in Module 1. Module 2 presents the first three steps, where you determine *what* to say. Module 3 then presents the last three steps, where you work out *how* to say it. This six-step process is then carried forward through each rhetorical mode module. While the immediate applicability of this process to your interests may seem a bit distant in these first modules, this is the general foundation for your later particular applications. Once they are mastered, you will see how these steps both adapt easily to every form of writing and adjust simply to every practical application.

These six steps include a thinking tool called the Rhetorical Triangle, which helps you to focus your thinking visually and to address crucial planning questions before you commit your thoughts to the page. Together, the rhetorical triangle and the other five steps provide an approach to writing that logically distinguishes writing tasks and stresses personal applications.

This book is modular; thus, each module is designed to stand alone. You should, however, work through the first three modules, since this is where the six-step process and the rhetorical triangle are presented in detail. After this, modules dealing with each rhetorical mode, which is an adjustment or modification of this writing and thinking process, will stand alone. The format of the rhetorical mode modules is consistent, moving from an overview and explanation of key issues through to examples and exercises. We even guide you through the application of the six-step model, highlighting issues unique to the mode in question. Our hope is that the user-friendly features can act as easy references for you not only within this subject, but also in your other classes and even in your career after graduation.

 TOP TEN OTHER FEATURES OF THIS TEXT

1. *Learning Outcome Statements.* Every module begins with explicit and practical learning outcome statements. These specify exactly what you will be able to do at module's end in order to show that you have mastered the content of the module. They are intended to be your road map and study guide: they indicate exactly what will be expected of you, and what the point is.

2. *Top Ten.* These lists stress the applicability of writing. As you work through each rhetorical mode, you will be asked to specify the Top Ten practical applications of it in your own field of study and in your chosen career. You will often be asked to think through and develop essays around these specific applications.

3. *Collaborative and In-depth Exercises.* Real writing does not happen in isolation. Collaborative exercises have been designed to involve you in the give-and-take process of written communication. At the same time, applications by students in different fields will be different, so in-depth exercises will have you focus on your own areas of interest. For distance and independent learning students, the collaborative exercises still will be completed, but we encourage you to discuss them with other people.

4. *Compusitions* (compositions written while using a computer). Computers are a reality in writing. Compusition sections address this. But rather than being tied to any specific word-processing package, compusitions look at the basic functions of word processors and show you effective ways of using them to enhance the essay-writing process. You will also find sections of the text that consider the applications of the Internet in writing and research.

Hypertext: a cross-referencing system that allows readers to take several different "routes" through a book. See Module 7, "Comparison and Contrast," Rhona Goldstein, p. 132.

5. *Icons and Marginalia.* These tools, incorporated throughout the book, are intended not only to give you a visual way to identify specific, important ideas within modules, but also to provide the entire text with a hypertextual approach, showing immediate cross-referencing to other areas and applications. See the Key to Icons that follows this Preface.

6. *Study Tips and Traps.* There are short-cuts and pitfalls in every aspect of writing and within every mode. Study Tips and Traps will highlight these in context. They are intended to be quick reminders and lessons to help you to master the forms of writing. They are signalled by icons so that, in a quick review of a module, you can easily locate them.

7. *Writer's Blocks.* Where specific grammatical difficulties can easily creep in and "block" your success, they have been highlighted with Writer's Blocks. These will often be particularly useful to students whose second language is English.

8. *Summary Skills Module.* The ability to summarize is an essential skill not only in English, but in every subject and career. Unlike many texts that assume this skill, we have made the process of summarization explicit in Module 4 and elsewhere.

9. *Checklists.* Every rhetorical mode module ends with a specific checklist. These are handy references that will help you to identify the key features of each mode and to insure that you have used them in your essays. General development and revision checklists that apply to every form of writing are also included on the inside front and back covers of the text.

10. *Appendices.* There are two appendices to the book. These cover documentation of sources, and grammar.

    • The documentation appendix presents the most up-to-date Modern Languages Association (MLA) and American Psychological Association (APA) formats. These are the two most common documentation styles that you will use for research essays or reports.

    • Grammar as Contract presents the top ten grammatical difficulties that English students encounter under the guise of grammar as a basic agreement between the writer and the reader. We have intentionally avoided much of the jargon of grammar, and instead we have used a common-sense approach to precision in writing. We assume that everyone who puts a pen on a piece of paper needs to own a decent handbook of grammar and usage; therefore, we have tried to avoid duplicating content. Instead, we have tried to provide ten user-friendly, tutorial-style explanations with exercises. These are appropriate for either individual work or brief classroom lessons.

As we say in the first module, writing is work, often hard work. We have tried to provide you with a useful and easily mastered process for addressing this reality, and a way to see the usefulness of thinking and writing in your own careers. We hope that you enjoy *Writing for Real* and that, after this course is completed, you enjoy or at least feel comfortable writing for real. Your success and comfort in a variety of writing tasks are the ultimate learning outcome.

Scott Sneddon, Larry Hopperton, and Lewis Fried
Seneca College

Acknowledgments

We would like to thank Dr. Patricia Probert, all of the authors' families, and our students at Centennial, Humber, and Seneca Colleges. Thank must also to to the following reviewers for taking the time to comment on this text: Anita Agar (Sheridan College), Brian Flack (Seneca College), Ingrid Hutchinson (Fanshawe College), Christa Jacobs (George Brown College/Sheridan College), Dorothy Kelleher (Centennial College), Karen Pancer (Humber College), Gail Rees (Canadore College), and Pat Rogin (Durham College).

Key to Icons

 Study Tip

 Time Saver

 Study Trap

 Rhetorical Triangle

 Compusition

 Top Ten

 Critical Thinking

 Collaboration

 Writer's Block

Writing: What's the Problem?

OVERVIEW

Have you ever watched a really awful television show and wondered how anything so bad could be allowed onto the screen? Well, the reasons for a bad program can be compared with the main reason for a bad piece of writing: being in a hurry. We may know how to write, but we often make the error of trying to do everything at once. Writing should be approached as a series of related tasks. The key is to address them one by one, in an orderly fashion; that way, they become more manageable.

WRITING: WHAT'S THE PROBLEM?

You have written before—probably many times: thank-you letters to your aunt, essays on your summer vacation, or reports on a variety of subjects. You may not like it, but you have an idea of how to do it. You get a topic; you write. Or maybe you have learned not to jump immediately into the actual writing, so you brainstorm some ideas for a few minutes, and then you write. Then you look your paper over carefully.

Let's take a specific example of this. It is the first day of your English class. The assignment is to write a 1000–1500 word essay on the subject of television. No problem, right? Take a look at the brainstorming generated by Bruce Lau, a student, in response to this question:

- television stations—giving us the news of the day
- comedies, dramas, documentaries
- people like to laugh—infantilistic escapism
- talk shows like Geraldo/Ricki Lake: dig up the dirt on people
- Melrose Place!!! No one lives like that (but sexy people)
- trashy shows some people don't like
- "educational programs" Dad wants me to watch
- CABLE TV—big business—lots of talk in the news
- my favourites: talk shows and MUCHMUSIC
    - music videos beat regular programs
    - turn them up for a while and be entertained

Now take a look at the five-paragraph essay written by Bruce from his brainstorming.

Exercise 1

Have your pencil in hand while reading the essay that follows. Make brief notes (by underlining, noting in the margin, or taking down notes) of any problems you identify with its structure, organization, content, or style. Included are some of the marginal notes made by Kim, Rajiv, and Tracy, classmates of Bruce who read his essay as part of some group exercises. There are, however, many more issues to address. Note as many as you can for discussions with a group or your class.

Sample Essay

Television gives us lots of different things, like news, sports, movies, comedies, and dramas. Not everybody watches the same programs.

Shouldn't there be MORE in an introduction?

Some people like so much comedies. They watch *Friends*, *Martin* or *Air Farce*. People like to laugh because their lives are boring, so this provides us with <u>infantilistic escapism</u>. Comedies like *Seinfeld* are relief from murders and traffic accidents and natural disasters on the evening news. Or bosses at work. (1)

What does this mean?

Talk shows are popular with other people because they like to hear the dirt about other people's lives. Because it makes them feel better when they see how mixed-up they are, and when they see people making fools of themselves like on "<u>Stupid Human Tricks</u>." I saw *Geraldo* once; and they showed a man before he had an operation that turned him into a woman and they showed it afterwards, to. Soap operas like *Melrose Place* are very sexy and steamy people can't get enough of the action that gives them a vicarious outlet for their own repressions and their unfulfilled <u>id</u>. Lots of people watch them but they are embarrassed that they watch

Who are all these "theys"?

What is this?

I thought this paragraph was about talk shows. What is the "id"?

What is the point of this example? I don't get it.

them because they are not very good. (2)

What is the connection with the previous paragraph?

Cable television lets people watch almost anything you want to. Lots of teenagers watch *MuchMusic* because it has videos you can watch for a while if you want but you don't have to watch a full program if you don't want to because the videos are short and you don't have to pay a lot of attention if you don't want to. Or just fills the time. Most people watch television from the United States because the shows are better, <u>their</u> more interesting and better filmed. Canadian television is different. (3)

RUN-ON. I can't catch my breath!

Spelling! I think...

Why? Do we need some explanation here?

As I have shown, there are lots and lots of different programs that different people like to watch. Some people like comedies, talk shows or other things offered on cable television. Television has something for everyone. (4)

So what? Shouldn't there be a <u>point</u>?

Exercise 2

While you read this essay, you made a series of notes on its problems. In groups of four to six, discuss the errors in each paragraph. Now write one paragraph in which you give Bruce, the author of this essay, your advice on how to improve it.

WRITING: WHAT ARE THE PROBLEMS?

You have no doubt noticed some difficulties with Bruce's essay. The essay demonstrates many problems, but at the root of all of them lies a failure to understand writing as a process that involves several different steps. Whether you write your first draft immediately or begin by brainstorming and then do your draft (as Bruce did), you place yourself under enormous stress by trying to solve two distinct problems at the same time. You are trying simultaneously to decide

1. *what* you want to say; and

2. *how* you want to say it.

To be a successful writer, you should separate these steps. First, make decisions about what ideas you want to present and in what order. Only then tackle the question of exactly how you want to say them—that is, start figuring out the words, the sentences, and the overall structure.

Treating writing as a one-step problem is like trying to watch several different television programs at the same time. You may be able to follow the various programs, but it is extremely difficult and requires constant, total concentration. Moreover, you are automatically missing out on large chunks of each program. Similarly, trying to perform the major tasks of writing at the same time means you are missing significant opportunities for shaping your essay. As a result, you may end up writing an essay like Bruce's.

WHAT TO SAY: FOCUS OF TOPIC

See Module 3: How to Say It, The Thesis Statement, p. 53.

The first, most obvious question about Bruce's essay is "What is the point, or **thesis**?" What is Bruce trying to accomplish? Bruce does not seem to have a clear focus here: the essay discusses several different kinds of programs on television—comedies, talk shows, soap operas, *MuchMusic,* Canadian television—but it does not have much to say about anything. The conclusion states the obvious: different people watch different programs.

   Bruce has brainstormed about the spectacularly huge topic "television," but there are as many things to say about television as there are television channels on cable. In reality, Bruce cannot say everything, nor should he try. This is why he needs to limit his topic either before writing down ideas or while writing them down. Bruce should choose a single element, like violence on television or the way "Canadian television is different" (whatever that means). He should tell his readers clearly what his focus will be in a single sentence, or **thesis statement**, and then develop

See Module 3: How to Say It, Body, p. 57.

his thoughts on that focused subject in the **body** of the essay. By saying more about a smaller topic, he can develop a more coherent and more significant argument.

Exercise 3

Here is a series of general topics. In groups or individually, identify the general topic in each statement. For each topic, write one or two sentences in which you specify how you would focus the topic and what your "point" would be. By doing this, you are working on the development of your thesis statement, which will tell your reader what your essay will discuss.

1. Women's rights have been violated for thousands of years.

2. Only rich kids can get good jobs.

3. Government is too big.

4. English is difficult.

5. Religion is right.

6. Quebec is different from the rest of Canada.

7. We need better day care for children.

8. The nightly news is sensational.

9. Welfare is a problem in Canada.

10. Education needs to be changed.

AUDIENCE

From the informal language and the personal story about how he "saw *Geraldo* once" (paragraph 2), Bruce seems to have written his essay for an audience of fellow students. However, did you find yourself a little confused by the occasional complicated, specialized idea like "infantilistic escapism" (paragraph 1) and the idea of television as a "vicarious outlet for ... repressions and [the] unfulfilled id" (paragraph 2)? These passages may cause problems because they do not fit with the conversational, down-to-earth tone and simple ideas of the rest of the essay. This inconsistency suggests that Bruce does not have a clear sense of just who will read his essay.

No television program appeals to every viewer. Children may like *Barney* or cartoons because these programs address subjects in a language children understand and to which they respond. Many adults, however, find these shows unwatchable. Think of the programs that your parents or grandparents watch, as well; you likely do not share all of their tastes. This is entirely normal: television producers and advertisers decide exactly which audience they are trying to address, and they tailor their product or message to the interests, language, and attitudes of the target audience. It is a mistake to assume that when you write, you write for everybody, for one big audience. If you try writing for everybody, you often end up reaching nobody, because everyone is bored or does not understand what you are saying. There is not one audience, but numerous audiences. Select yours specifically.

As the people who bring you the THX sound system in theatres like to remind you, "The Audience Is Listening ... "

Exercise 4

Working in groups or individually, take three of your focused topics specified in Exercise 3. Discuss each focused topic, and write at least three statements of one or more sentences about the reader of an essay on that topic.

1. Describe what you think your reader knows about the topic.
2. Describe what your reader does not know about the topic.
3. Describe how you will adjust your writing so it will meet the needs of your reader. Keep in mind that the needs of the reader are defined as the difference between what the reader already knows and what the reader needs to know.

POINT OF VIEW

When you have a conversation with someone, you relate to the other speaker from a specific point of view. Sometimes you are one friend talking to another friend; sometimes you are an employee talking to your boss. At other times, you may be a parent talking to your child; at still other times, you are the child talking to your parents. An essay, like a conversation, needs to address its audience from a specific point of view. Bruce's essay often seems to be a personal, general account of his observations as a television viewer, but at other times it sounds as if Bruce is an expert with specialized knowledge to communicate. For instance, this is suggested by his use of psychoanalytic terminology such as "id" and "repression."

Psychoanalysis: the study of the workings of your unconscious mind. The "id" is the unconscious mind, which is filled with unruly desires and ideas. "Repression" is the suppression of or refusal to think about painful memories or desires.

The unexplained reference to "Stupid Human Tricks," a comedy segment that frequently appears on *The Late Show with David Letterman,* suggests that Bruce watches a lot of television and assumes that his audience also watches a lot of television. So, is Bruce an average student-age viewer? A psychoanalytic expert? A TV junkie who knows everything about every program? Bruce needs to clarify his point of view; otherwise, his reader will be confused.

When you are having a conversation with someone, and that person makes a statement you do not understand, you might ask, "Where is that coming from?" When writing, you should try to know exactly where you are coming from. Are you an expert on your subject because of research or accumulated knowledge? Are you someone with relevant personal experiences? Are you an average person who has done some thinking about a topic? Are you someone who uses writing to explore what you do not understand? In each of these different points of view, your entire essay will be organized differently, presented in different levels and styles of language, and aimed at achieving something different.

Exercise 5

Given your three focused topics of Exercise 3, discuss and then specify how you would define your viewpoint in relation to the audiences identified in Exercise 4.

1. Write a sentence for each topic that begins "I am … " and defines exactly who you, as a writer, are in relation to the topic.

2. Given this point of view, write a second statement defining your purpose in relation to your audience. For instance, are you trying to educate, entertain, persuade, or have another effect on this audience? Begin that sentence, "My purpose is to … "

CONTENT GENERATION

With a world of possible information, Bruce began from a very small quantity of brainstormed material, and then simply wrote it out in the same order in which he thought of it. His brainstorming is undeveloped; it simply tells you what you already know if you have ever picked up a *TV Guide* or watched a little television—that there are many different kinds of programs that are watched by many different viewers. This is like a television studio spending millions of dollars to produce a brand-new weekly television show, and basing the show on the notes that happen to be in the briefcase of the next writer who walks through the door. A more prudent business decision is to bring several different writers together and hear what each has to say. Then, the studio can sift through the material to find, organize, and develop only the best ideas.

When you are developing content for the body of an essay, you need to use a similar approach. Like the television studio executives, you want to begin with *too much material* in order to be able to select and develop only what is most appropriate and useful for your topic. In order to generate this excess, you do not rely upon only one method like brainstorming; instead, you use several methods of generating and developing ideas. This also allows you the opportunity to develop your initial random thoughts into something original, interesting, and intelligent.

Exercise 6

Given your three focused topics of Exercise 3, the audiences that you specified in Exercise 4, and the points of view you established in Exercise 5, each member of the group should write down five major points on each topic to discuss with the reader. Then, share your thoughts by discussing and passing around your rough ideas; your group should now have an excess of ideas.

See Module 2: What to Say, Step 3: The Outline, p. 36.

OUTLINE

Content generation means creating raw material. Think of writers and producers sitting around exchanging random ideas about possible new television shows. Suppose the network executives want a soap opera. Some of the writers want the show to be a medical soap opera, like *General Hospital* or *ER,* but others want it to be a show based on characters in their twenties, like *Melrose Place* or *Liberty Street.* Still others want a police drama. What they have is a bunch of ideas in different categories. It would be crazy to try to combine *all* of these ideas. The writers and producers need to pick only the most promising and useful ideas, blend them, develop them further, and organize them into a series outline.

As you have seen, Bruce has not done this for his ideas. He has simply included every point in the same order in which it occurred to him during his brainstorming. This makes for extremely poor organization and a clear lack of development. For instance, why are talk shows discussed in paragraph 2 and then again in paragraph 4? Would it not make more sense to discuss them in depth in only one place? And why does the third paragraph jump from cable television to *MuchMusic* to Canadian television—all independent but overlapping categories? Rather than thinking about the presentation of his points, Bruce has committed to a pattern of organization that is purely accidental and that includes every random thought.

COMPUSITION

Composition by computer—compusition—is both a similar and a very different process. It is important to try to learn *by means of* the computer, not to depend on the computer to do things that you do not know how to do, such as solve spelling or grammatical errors. The computer is a very effective tool if you use it consciously and purposefully through the entire process of writing, not simply as a crutch to cover up weaknesses.

Remember that, unlike paper, the computer will forget what you write completely if you want it to do so. This is the strength of compusition—it takes the threat of permanence away until you save or print. Using a word processor, therefore, can be particularly suited to "messy thinking" like brainstorming, since the mess can be tidied up easily. The computer is also a major aid in deleting or moving around ideas as you create an outline.

Do not let the accident of when the ideas occurred to you determine when you present them. Do not let the fact that you wrote something down commit you to keeping it for the essay. You must make conscious, deliberate decisions about what your main argument is, what points you will eliminate because they are not relevant, what points you will include to support your argument, and in what order you will present these points. This is **point-form outlining**. Clear outlining means finalizing the clear thesis (the main point of the essay, which usually appears at the end of the introductory paragraph). It also means deciding upon several subtopics, each of which occupies a paragraph of the body of the essay, and each of which begins with a clear topic sentence. The topic sentence simply indicates what the paragraph is about; if you examine any paragraph in this book, you can see it begins with a topic sentence that clearly tells you what will be discussed in the paragraph. Some of Bruce's topic sentences, by contrast, are misleading and confusing. For instance, the topic sentence of paragraph 2 in his essay indicates that the paragraph will discuss talk shows, but the second half of the paragraph deals with soap operas.

See The Thesis Statement, p. 53.

See Body, p. 57.

You will notice that in the revised version of Bruce's essay reproduced on page 9, significant ideas (like the *MuchMusic* discussion, the undeveloped *Geraldo* example, and the idea that Canadian television is different) simply disappear because they are not relevant to the thesis. Note also how what is a throwaway reference to *Seinfeld* in the first essay is developed at length into a useful illustration of Bruce's point in the second paragraph.

Exercise 7

In Exercise 6, each member of your group identified five major points to discuss with your readers for each of the three topics. Examine each group member's five points.

1. Since you have too much material, carefully eliminate any points that do not seem useful or entirely relevant to your thesis or main point.

2. As a group, rank the remaining points on the basis of most to least important. Remember your readers. How does this ranking appeal to the readers whom you defined in Exercise 4 and fit with your established points of view from Exercise 5?

HOW TO SAY IT: DRAFTS AND EDITING

After the writers of a television show have produced a series outline and the script for an episode, it is time to produce the actual program that will be viewed. Now the director takes over; she or he makes the script come to life by directing the actors. Writing the first draft of your essay means that your role also shifts. After completing the stages above, you have decided exactly *what* you want to say and in what order. Now, and only now, do you turn to the task of actually deciding *how* to say it. Now you decide exactly how your actors should deliver their lines.

This is a tremendous luxury: you now spend all of your time ensuring that you find the perfect words, that you structure your paragraphs and sentences correctly, and that you clearly link your examples and arguments. You can ensure that the ideas are presented in the most effective manner possible, and also that the writing is grammatically and structurally correct.

By trying to figure out what to say and how to say it at the same time, Bruce ended up not saying much, and saying it with numerous structural, grammatical, and punctuation problems. For example, Rajiv noticed the vague pronouns in paragraph 2, and wrote down "Who are all these 'they's'?" You might also notice such items as the misused semicolon and spelling error (to/too) in sentence three of paragraph 2, or the general lack of clear connection between individual paragraphs (such as Kim noted between paragraphs 2 and 3) and between individual sentences and ideas. And these are only a start—you likely identified many more problems.

In the end, with the aid of the questions and suggestions of Kim, Rajiv, and Tracy (the other members of his group), Bruce rewrote his essay, this time thinking carefully about what he wanted to say, and then deciding how to say it. Bruce carefully followed all of the necessary steps of

1. focusing the topic;

2. targeting a specific audience;

3. adopting a clear and unified point of view;

4. generating an excess of well-developed ideas;

5. outlining a coherent plan; and

6. writing and editing a grammatically, structurally sound paper.

When you read it, you will recognize only certain sections and basic ideas.

Have your pencil in hand while reading the essay that follows. Make brief notes (by underlining, noting in the margin, or writing down comments) of any improvements you notice in its structure, organization, content, or style. Note as many as you can for discussions with a group or your class.

Sample Essay

YOU ARE WHAT YOU WATCH

BY BRUCE LAU

You are what you eat. No one questions the wisdom of this statement, so let's try another one: you are what you watch. You are your television. People gather each night around the TV, and it often becomes a key topic of discussion the next day at work or school. Depending on who you are, you and your friends may laughingly discuss *Friends* or *Martin* around the water cooler. Maybe you and your friends chat about this week's episodes of *The Young and the Restless* or *Days of Our Lives*. Maybe it's whichever *Star Trek* series is currently going, or the hockey or football game. These are the programs that you and your friends all watch, the ones you all agree are worth watching. These aren't the ones I'm interested in. I think we can learn more about who we are by examining all the other television programs out there. These fall into two basic types. (1)

First are the shows we watch but won't admit we watch: for me, as a guy, it's generally soap operas. I'm always the first in line to bad-mouth the bad acting and slow pace of your average soap opera—but in at least some cases, I watch enough to be able to tell you what's going on. Can I admit it? I've been watching *The Young and the Restless* for ten years. I feel a bit like Jerry Seinfeld. On a 1995 episode of *Seinfeld,* Jerry's policewoman girlfriend makes him take a lie-detector test in which he breaks down and admits that he watches *Melrose Place.* Well, I'm admitting my embarrassing little habit. Do you have an ugly little secret, too? (2)

The second type of program is the shows we don't watch but say we do. Again, these can fall into various categories, but in general resemble the vegetables our mothers make us eat for dinner. We know they're good for us, but they don't taste as good as dessert. Maybe it's all those "quality" shows that are good for the soul: the arts programs on Bravo, or the documentaries on PBS, the Learning Channel, and the Discovery Channel. If you don't have cable, a lot of the documentaries or "responsible journalism" on the CBC's *Prime Time News* or *The Fifth Estate* fall into this category. "Yes, yes, I'm looking forward to the documentary on the budget deficit," we murmur when one of these important programs comes on. But, whoops, look what happens to be on at the same time: *Melrose Place.* Without even really consciously thinking about it, I know what program I will end up watching. I make the switch in favour of the sex, sizzle, and stimulation of a show I watch but won't admit to watching. But when I'm talking with someone the next day, I may lie: "Yes, yes, I saw the report on the deficit crisis ... " (3)

I guess that as a nineteen-year-old Canadian student, my television viewing habits are filled with denial and fear: I like some programs, but won't admit it; similarly, I sometimes claim to watch other programs because they're "good for me"—but that doesn't mean that I do. If we are what we watch, it's time I faced up to these other parts of myself that I see through television. And when I do, I discover I'm overly interested in titillation and underinterested in intellectual challenge. Now it's your turn: come clean about what you really watch, and why. Who knows—it may pay off for you. I can just see it now: Shocking Secrets of the Viewing Habits of the Canadian Student on the next *Ricki Lake.* Your friends will all be tuned in—though they may not admit it. (4)

Exercise 8

In groups or as a class, briefly discuss the following questions:

1. What do you like about this essay?

2. What do you dislike about this essay?

3. What is the focused topic of this essay?

4. Using specific examples of the language, the tone of voice, and the writer's examples, who would you say is the target audience of this essay, and why?

5. Using specific examples, describe the writer's point of view or perspective in this paper.

6. What purpose is the writer trying to achieve?

7. What is more (or less) interesting, original, or imaginative about the second essay's analysis of types of programs on television as compared with the first essay's?

8. What is the thesis or sentence that makes the main point of this essay?

9. What are the topic sentences of the two middle paragraphs? How do they relate to the thesis?

10. How are the individual paragraphs dealing with different ideas clearly linked?

11. What overall point does the writer leave you with?

SUMMARY

As Bruce discovered with the help of his friends, writing is hard work. We are not going to try to convince you that writing is always fun, nor are we going to try to convince you that by the end of this book you will be a first-rate writer. While we will be happy if you enjoy responding to any of the problems and assignments in this book, our goal is more basic. We want to give you ways of methodically and logically approaching and executing a writing task. We want to help you get the job done, and, to do that, you need to start by viewing writing as a job. This job does have its payoffs: it may lead to enjoyable, creative self-expression that will certainly give you some satisfaction, but like any job, you are paid only in exchange for an initial commitment of your time and energy.

Through the exercises in this module, you have already started to approach the logic and method of writing. Whether you are writing a report at work, a letter to the editor of your local newspaper, or an essay for your English class, writing always presents the series of problems discussed in this module. In this textbook, we are going to equip you with simple strategies that will help you to solve each of these problems and accomplish your specific task. Eventually, for the experienced writer, many of these specific tasks become part of a mental process; for example, the experienced writer may not write down as much preliminary material. It takes a long time and a lot of practice to achieve this level, however. Until that time, these stages are physical tasks that you should complete in sequence as part of the writing process.

Now it is time to get to work. Module 2 establishes the stages and strategies for deciding *what* to say. Module 3 establishes the stages and strategies for deciding *how* to say it.

The Essay: What to Say

By completing a series of written and oral exercises and producing the clear, complete outlines for two essays, students will

1. *distinguish between personal and formal modes of writing, and the topics and voices appropriate for each;*

2. *utilize each of the first three steps of the six-step essay-writing process to make necessary decisions about what to say;*

3. *determine a focused topic, specify and analyze an audience, and adopt a coherent point of view for an essay, using the rhetorical triangle;*

4. *utilize five different methods of generating content to produce ideas for the body of an essay.*

OVERVIEW

As discussed in Module 1, creating an essay is like creating a new television program. In both cases, to end up with a quality product requires a variety of programming decisions. The television program's producers need to decide first on the type and purpose of the program, its target audience, and what personnel and processes will be used to create the program. This module describes the programming decisions you must make when you write an essay, and suggests strategies for developing a clear picture of what you want to say.

PURPOSE AND FUNCTION OF THE ESSAY

An essay is a fully developed piece of writing that deals with a topic in an in-depth manner. Moreover, the essay has a very structured format, with a definite introduction, body, and conclusion. As such, the essay is the most sophisticated form of writing most writers will do. But what exactly is an essay, and why would you write one?

Exercise 1

In groups of four to six, complete the Top Ten List with the group's suggestions. Which of these, if any, do you agree with? Why?

TOP TEN ANSWERS TO THE QUESTION "WHAT'S AN ESSAY?"

1. A chance to express myself
2. Hard work (at least that's what it said in the last module)
3. About five paragraphs
4. A way for me to communicate with a reader
5. Two or three hours
6.
7.
8.
9.
10.

In fact, the word "essay" derives from two related French words. The French verb *essayer* means "to try" or "to make an attempt." The French noun *essai* means an extended composition that is usually focused on a single topic. When thinking about an essay, you should keep both definitions in mind: in your essay you "try out" or explore various ideas on a specific subject that you consider in some depth. This initial definition does not, however, fully capture the wide range and scope of possibilities that the essay form opens to you. To consider these possibilities, it is necessary to understand the two major categories of essays: personal and formal.

THE PERSONAL ESSAY

See Appendix A, Contract #6: Pronoun Reference and Agreement.

A **personal essay** is like a local cable television show: you never know what might show up in it because there are few rules governing what you may say or how you may say it. The personal essay, as its name suggests, is based wholly on your own experience. It involves your personal feelings, emotions, opinions, beliefs, and responses to a subject. In personal essays, you let your "I" speak; indeed, the pronouns most commonly used for this type of essay are "I," "me," "my," and "mine."

See Appendix A, Contract #2: Sentence Fragments.

Often this type of writing uses a less formal, more conversational voice in which slang and other informal or colloquial expressions are acceptable. Sentence fragments and other "incorrect" sentence structures may be used to achieve a desired effect. A letter to the editor of a newspaper is a miniature personal essay. Thus, in this type of essay you might offer your opinion on a controversial issue such as capital punishment. You might express your feelings about a particular local, national, or international event: for instance, your views on how Christmas is too commercialized. The personal essay is an important and valuable tool for reflecting on and expressing your personal opinions on a wide range of issues, problems, and concerns.

PERSONAL ESSAY:
1. "I" voice
2. Personal
3. Conversational

THE FORMAL ESSAY

The **formal essay** is more like a television program broadcast by a major television network. Such programs are governed by special rules on content and format. For instance, the government regulates the amount and type of violence, nudity, and profanity on major television programs. Just like a program on a major network, the formal essay is subject to a number of regulations or restrictions that distinguish it from the personal essay. When writing a formal essay, you are not relying solely on your own experiences. More often than not, you are responding to a piece of writing (such as an essay, a study, or a work of literature) by someone else. While your opinions and feelings remain important, they are not the exclusive focus of a formal essay.

As this is not personal writing, a more formal voice and a more objective approach are required. The pronoun "I" is rarely used; instead, the third-person form is utilized, along with a more formal tone and diction. Conversational phrases and colloquial expressions should be avoided, as should contractions (*can't, don't, they're*): spell these out in full (*cannot, do not, they are*).

FORMAL ESSAY:
1. No "I" voice
2. Objective
3. Formal

 SEARCH FEATURE

One of the advantages of using a word processor to write an essay is that you can use the Search feature to check to see if you have overused personal pronouns in a formal essay. If you have, you can quickly change them to the third person.

This type of writing is designed not merely to present your views, but instead to examine, incorporate, and sometimes critique the concepts, ideas, and thoughts of others. So an agriculture student might write a formal research essay comparing various methods of irrigation in Canada; an aviation technology student might write a formal essay analyzing computer applications in her vocation; a dental hygiene student might write a formal essay on applications of new technology in clinical practice. The formal essay provides you with an opportunity to explore topics and react to ideas from a broad perspective, often incorporating ideas and material from secondary sources. This second type of essay is often associated with the idea of **expository** writing, which explains or comments upon something.

See Module 12: The Research Essay.

Exercise 2

1. Turn back to the essay on television viewing at the end of Module 1. Is it a personal or a formal essay? Provide at least five specific examples to back up your answer.

2. One of the following excerpts is from a formal essay, while the other is from a personal essay. Providing at least five specific reasons, explain which is which.

   a. Stress management teaches skills for mastering, reducing, or tolerating the demands created by stress. Some approaches are aimed at reducing the sources of stress through problem solving and communication skill training, while others deal with coping with the reaction of stress emotionally and physically. Skills can be developed through regular practice of systematic relaxation techniques or aerobic exercise. Significant correlations were observed between functioning and stress measurements of depression, locus of control and self control measures in studies by Brandon et al. (1991). These findings suggest a link between physical fitness and improved emotionality. [From Ann Trick, "Can Stress Be Managed?" *OOHNA Journal* 14.1 (Spring 1995):10.]

   b. Normally this type of information wouldn't make me feel uncomfortable, because famous people throughout history have died by the millions at every conceivable age. So 33 shouldn't make all that much difference. Theoretically. [From Drew Hayden Taylor, "Don't Count on My Dying Any Too Soon," *The Toronto Star* 7 Aug. 1995: A11.]

Exercise 3

In groups of four to six, identify each of the following topics as more appropriate for a formal or a personal essay. Briefly explain your decision.

1. Describe the accounting procedures used in a small business.

2. Should euthanasia be legalized by the Canadian government?

3. Evaluate the day-care crisis and possible solutions.

4. Would you recommend to a friend the last novel you have read or movie you have seen?

5. Is sexual deviance the result of an immoral society?

6. Compare and contrast the relative advantages of higher and lower speed limits on Canadian highways.

7. The Internet has revolutionized human communication.

8. Ongoing professional development and education are essential if Canadian industry is to remain competitive in a changing global marketplace.

9. Everyone should have a pet.

10. Sales is the process of defining and fulfilling customer needs.

ESSAY WRITING: A SIX-STEP PROCESS

A key aspect of making essay writing more manageable is breaking the process down into a number of distinct stages that build on each other. The following six-step approach—**rhetorical triangle, content generation, outline, rough draft, revision,** and **editing**—will help you see the essay as the outcome of a number of distinct but interrelated steps that should be performed in order. In particular, the first three steps are strategies for deciding *what* you will say; the last three steps concern decisions about *how* to say it. These are two different mental operations, so it is essential to keep them separate.

MAKE THE PROCESS YOUR OWN

There is always a danger in using someone else's process without adjusting it to your personal strengths and weaknesses. This six-step process is a guideline, but not a set of absolute rules. Keep in mind that the first time you cook something according to a recipe, you usually follow the recipe exactly; the next time, you adjust some ingredients by adding a little more or a little less, according to your preferences. Whatever you decide, however, what is important is tackling the question of what to say and how to say it in separate steps.

Step 1: Imaging the Essay with the Rhetorical Triangle

For many writers, the biggest problem is the first one: where and how do you start? You may solve this problem by jumping right into furious production of a first draft. This may result in a significant chunk of text, but in all likelihood, this is text without a clear focus or purpose. Like Bruce in Module 1, you eventually slow down, become confused and uncertain about where to go next, and are dissatisfied with what you have produced.

Often, the opposite problem occurs: you stare at a blank sheet of paper or a computer terminal trying to figure out how to begin. This is because you find it next to impossible to figure out exactly where it is you are heading with your writing. One solution to this problem is to "image" the essay you are about to write. To do this, you can use a tool called the rhetorical triangle.

THE RHETORICAL TRIANGLE

The *Gage Canadian Dictionary* defines *rhetoric* in the following manner:

> 1 the art or skill of using words effectively in speaking or writing.
> 2 a book about this art. 3 language used to persuade or influence others: *The crowd was impressed by the speaker's rhetoric.*

A good essay depends upon your effective use of rhetoric—that is, how "effectively" you use words to achieve your purpose. The rhetorical triangle is a method of mapping out your strategy to "persuade or influence" the specific audience you are addressing in your essay. The triangle's components are as follows:

Because of the rhetorical triangle's fundamental importance in any writing situation, the issues of topic, audience, and point of view will recur as you proceed through the text. Wherever you notice the following triangle icon, some corner of the triangle is being considered.

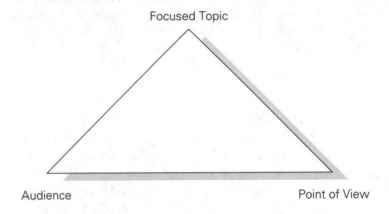

Focused Topic

Audience

Point of View

There are three central elements of the triangle: **focused topic, audience,** and **point of view.** You must make specific decisions about each of these three elements when you do any type of writing, whether an English essay or a report, a personal letter, a memo or report at work, or another task. Each of the three corners of the triangle greatly influences how and what you are going to write. Any time you change any of the three elements, you change the entire nature of the writing assignment. The best way to keep track of this is to draw your own version of the triangle when you are ready to start writing. Then write down in point form the relevant information outside each corner.

 ## USING THE TRIANGLE

If you look at the shape of the triangle, you can see that any time you are working in one corner of it, the two lines forming that corner are pointing to the other corners. This should remind you that while you start filling in data in, for example, the audience corner, you should also be thinking about how to focus the topic for this audience, and what your point of view is in relation to that audience.

Suppose you are a pharmacy student working in a senior citizens' retirement home. You have been asked to contribute to the newsletter something about drugs, a hot topic. You think about how to appeal to your audience, and you realize that rather than follow your first instinct and discuss illegal drugs, it would make more sense to discuss legal pharmaceutical drugs. This will permit you to share your

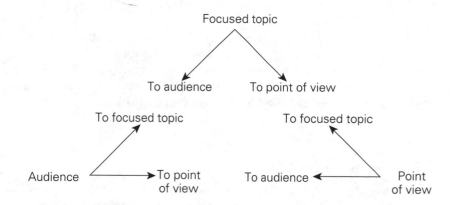

expertise and say something meaningful to your readers who, given their ages, likely do take some form of prescription drug.

As you fill in this information, you start to become aware of appropriate ways of focusing your topic ("I'll explain the dangers of overmedication and the importance of having all your medication reviewed annually"), and of an effective point of view to adopt ("I'd better not sound like a know-it-all expert. I should try to relate to them as a student who knows what it's like to struggle with doctors' explanations and jargon"). Thus, you fill in points simultaneously in all three corners while they occur to you. When you do this effectively, you actually start generating ideas about what to say, which gives you a head start on the next stage of essay writing.

Consider a specific example. Imagine that, like Bruce in Module 1, you were given an assignment asking you to write a 1000–1500 word essay analyzing how television has influenced modern society. By addressing the three key areas, you will create a rhetorical triangle that will image this essay.

Focused Topic

One of the primary things you have to do is figure out how much you are going to be able to say in the time and space allowed for the specific assignment. In other words, you have to narrow your topic and focus it so that you can say something meaningful within the limits given to you. How many words do you have (300? 500? 1000?), and how much time do you have (90 minutes? 3 hours? 5 days?)—these restrictions will have a direct role in determining the topic and scope of your essay.

See Modules 5–11, each of which explains how to write an essay in a different rhetorical mode.

If you are assigned a topic, there are generally two possibilities: you may get a very specific topic and accompanying **rhetorical mode**, which is simply the category or type of essay. These modes include **description/narration, process, comparison/contrast, definition/classification, cause and effect, persuasion,** and **analysis.** Examples would be topics like "Examine the causes and effects of alcoholism in married men," or "Compare Intel's and Motorola's manufacturing process for making computer chips." The second possibility is that you receive a very broad topic and an accompanying rhetorical mode—for example, the old favourite, "Classify types of cars."

In the first cases, you do not have to do much to make the topic manageable. In the second example, you clearly have a much greater task in narrowing the topic. For example, how are you going to classify cars? Are you going to do it by category, and therefore classify sports cars vs. luxury cars vs. family cars? Are you going to judge by reliability? Are you going to judge by price, or by safety, or by your personal likes and dislikes? You would decide your focus now, and note your decision at the top of the triangle.

Exercise 4

Examine the following topics. Discuss which ones would need to be more tightly focused, and some ways in which you might focus them.

1. Compare college vs. university.

2. Define happiness.

3. Write a sales letter to persuade the reader to buy energy-efficient light bulbs.

4. Describe your home town.

5. Analyze the effects of cuts in government spending.

If you are given a free range of topics, it will be completely up to you to do the work of finding a subject to write about and figuring out what specific aspect of that subject you will examine in your essay. Once again, this is the time to consider the specific requirements of the assignment, which are to write an essay of 1000–1500 words. Bruce in Module 1 had these same limitations, which meant that discussing all of the effects of television on North American culture was impractical.

PLAY YOUR STRENGTHS

Regardless of whether the topic is assigned or not, you should always try to focus it in such a way that you will be writing on something about which you are knowledgable or interested. Taking into consideration both these factors will make writing essays less stressful, less time-consuming, and, ultimately, less problematic.

You cannot say everything, nor should you try. Given your own interests and viewing habits, perhaps you choose to focus on the entertainment programming that many students watch—and more specifically on the physical and mental effects of this entertainment programming on the viewer. You pencil this in at the top of the triangle.

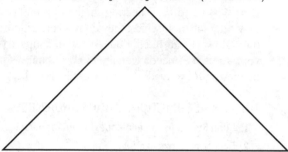

Physical and Mental Effects of
Entertainment Programming on Viewers (Cause/Effect)

Exercise 5

Fill in the Top Ten List below with essay topics that you expect to write on or that, given your interests and knowledge, you would like to write on for courses in your program.

TOP TEN ESSAY TOPICS I EXPECT OR WANT TO WRITE ON IN MY PROGRAM

1. The changing job market in my field
2.
3.
4.
5.
6.
7.
8.
9.
10.

Exercise 6

1. From your Top Ten List, choose the four topics that interest you the most.

2. Draw four rhetorical triangles. At the top corner, write in a focused version of the topic that reflects your particular interest in the subject. If the topic is a question, make your focused topic your basic answer. If it is a general statement or broad topic, try to make the statement your main point. Ensure that two of your focused topics lend themselves to personal essays, and two lend themselves to formal essays.

Audience

In order to give your essay a strong focus, it is best to pick a very specific audience. Think of your favorite band performing in concert. Imagine paying $30 or $40 for your ticket and then hearing the band members say in an interview that since they play only for themselves, they do not care whether or not the paying audience enjoys their show. In all likelihood, this would upset you. If you fail to consider carefully your audience's needs, you are likely to have a similar effect; your "performance" may be met with the reader's disinterest or hostility.

10 TOP TEN ASSUMPTIONS ABOUT AUDIENCES

1. I don't write for an audience; I write for myself.
2. Everyone thinks like I do.
3. Same class, same ideas.
4. You look different; you think differently.
5. Essays do not make a difference in the way a reader feels about a topic.
6. I'm more important than my audience.
7. I have to know more than my audience to write about a subject.
8. Why would I change my essay just because of a different audience?
9. Women like essays about love; men like essays about violence.
10. If the audience puts in half as much work as I do, then they'll understand.

Exercise 7

Respond briefly to the assumptions and attitudes in the Top Ten List. Are they correct or not? Do you see any problems? Discuss your ideas with group members.

Defining an audience for an essay always involves asking yourself several fundamental questions. If your writing is going to be effective and worth reading, it should be aimed at the people who are most naturally going to be interested and involved in whatever you are writing about, and it should be packaged in such a way that it will achieve your purpose.

Some of the questions you should ask yourself include the following.

Acronym: a word made from the first letters of other words, such as RAM (Random Access Memory), ICU (Intensive Care Unit), ECE (Early Childhood Education).

1. Familiarity. How familiar is my audience with my topic? For instance, if I am writing about computers, am I writing for beginners or experts? This will affect both the sophistication of my language and the complexity of my topic. Can I use acronyms and computer jargon freely, or will I need to explain things in more detail and in everyday language?

2. Attitude. What is my audience's likely attitude toward my topic? Are they eager? hostile? uncertain? Do they have any preconceptions about the subject? Do they have a personal or professional interest in my topic? Are they reading the ideas and information in my essay for pleasure, or do they need to do something with this information? If I am writing an essay on computer use in the workplace and my audience

Jargon: the specialized language of a particular group or profession. Computer jargon would include words like "software" (programs that run the computer) and "hardware" (the computer itself).

consists of older workers worried about their job security, I will need to speak in simple, accessible, and reassuring language in order to reach them.

3. Cultural Factors. Consider a variety of cultural factors in assembling your audience profile. These include

a. AGE. Your approach to a topic such as computers in the workplace will be very different if your audience is the older workers cited above or is predominantly young adults who are likely very familiar and comfortable with computers and their uses. Think carefully about the specific impact of your topic on your specific audience.

b. GENDER. You must be careful not to stereotype, but an essay written primarily for female readers may tackle a subject very differently from an essay written for male readers. For instance, a description of cable television's The Women's Network might be received differently by the readers of a women's magazine and by the students in a mostly male class. A recent television commercial for feminine hygiene products takes a lighthearted approach to the question of gender in the audience. Since male viewers presumably have no interest in the commercial, the female announcer immediately directs the attention of male viewers to a small television screen that appears in the bottom right-hand corner of the actual television screen. On this small screen, viewers see a football game. It is, of course, a stereotype to suggest that all men love football, but the commercial humorously acknowledges that part of its audience will not be interested in the product. In general, try to make gender-inclusive language choices and to select examples that both men and women are aware of, are comfortable with, and will respond to.

Aquaculture: fish farming, or the care and management of fish stocks.

c. NATIONAL/RELIGIOUS/ETHNIC/POLITICAL BACKGROUND. The country or part of the country a person is from will influence her or his attitudes on a variety of subjects. Imagine an essay on why government subsidies of aquaculture programs should be slashed. Now imagine how differently this essay would have to be written for an audience of Maritimers as opposed to an audience of Manitobans. Religious and cultural background will also influence attitudes about certain topics, and therefore must be considered. Being aware of the audience's background does not mean that you have to avoid being controversial or honest in your opinions. It also does not mean that you should be paralyzed by the idea that you have to appeal to every member of every potential audience. An awareness of these issues, however, will help you to reach the maximum number of audience members in the most effective way.

d. EDUCATION. The level of your audience's education will affect the sophistication of your language, the approach you will take, and the subject matter you will choose. Think about an automobile technician's essay on automobile design. Now imagine how different this essay looks depending upon whether it is aimed at fellow auto tech students, university or college engineering graduates, or high school dropouts. All three corners of the rhetorical triangle will be radically affected by each different audience's level of education. This will, in turn, affect vocabulary, strategies for capturing the interest of the audience, and the essays' purpose.

VISUALIZE A READER

It may be helpful to visualize a specific reader for your essay while assembling your audience profile. For instance, perhaps your grandmother or your next-door neighbour fits the profile of the kind of reader you are hoping to reach. Perhaps a friend or fellow student fits the profile. If you can plan and write the essay with this specific reader in mind, you will help yourself make good decisions about how to approach your subject and what kind of language to use—the same decisions you automatically make when speaking to that person.

In the case of the television topic, since virtually every home in Canada has a television, this is a subject of broad interest and relevance. You still, however, have a decision to make in terms of the audience. Are you going to attempt to write for every possible Canadian television viewer? Or are you going to focus in on a more specific group, such as people from a certain part of the country, age group, economic class, or level of education? Analyzing your audience is crucial, because any change in your audience is going to have an impact on everything you do leading up to the finished product.

Exercise 8

1. For each of your four rhetorical triangles from Exercise 6, fill in the relevant characteristics of a very specific audience in the lower left-hand corner. Briefly justify each choice.

2. Rewrite/revise/clarify your topic corner in light of your specific audience.

Point of View

Determining a focused topic and identifying a specific audience are very important elements in the essay-writing process. Equally important is understanding exactly why you are writing—in other words, your point of view and purpose. Here, again, each and every writing task differs, but you should follow these general steps:

1. Figure out your purpose for writing on that specific topic.

2. Determine where you stand, or your point of view, in relation to the topic you have chosen.

3. Take into consideration how much knowledge you have about the subject at hand.

Knowledge

Point of view

In our example, you are not an expert in the sense of having a specific educational background in television and other media. However, you are a well-informed average citizen who reads the newspaper regularly and is aware of certain studies conducted on the effects of television viewing. You are also an occasional viewer of

Purpose

various television programming but perhaps a more critical viewer than some. You are aware of a variety of negative effects television viewing has on the viewer, and your purpose in writing is to make other viewers like yourself consider these effects.

After you have done the groundwork, you should have something to place at all three points of the triangle. Your rhetorical triangle in this situation would look something like this:

Notice that the topic is more focused (on negative *effects) after triangle construction.*

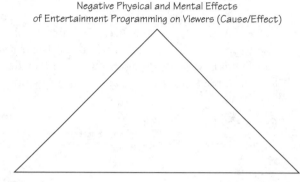

Negative Physical and Mental Effects
of Entertainment Programming on Viewers (Cause/Effect)

Audience

— Average Canadian cable television viewers of ages 18-45 approx.

— very familiar with television; will recognize program references

— likely enjoy it, at least certain types of programming; may have misgivings about it, particularly if have children

— average education; culturally diverse; men and women

Point of View (perspective)

— I am a fairly average viewer familiar with TV programming and its good and bad effects, and well-read in terms of newspaper television studies—I am a critical viewer.

— I would like to point out to others some of the pitfalls of television, using examples that will be familiar to them.

— I must use no specialized vocabulary.

Expository writing: writing that explains an idea in detail.

By fixing the three elements of the triangle in this way, you have committed your-self in some real ways to delivering an expository essay. This essay must have enough detail and clarity that an average Canadian television viewer in Nanaimo or Fredericton can understand your information and argument. Notice that by chang-ing any of the three elements, you change the focus and aim of the essay consider-ably. For instance, consider the difference it would make in your essay to substitute only one of the following elements:

TOPIC: Positive Effects of Television

AUDIENCE: Political Candidates in an Upcoming Election

POINT OF VIEW: Media Expert

Exercise 9

1. Return to your four rhetorical triangles from Exercises 6 and 8. Taking into account your level of knowledge and your interest in each subject, and considering your audience and specific topic, define carefully your point of view and purpose in the bottom right-hand corner.

2. Rewrite your topic/main point in light of your audience and point of view.

THE RHETORICAL TRIANGLE AS PROPOSAL

See The Thesis Statement, p. 53.

You can use the rhetorical triangle to create a **proposal** for yourself. This proposal consists of three short sentences. The first details your topic/main point. This will lead to your thesis statement. The second specifies your audience. The third explains your point of view. By doing this, you can provide yourself with the specific, logical focus you need to get started on the road to writing a solid essay.

Exercise 10

Turn each of your rhetorical triangles from Exercise 9 into a three-sentence proposal.

Exercise 11

You have now written four versions of your topic. In groups of four to six, briefly examine and discuss how your topic or main point has changed in light of your specific audience and point of view.

SKIPPING THE TRIANGLE

Anxious to get on with the "real" business of writing, you may find yourself tempted to race through the rhetorical triangle stage. Resist this temptation. Five minutes of work on all three corners will give you a very clear image of what you are trying to accomplish, and will also begin to give you ideas for the next stage. Failure to give a careful consideration to these issues almost inevitably results in an unfocused topic and an essay that is a series of disjointed minor points without a major point. Remember Bruce's first essay in Module 1.

Step 2: Content Generation

Now you are in the situation of the network television executives who have decided what kind of program to produce, who the target audience is, and what the program's purpose is. Like the executives, you now need some specific ideas about what to say. Obviously, the more you have to say on a given topic, the easier it will be for you to write a good essay. The key, then, is to create an excess of content so that you can sift through it and pick out what is most relevant and useful for the topic you have chosen. In order to generate too much content, you will need to employ a number of techniques. Some methods include **brainstorming, clustering, the dictionary method, the five "Ws" and one "H,"** and **research**.

BRAINSTORMING

Brainstorming is probably a technique that you have relied on at some time in the past, either in writing or in business meetings. If you break down the word "brainstorming" itself, you get a clear picture of the basic process. Think of a storm's violent downpour of rain, mixed with wind. Brainstorming is a similar frenzied burst of ideas from your brain to the page. A storm brings rain that nurtures new life, but also leaves debris and wreckage. Similarly, brainstorming creates a fertile group of ideas that can later grow into an essay, but also leaves a physical mess on your page that you will have to sift through.

There are several variations on this method, but brainstorming generally involves writing down (or typing) all your ideas on a specific topic without paying much attention to exactly what you are saying or how it looks on the page. This technique can be based on word association; for example, in the case of your essay, you might write down everything you think of when you hear the word "television." Or brainstorming can have a slightly more structured basis: every problem you can think of in regard to television viewing.

Ignore sentence structure.

While brainstorming, you must let your mind work freely and not worry about the relevance of your material. Do not worry about writing in complete sentences or paragraphs; simply get the ideas down in point form. You are concerned exclusively with what the ideas are, not with how you are expressing them—that comes later. At the same time, it is also important to set a definite time limit on brainstorming sessions because otherwise they are potentially endless.

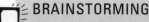 **BRAINSTORMING**

Using a computer when you are brainstorming can give you a decided advantage when it comes time to sift through and organize the material you have generated. This is because by using the Search function of your word processor, you can find and move similar information into a separate file or location so that you can work with it more easily and quickly.

Exercise 12

Take one of your four complete rhetorical triangle proposals from Exercise 10, and brainstorm for ten minutes on the subject. Pay no attention to the form or structure of the ideas; simply get them onto the page as they occur to you, with no concern for sentence or paragraph structure. When you are done, your page(s) should look like a mess, as if an ink-storm just happened.

CONTENT GENERATION WITH A WORD PROCESSOR

Students should be familiar with how to cut and paste text in their word processor.

1. Open a document in your word processor. Now, just as if you were brainstorming on paper, type anything that comes into your mind as you think about one of your topics. Do not worry about spelling or capitals, grammar or order, or even hitting the Enter key. There will be time for all that later. Set a time limit—say, twenty minutes—and then relax and let your fingers dance across the keyboard. Make a mess.

2. Once this is done, save the mess on a disk. This way, you can make any changes you want and even change your mind without losing what you have done. It will always be on your disk until you want to get rid of it.

3. Now, isolate each idea on its own line. If ideas are run together, you may need to flesh them out a bit. For instance, "television is mind-numbing and sore bum" might need to be changed to

   • watching too much television can be mind-numbing

   • also numb bum

   No matter what, add enough to each thought so that it makes sense to you. This just means adding a few words that can be deleted easily later. Keep in mind the old adage that it is easy to change something once it exists. Making it exist in the first place is the difficulty. So you may want something like

   • sitting and watching TV for too long can give you numb bum

   All you are trying to do at this stage is write "tag-lines" for your ideas. Do not spend much time thinking. Talk out loud, or, even better, talk through your fingers. This is a new twist on thinking out loud.

4. Now that each different idea is isolated on its own line, type one quick sentence or a short series of point-form notes explaining what you mean by each idea. Do not worry about any order at all yet.

   Watching too much TV can be mind-numbing

   • hours go by and you can't remember what you saw

   • you find yourself watching stupid stuff like *Barney*

5. Save this new mess. You may want to call it by a different name (for instance, "MESS.2") than your first mess ("MESS.1"). This way, if you need to, you can always back up to the beginning again.

Your compusition is now well under way. Bear in mind that each of the following modes of content generation can also be approached through the computer in the same fashion. We will return to this at the outline stage.

Whether you are aware of it or not, brainstorming is a very limited and limiting way of getting ideas. It is influenced a great deal by factors such as how well your mind is functioning on that day, your previous knowledge of the subject, whether or not you feel inhibited for any reason, and other similar factors. Thus, no matter how adept you are at brainstorming, it is essential that you use more than this single method for producing content. To generate a broad and useful range of content, it is necessary to expand your search for material.

CLUSTERING

Clustering is a more visual way of generating content. When you cluster, you begin by placing your focused topic in an oval in the centre of your page:

At this point, you produce ideas that are related to your main topic. You place each idea in an oval of its own, and draw a line from it to your central idea to show the connection.

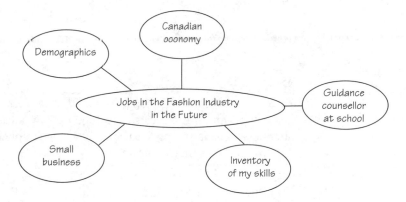

Now you produce ideas related specifically to your subideas. Once again, place each in an oval, and draw the lines to the subidea to which the idea is connected (see the diagram on the next page).

As you can see, clustering not only produces a number of ideas, but visually maps out the organization of these ideas for you. For instance, see the "Canadian economy" section. All of the ideas related to this topic are clustered together in the same area. Often, you will develop only one particularly good area of your cluster into an essay. Some of the areas of the cluster may not lead you anywhere (see the "small business" and "guidance counsellor" clusters); these can be abandoned.

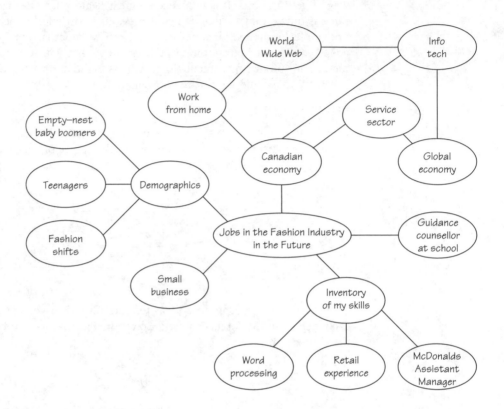

Exercise 13

Take a second rhetorical triangle proposal from Exercise 10. Bearing your triangle's contents in mind, use a cluster to produce raw ideas for fifteen minutes. Pay no attention to the form or relevance of the ideas; simply get them onto the page in the various groups as they occur to you.

THE DICTIONARY METHOD

A good writer always has a dictionary on hand to check word meanings and spellings. But the dictionary is also a handy tool for content generation. Very simply, you can look up the key word(s) in your topic, and copy out the definition(s). Within the copied definition will be other key words that you can either brainstorm or cluster about, or that you can look up to find other definitions (and therefore other ideas). For instance, for an essay on racism, you might look up the word "racism" and discover key words to think about, like *prejudice*, *bias*, and *belief*. You can use your thesaurus in a similar way.

THESAURUS

When using your computer, type in a word related to your topic and look it up in the thesaurus of your word-processing software. This is another route to generating ideas.

Exercise 14

Take a third rhetorical triangle proposal from Exercise 10, and use the dictionary method to generate rough ideas on the subject. Use this strategy for ten minutes. Pay no attention to the form or structure of the ideas; simply get them onto the page as they occur to you.

THE FIVE "Ws" AND ONE "H"

Even the use of brainstorming, clustering, and the dictionary do not exhaust the potential sources of content. Every imaginable topic can also be explored by using the six basic questions that a good reporter asks when covering a news story: **who, what, why, when, where,** and **how.** These questions are tremendous vehicles for creating content because almost all of them can be posed from different angles and perspectives. For example, for the television essay you could ask not only the obvious question "Who watches television?" but also questions such as "Who does not watch television?" "Who suffers because of the effects of television on viewers?" "Who determines the kind of programming we see on television?" and so on.

Exercise 15

Take your fourth rhetorical triangle proposal from Exercise 10, and use the five "Ws" and one "H" to generate ideas for ten minutes. Pay no attention to the form or structure of the ideas; simply get them onto the page as they occur to you.

RESEARCH

Another possible source of content is research. You may think of research as something you do exclusively at a library—and there is no doubt that a good portion of research involves finding material at libraries—but do not forget that your home or office can be a valuable source of information as well. Newspapers, magazines, a dictionary of quotations, and people are all valuable resources that should not be overlooked or ignored.

See Module 12: The Research Essay.

Formal and Informal Interviews, Polls, and Questionnaires

Speaking directly with people about your topic can also be an enormous help when generating content. Very often someone else will have a perspective, insight, or idea about your topic that will lead you in a direction that you might never have explored on your own. Discussing ideas with people who have expertise or knowledge about your subject may also help you generate information or formulate specific approaches to your topic. And even if you cannot speak to one or more people directly, you can have them fill out a brief survey or questionnaire. Later this information can be presented as factual or statistical evidence (if you make certain that you clearly document the source) in your essay.

See Appendix B: Documentation Styles.

On-line Research

More than ever, you have a wealth of resources at your fingertips in the form of a computer and modem and/or fax modem. The amount of information available is almost infinite.

There is a variety of ways to use a computer for generating content and ideas:

1. library catalogues available through the Internet;

2. databases of articles in various fields, professions, areas, and media (such as business, architecture, science, history, literature, and newspapers and journals);

3. World Wide Web pages and their hypermedia links;

4. text-based Internet resources and accessible CD-ROMs.

All of these sources can be effectively used both in getting an essay started and in generating useful content.

The best way to think about this is through a specific example like the television topic. After generating your rhetorical triangle, suppose that you do a quick check of a database containing articles from journals, magazines, and other sources easily accessible on the Internet. This reveals over 5000 articles on television. This is far too much information, so you use **Boolean operators** to narrow the search by adding a word that reduces the number of matches. In other words, you are now searching for "television and violence," or "television and behaviour." The following is only a partial list of the articles found in this database. Note that some of the article titles are not complete, but this is exactly how they appear in the database under "television behaviour."

Boolean operators are logical controls you can add (words like AND, OR, and NOT) that allow you to join different conditions in a computer search.

> **And the moral is ...**
> **Why watch it, anyway?**
> **Connie Chung incident**
> **Little dish TV**
> **Picks & pans: Does TV Kill?**
> **Shopping by television**
> **Teaching about television in the classroom**
> **Television: What Can We Do About Violence**
> **Channel surfing's new wave**
> **The glamorization of violence**
> **Influence of TV on daydreaming**

 ## USE TITLES TO GENERATE CONTENT

Just the titles of these articles are a gold mine of ideas. If you have not focused your topic before starting your on-line exploration, think about all the possibilities offered to you here—channel surfing, does television kill, violence on television, myths of television, interactive television, gender bias, fame and television, teaching and television.

The titles of these articles are not only helpful for finding specific useful information, but also for producing content for an essay already underway. For example, below is a partial list of books on television from the computerized card catalogue at a regional library.

Children in Front of the Small Screen
Television and Aggression
Changing Channels: Living Sensibly with Television
Four Arguments for the Elimination of Television
Teleliteracy: Taking Television Seriously
Television and Human Behaviour
TV's Image of the Elderly

Take the title "Television and Human Behaviour." What is the relationship between television and human behaviour? Does television reflect human behaviour? Does human behaviour control what gets on television? Or consider "Four Arguments for the Elimination of Television." What could these arguments be? What would be the impact of eliminating television or even reducing the amount of television available for viewing? Naturally, you should read any useful materials uncovered in your research, but the first stage of the research, the title search, can also be used to stimulate your own creative content generation.

USING MORE THAN ONE METHOD

No matter how good one writer may be, a television studio always hires a team of writers to produce a television show because several minds are better than one. We are not telling you to hire other writers to do your assignments, only that the same principle is true for content generation—several ways of thinking are better than only one.

Since your goal is to generate an excess of ideas quickly and efficiently, it is important to see how shifting mental gears from one method to another creates a spinoff effect. Examine the following sequence of different methods used to generate ideas about television. As you will see, this chain reaction of ideas leads to a great deal of content in a relatively short time. Notice the way each method takes the materials generated by a previous method and elaborates/expands them in new directions.

Sample Content Generation

1. Research. In the case of your particular topic, a combination of library and personal research seems to be a good place to start. At the library, you discover a recent survey of North American entertainment habits that states that the typical North American adult watches four hours of television per day. You also discover an article

See Module 12 for more information on library research.

in the latest issue of *Psychology Today* that describes in detail the effect of extended periods of television viewing on the brain.

You examine a newspaper article from *The Globe and Mail* entitled "New Broadcast Code Aims at Curbing Television Violence." This article yields information on the broadcast code implemented by the Canadian government on January 1, 1994. This code specifically seeks to reduce "gratuitous violence" on television and is particularly concerned with reducing violence in programming for children. You then read a variety of other articles concerning the implementation of this broadcast code, and track down a copy of the government report that discusses it.

Development of the content is a process. The research becomes a starting point from which you apply the other methods of content generation.

In light of this apparently widespread concern over the effects of television violence, you then discuss the issue with people you know. You learn from your parents that, as a child, you would often become very aggressive after watching a violent program. You also learn from your friend Minia, a teacher, that her students emulate the violence of certain programs on the playground.

2. Brainstorming. Now that you have your research, you use it as a basis for brainstorming, which takes the following rough form:

- VIEWERS: 4 hours per day watching television = 1/6 of entire life = 1/4 of life while awake!! Wow!!
- enormous amount: effects?
- new Canadian Broadcast Code
- government and researchers scared by effects of this overexposure
- people take this problem of effects on viewers very seriously
- who should be responsible? government? viewers? parents of children?
- conclusions? television's net effects bad? or simply a function of individual responsibility?

3. Dictionary. As a third method of content generation, you look up the word *television* in the *Gage Canadian Dictionary*, and then brainstorm about key words in the definition.

> Television: *n.* **1** the process of transmitting the image of an object, scene, or event by radio or wire so that a person in some other place can see it at once.

- "image" idea: people are watching IMAGES of reality, not the "real thing"
- people mistake television for reality: very dangerous
- television presents distorted view of world (only glamorous, sexy people; lots of violence; all programming reflects bias of some kind, so it is dangerous for people to see television as presenting "the truth")
- television becomes reality for a lot of people
- it's easier to deal with television (it's always there; it never lets you down or talks back to you)

- most important source of entertainment and information
- so difference between the two is blurring more and more every day

4. Continue Brainstorming. From the assembled material, you then continue brainstorming.

GROUP RELATED IDEAS TOGETHER

It is helpful, when you reach a pause in your ideas, to start joining similar or related ideas together with lines and placing them under headings or categories. Starting to do this will lead you to other categories and other ideas.

Effects of Television

MENTAL: hypnotic; like a narcotic drug; brain-wave activity reduced — puts you to sleep; dulls your analytical, active mind

- advertising manipulates viewers who are already in a suggestible state

PHYSICAL: "couch potatoes"; people out of shape

- eat while they watch: chips, candy
- living vicariously through athletes on the screen
- statistics on growing numbers of overweight people in North America

BEHAVIOURAL: viewers imitate what they see

- viewers desensitized to what they see
- violence a big problem (see research)
- emotional problems: television may oversimplify emotional/sexual situations and therefore foster emotional immaturity in viewers
- children

FAMILIAL: television is the electronic babysitter

- family members don't talk to one another, just let the television babble
- years ago entertainment would take form of an active, collective activity (reading aloud; outdoor outings)
- even in the early days of television, families would watch together
- now, with hundreds of channels, lots of families have several televisions so family members can watch separate programs

Exercise 16

1. Choose two of the content generation exercises that you have completed for Exercises 12–15, one of which will become a formal essay and the other a personal essay.

2. For the formal essay,

a. Look up the key words of your focused topic in the dictionary, write down the definitions, and brainstorm, cluster, or ask questions based on them.

b. Conduct an informal telephone survey of at least four different people, asking for their answers to specific questions on your topic.

c. Use the Internet and/or your school library's database or card file to generate a list of article and book titles for your topic. Brainstorm, cluster, or ask questions to generate ideas from these.

3. For the personal essay,

a. Apply at least one other method of content generation (brainstorming, clustering, dictionary, five "Ws" and one "H") to the content you already have.

b. Do this for fifteen minutes.

Once we have all this information, however, what do we do with it?

Step 3: The Outline

⚡SKIPPING THE OUTLINE

The very word *outline* may make you want to skip ahead and ignore this section. Do not! If you have ever made a travel schedule, itinerary, or daily schedule, or if you have ever planned a date, traced an image you wanted to draw, or arranged a delivery, you already know the importance and value of an outline.

The best and most interesting information in the world is of no value if it is not organized in a way that makes it understandable to your readers. This is precisely the function of an outline. The outline is the place where you decide your main point or thesis, put your ideas in order, and map out in some detail what you are going to say in each paragraph of the body of your essay. While every writer has a different conception of what an outline should look like, there are good reasons to heed the advice that a good outline is a detailed outline.

What to leave out.

Some of the most important decisions you will make during the outlining stage are about what material to leave out of your essay. Including everything you write down, like Bruce did in Module 1, is an indication of either inadequate content generation or a failure to focus your subject. Your content generation is a deliberate mess; when you put together an outline, you clean up the mess. To do this, remember to take out the trash.

See The Thesis Statement, p. 53.

Outlines are personal to every writer, so the following is general advice concerning what should go into an effective outline. Write your main point, or thesis, at the top of the page. Group significant and similar, but smaller, ideas together below it. Each idea will likely be expanded into a paragraph. For every paragraph of the essay,

See Appendix A, Contract #10: The Paragraph.

you should produce an outline that specifies a rough **topic sentence** that indicates the paragraph's subject and clearly relates to your thesis statement. You should then list the supporting points, examples, and arguments you want to make in the paragraph. The exact method for this will vary. Some people will create sketch outlines that have only a couple of words to remind them of what they are going to write; others will create very detailed and substantial outlines.

EXACTLY WHAT YOU WANT TO SAY

See Module 7: Comparison and Contrast for two more examples of full outlines.

Regardless of the type of outline you use, remember that the purpose of the outline is to solve *all* questions about *what* you are going to say. When you look at your finished outline, you should understand exactly what you intend to write about and in what order you will be presenting your points and examples.

TYPES OF OUTLINES

See Body, p. 57.

Utilize the type of outline that will help you to clearly and methodically organize your ideas. A detailed outline of one paragraph from the body of an essay could look like this:

Topic sentence establishes new topic (mental defects) by linking it to the previous paragraph's subject (physical effects). This is an effective transitional device, reinforced by the rhyme of defects/ effects.

A. Topic Sentence: Worse than physical effects are mental defects television creates

   → 1. Researchers: viewing TV is like taking narcotics; brain-wave activity is reduced

      2. A mindless, numbing pleasure experienced

      3. Example: *The Simpsons'* Homer Simpson—belly, beer, drool, glazed eyes

      4. TV gives impression of "being there"

      5. People don't think — they mistake television for reality

   → 6. Reading encourages mental activity: we interpret, imagine words and ideas for ourselves

The Homer Simpson example adds nothing to the actual argument being assembled, but by presenting such a vivid visual image, you can give your reader a concrete example of the entranced viewer being discussed.

Notice how point 6, about reading increasing brain activity, will balance point 1, about television reducing brain-wave activity. Good outlining allows you to create such balances and contrasts, which would almost never occur without such planning.

Notice how each point is sketched out in detail. A given point may end up as more than one sentence, but this is not a major concern when you assemble your outline. All you are worried about is deciding exactly what points you wish to raise and in what order. A much sketchier outline could be as simple as this:

— TS: Mental defects: narcotics

— Example: Homer Simpson

— Mistaking TV for reality

— Contrast: reading

The level of detail you employ in creating your outline is up to you. Just remember: the outline must have sufficient detail to tell you exactly what you want to say, so during the next crucial stage of the process (producing your rough draft) you can concentrate instead on how you want to say it.

Exercise 17

1. Take your two detailed content generations from Exercise 16.

2. In each case, write your main point or thesis statement at the top of the page.

3. Read through your content generations, underlining or using a highlighter to emphasize ideas that are important and related to your main point.

4. Group significant, similar, smaller details and ideas together into potential paragraphs.

5. Put an "X" beside any ideas from your content generation that do not seem related or that you did not develop.

6. Examine the groups of ideas, and try to establish a logical order for these ideas. Number the groups in the order in which you will want them to appear in the essay.

7. Copy these out in point form in the correct order, indicating at the start of each group the topic sentence, and below it the examples, supporting arguments, or explanation that will flesh it out.

8. Expand the points that need clarification.

 OUTLINING WITH A WORD PROCESSOR

Continued from page 28, "Content Generation with a Word Processor."

6. Establish your main point or thesis. Place this at the top of your notes. This will be the guideline for what follows.

7. Now comes the cutting and pasting:

   Read through your list of ideas. Ask yourself, "What in this mess should come first in my essay?" Cut it out and place it at the top of your screen, under your thesis statement. Number this as "1."

8. Now go through your list again and pull out any ideas that go with your #1 idea. Cut and paste these under your #1 idea. Later, you can come back and put these in order. You may want to indent these secondary ideas just to keep them clear on the screen.

9. Keep going through steps 7 and 8 until all ideas have been grouped together. Leave out anything that does not fit. You will find that these irrelevant ideas naturally fall to the bottom of the screen.

10. You are close to your outline, so save this semi-mess once again. You probably will want to use a new name.

11. You may want to print out your semi-outline and make notes on the page before returning to your word processor; alternatively, you may wish to go back and expand each of your ideas and subpoints in the original computer file. This is the revising stage of outlining.

12. Finally, consider the transitions between sections of your outline. Do ideas flow together logically or should they be expanded further? You probably should write a transition sentence between each major idea. Draft these into your outline. They will make the final writing simpler.

You now have your compusition outline. The beauty of the word processor is that you can add or subtract as much as you want without committing to a final product. You can insert or delete anything that you want. This is important to remember since the process of generating ideas and outlining is iterative; in other words, it is a process that you go through repeatedly until it is complete. Only you will know when it is complete, but you can always expand on what you think. After all, you are not wasting paper.

Exercise 18

In groups of four to six, examine, compare, and discuss your outlines. Do you find other students' outlines sensible? Do you understand how they are organized, and why? Would you suggest changes, such as elaborations and deletions?

Exercise 19

In groups of four to six, complete the Top Ten List that follows with other "myths" about essay writing based on what you have learned in Module 2 and elsewhere. Why are they myths? Discuss in groups or as a class.

TOP TEN ESSAY-WRITING MYTHS

1. I write for myself.
2. I write for my English teacher; no one else marks my writing.
3. Ten pages of rough notes = twenty pages when I write them out in full!
4. My outline? It's in my head.
5. I write good. You don't read so good.
6.
7.
8.
9.
10.

SUMMARY

You have completed the first half of the essay-writing process. You now possess strategies for arriving at a clear understanding of *what* you want to say. You accomplish this in three stages:

1. rhetorical triangle (focused topic, specific audience, point of view/purpose);
2. content generation (brainstorming, clustering, dictionary, the five "Ws" and one "H," research); and
3. outlining.

Now you shift to a different aspect of the process: deciding *how* to say it. This will be addressed in Module 3.

The Essay: How to Say It

By completing a series of written and oral exercises and using steps 4–6 of the six-step method to turn an outline into a finished essay, students will

1. *draft, revise, and edit an essay;*
2. *identify and write effective introductions;*
3. *identify and write effective thesis statements;*
4. *write a well-organized, coherent, and unified body;*
5. *identify and write effective conclusions.*

OVERVIEW

All of your work until now has been "behind the scenes." Now it is time to think about the product that your audience will actually be seeing. When television executives have the outline for their television series, it is time to hire producers, directors, and actors. Since you have already generated content and outlined your essay, you, too, are ready to take the next steps. You are no longer a planner; now you are a director, thinking about how specific words, sentences, and paragraphs will be received by your audience.

Another way of thinking about it is to remember that your essay is really just an expansion of your outline. Your outline is the skeleton of your essay. Now it is time to put the flesh on the bones, and then to make the overall body attractive. You know *what* you want to say; now all you need to worry about is *how* to say it.

Exercise 1

Working in groups of four or five, discuss and write down your responses to each of the following statements. You may agree, disagree, or use each statement as a starting point for your own idea.

1. Never change anything in your first draft. It will destroy the flow of your thoughts.

2. I have a spell checker and a grammar checker on my computer. Who needs proofreading?

3. Nobody talks this way! My grade 10 teacher told me to use the "ear test." He said, "Write the way you speak. This will get your ideas down on paper." So I write the way I talk and I'm passing, mostly.

4. Writing essays is very hard for people from other cultures. Teachers should use different marking criteria for them.

5. Essays are easy once you know the formula.

    a. Each essay has five paragraphs: introduction, three supporting paragraphs, and conclusion.

    b. In the introductory paragraph, the first sentence sets up the thesis, the second sentence is the thesis, and the third sentence says what the three supporting paragraphs will be about.

    c. Each supporting paragraph is three sentences long. It begins with a topic sentence, which is lifted from the last sentence of the introductory paragraph. The second sentence supports the topic sentence, and the third sentence provides a transition to the next supporting paragraph.

    d. The concluding paragraph is three sentences long. The first sentence summarizes the topic sentences of the three supporting paragraphs. The second sentence states the conclusion. The third sentence provides a snappy closer.

ESSAY WRITING: A SIX-STEP PROCESS CONTINUED

Step 4: Writing the Rough Draft

The rough draft is the stage at which you are ready to put all your ideas and information into sentences and paragraphs. You should never, however, lose sight of the word "rough" in rough draft. What you want to produce is a document that is not perfect, but has everything in the correct place:

1. a clear introduction with a thesis statement;

2. complete body paragraphs with topic sentences, adequate development of examples and arguments, and clear transitions between them; and

See Parts of the Essay, p. 49, for more detail.

3. a conclusion that is part summary and part extension of the ideas of the essay.

For the most part, the sentence structure, grammar, and punctuation should be correct, but these are not the primary focus of your efforts. You can always fix them later. This suggests that you will rework your draft once it is written, and that is exactly true because writing is a process.

THE ROUGH DRAFT AS PROCESS

There are several key issues in writing a rough draft. First, *never aim for perfection*. You can change anything once it is written down, but until it is written, there is nothing to change. The aim of the rough draft process is to develop text that you will change later in the revising and editing stages.

THE CURSE OF THE "PERFECT SENTENCE"

The curse of the "perfect sentence" is the bane of many essay writers at the rough draft stage. When doing your rough draft, never get caught up in the vicious circle of trying to make one sentence absolutely perfect before moving on to the next. Keep in mind that you do not learn to hit the ball perfectly *before* you play golf, tennis, squash, cricket, or baseball; you learn and improve by actually hitting the ball in a game.

Second, *keep your outline handy and follow it. It is the road map for your essay*. You have put a great deal of effort into developing the outline. You have thought through the relationships of paragraphs and related every thought to your central idea. Do not waste this work now! If you have developed a thorough outline, the process of drafting should be like connecting the dots, where the dots are ideas that can already stand by themselves. Work directly from your outline, but now, instead of developing points, write sentences and paragraphs that make your points hold together logically.

If you are unsure of the spelling of a word, mark it out and look it up after you have finished your rough draft. The same goes for sentence structure or other elements. If you are unsure of whether you need a semicolon or colon in the sentence, for example, *do not interrupt your writing* for fifteen minutes to look up the rule in a handbook. Mark out the problem piece of punctuation with a highlighter or regular pen, and come back to it. The less you break up the rhythm and flow of your writing during the rough draft phase, the more likely you are to produce coherent, unified prose.

DO THE WHOLE DRAFT

Give yourself adequate time at a single sitting to write a complete rough draft of an in-class essay, and either the whole draft or a very substantial portion of the draft of a take-home assignment. It is easier, more efficient, and therefore more effective to do your rough draft as a whole than to try to write it in small snippets. Your thinking will be more focused, and the writing will make more sense.

In order to keep the flow moving, you should set up a method for marking out the problem areas of the rough draft that you want to go back and change. Whether you are writing your essay longhand or using a word processor, you need to design a set of symbols, colours, and/or marks to distinguish things from one another. If you are handwriting your rough draft or printing drafts, you can designate problems by using highlighters or different-coloured pens or pencils, and by making marks such as asterisks. Develop a code to make it easy to find individual problems.

PROBLEM SYMBOLS

If you are typing or word processing, you should employ symbols such as @, #, ^, &, *, { , }, | to draw attention to problem areas during the creation of your rough draft. You can later use the Search function to locate and work on these.

Once you have a completed rough draft that is in decent shape but has some areas needing attention, you are ready to move on to the next steps: revising and editing.

Exercise 2

Take your detailed outlines from Module 2, Exercise 17, and write a rough draft for one or both. Flesh out your point-form outline(s) into complete paragraphs with clear topic sentences and fully developed supporting details. Be sure to allow yourself sufficient time to complete the draft(s) at one sitting.

REVISING AND EDITING ARE NOT THE SAME THING

After your first draft, you are ready to begin revising and editing. You may think of them as the same thing, but this is not the case. **Revising** is a complete reassessment of the essay from beginning to end to see where it needs changes in content, ideas, and organization. By contrast, **editing** is the process of correcting grammatical, syntactical, and mechanical errors.

Step 5: Revising

You may hate to revise your work. After generating content, considering audience and purpose, developing a complete outline, and, finally, writing the essay, the last thing that you may want to do is make a change on your paper. This is natural, because making changes means that your job is far from complete. Suddenly your essay has notes scrawled in the margins, and whole sentences—even paragraphs—are scribbled out. You know that the changes will make your essay better, and you know that the instructor insists that your essay be neat, but you also know this means retyping or rewriting. You may even settle for a poor mark rather than go through the revising process.

Revising has a crucial function, however. Revising literally means "seeing again"; this means you are taking a fresh look at your paper and making changes based on this. When you think about it, in revising you add to your essay by rearranging its elements and substituting words and phrases. Revising strengthens what you say and how you say it, and ensures the consistency of your topic's focus, point of view, appeal to audience, and organization. Ultimately, this shows up in the effectiveness of your essay (for a student, this means your mark).

Disconnect from the draft.

Revising is a substantial and time-consuming process. To revise, you must be able to step back from your work. Put away your rough draft; forty-eight hours is considered by many to be the minimum time you need to "disconnect" yourself from your rough draft and really be able to see it in a more objective light. After this period of time, you can re-view it critically and evaluate its organization and content. Ask yourself these questions:

1. Do I have sufficient examples?
2. Are the examples elaborated in sufficient detail?
3. Are the development and organization of my argument clear?

Everything is open for revision.

If possible, ask a friend or colleague to read your writing and make suggestions before you attempt to look the piece over. When doing a revision, everything is open to reconsideration and reworking. A good revision does not change the text merely for the sake of change, but rather because you have discovered a flaw or you have hit upon a better way to express the same idea. Perhaps you uncover a problem with the order or the presentation of ideas, and therefore develop a more appropriate order or presentation.

REVISION WITH A WORD PROCESSOR

When you use a word processor, revising becomes relatively painless. Your computer will let you add ideas and text wherever useful, move paragraphs around, and reprint a clean copy.

Tips for Revising with a Word Processor

1. Manipulating text on the computer screen can be fun, but there is a danger of over-revising. As you start into revising, you should know your goals; for example, know your own common errors and, in successive passes, look for and correct these. Look at the transitional statements that link one paragraph to the next, and make sure that they show the links clearly.

2. Although it is very easy to make changes when you are working with a word processor, most writers like to work from a hard copy. There is a simple reason for this. While the word processor makes changes easy, particularly at the "micro" level (sentence and paragraph), your computer screen will display only a limited amount of text. A hard copy or printed copy will allow you to work at a "macro" level, looking at the overall structure of the essay. Further, there is a comfort level in working with pen and paper, and you should never forget this. Besides, since your file has been saved, you can always print another copy.

Exercise 3

Revise your rough draft from Exercise 2; begin the process of reviewing your essay by completing some of these statements to stimulate your thinking.

CUES FOR ELABORATING

1. Another way to say the same thing is ...
2. In addition ...
3. Another reason that I think this is ...
4. A good point on the other side of the argument is ...
5. My own feelings about this are ...
6. I could develop this idea further by adding ...
7. This is true, but it is not enough, so I should add ...
8. An example of this is ...
9. An explanation of this is ...
10. I'll change this a little by ...

CUES FOR IMPROVING

1. To put it more simply ...
2. I could make my point clearer by ...
3. I could add interest by explaining ...
4. This is not exactly how it is because ...
5. I'm getting off topic, so ...
6. I could give the reader a clearer picture by ...
7. This is not very convincing because ...
8. I really think that this is not necessary because ...
9. A criticism that I should deal with in this paper is ...
10. I could describe this in more detail by adding ...

CUES FOR NEW DIRECTIONS

1. An important point that I have not yet considered is ...
2. A better argument would be ...
3. A whole new way to think about this topic is ...
4. An even better idea is ...
5. A different aspect would be ...
6. A consequence of this is ...
7. One thing that makes this different from other things like it is ...
8. My audience also wants to know about ...
9. An important distinction is ...
10. Something that is similar is ...

Step 6: Editing

No matter how pressed you are for time, you must do a thorough job of editing your essay. This means that you must eliminate any problems with spelling and punctuation, smooth out and rearrange sentences that have structural problems, and correct all other general grammatical errors. Once you have completed your editing, you should feel completely confident that your paper has a minimal number of mistakes that will have a negative bearing on your essay.

✳ SPELLING COUNTS

People who have difficulty with spelling sometimes treat their spelling errors as something inevitable and trivial ("They're just spelling errors"). Do not make this mistake. Nothing makes your reader less receptive to your argument than evidence that you have not bothered to edit carefully. However unjustly, most readers will associate sloppy spelling with sloppy thinking—which means they will not take your message seriously.

HAVE A PLAN WHEN YOU EDIT

Editing is a much more useful process when you have a plan. In a given essay, you probably do not make twenty different errors; instead, you likely make certain errors repeatedly. If you have a tendency to make the same grammatical error (for example, sentence fragments) or spelling error (such as confusing "its" and "it's"), or if you overuse a particular word or phrase (such as "however" or "really"), you can do a search, either with the computer or by hand, to find each occurrence of the word, phrase, or grammatical error. By looking specifically for certain errors, you are much more likely to spot them.

See Appendix A, Contract #2: Sentence Fragments.

See Appendix A: Grammar as Contract for specific strategies for identifying and solving certain common grammatical errors.

This means that you need to be aware of your own common errors. Make a list of these. When you receive a graded essay back, examine your instructor's annotations carefully, and add to the list. Then, as you are reading your next paper in the editing stage, look for one specific listed error at a time. This means that you may read your essay over many times to catch all of your personal errors, but the payoff will come in your marks, and in the slow but sure elimination of these problems.

The importance of a thorough editing job cannot be overstated, as this is the last stage before producing the text that will be read and judged by your readers. This is the equivalent of the sound check before the concert performance: be sure you have done everything possible to ensure your audience's enjoyment and receptivity.

Exercise 4

1. Develop a common error list based on any assignments you have had returned to you in your English classes. The list should have three columns: on the left, write the name of the problem (you may also want to include your instructor's common abbreviations, for instance, "Sentence fragment—frag.") In the middle

column, write out two or three complete examples that clearly demonstrate what the error looks like. In the right-hand column, correct these errors. Keep a second list with the correct spellings of words you have misspelled. These lists, which you will update when assignments are returned to you, will guide you in what to look for in future editing.

2. Take your revised draft (or drafts) from Exercise 3, and edit it thoroughly. Conduct specific searches for your most common errors.

USING SEARCH TO CHECK AND EDIT SENTENCES

To check the style of your sentence structure:

1. Activate Search, and when you are prompted for a string to search for, type "." (period space). This will bring you to the end of each sentence.

2. Examine each sentence. Check in particular for the following:

   a. Underdeveloped sentences. These sentences need to be revised so that they become more concrete and provide more information to the reader.

See Appendix A, Contract #8: Parallelism.

   b. Parallelism. Are there nonparallel structures in your sentences that make your meaning ambiguous or difficult to follow? Are there elements that could be rhetorically stronger if they were made parallel?

   c. Is there any redundancy? Are there multiple sentences that say basically the same things? Can these sentences be combined?

   d. Is there a series of sentences that are basically of the same length? This is boring for the reader and should be changed.

FINAL COPY/PROOFREADING

In this final stage of editing, you are now producing the final document that will carry and convey your ideas. This means that all the hard work you have invested in this essay must now be reflected in the physical appearance of this copy. Readers form impressions of your writing on the basis of its appearance in much the same way as our initial impressions of people are based upon their appearance and demeanour. The golden rule of a good copy is that it should contain no evident errors or obvious signs of having been corrected.

"Keep up appearances whatever you do."
—Charles Dickens

Your good copy should not simply be free of visible mistakes. It must also conform to all length, formatting, paper size, and appearance requirements for the particular assignment. One thing to be aware of is that different schools, and even different departments within schools, may have different regulations for written assignments. A discussion of two sample formats—**Modern Languages Association** used in English essays and **American Psychological Association** used in social science essays—will be presented in Appendix B: Documentation Styles.

In short, be sure to adhere to the expectations for any given assignment. Remember that your essay represents you in the readers' eyes, and a positive impression created by a clean, well-presented rough draft can make a big difference in how your writing is perceived.

PARTS OF THE ESSAY: INTRODUCTION, BODY, CONCLUSION

Now that you have examined the essay-writing process from the imaging stage right up to the final copy, it is important to take a closer look at the components of the finished essay itself.

Introduction

The introduction, which is the first paragraph of the essay, leads the reader into the essay and must accomplish the following tasks:

1. capture the reader's attention and interest in a **grabber**; otherwise, it is unlikely that the reader will continue reading the essay;

2. provide the **background,** or context, necessary for the reader to understand the essay;

3. clearly establish the essay's **thesis,** or main point, and the rhetorical mode around which the essay is organized.

See Modules 5–11 for rhetorical modes.

The introduction should also attempt to establish your credentials as a writer, and it should establish the general tone and style for the essay.

ORGANIZING YOUR INTRODUCTION

In general, the introduction is like a funnel, moving from broad topics suggested by the grabber (the wide top) to the thesis, or very specific subject matter of the essay (the narrow bottom).

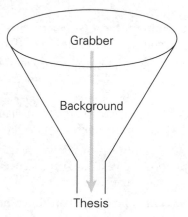

Grabber

Background

Thesis

The **general to specific** pattern, as it suggests, moves from large and broad concerns or questions down to the specific topic of the essay. Thus, in an essay on psychology, you might start out with some general comments on human behaviour, sketch out ways in which people throughout history have attempted to understand it, and end with a thesis statement concerning three specific psychoanalytic theories.

The Grabber: Capturing Your Reader's Interest

Your introduction is a failure if it does not create a spark of interest in your reader and generate a desire to continue reading. To accomplish this, your introduction should start with a grabber. Think about your topic. If you were speaking to another person, how would you start the conversation so that it would interest him or her? Think about your audience: why will your reader want to read everything that you have written? If your answer is, "My reader has to mark this thing, so my reader has to read it," your mark just dropped below a "C."

Here is an introduction from an essay in a computer magazine:

> I don't like Bob. I've yet to meet him, but I've seen his picture and I know his kind. Bob's the new guy from Microsoft, an add-on operating shell that will make your computer easier to use thanks to his tightly integrated mini-applications and a cast of animated friends that Microsoft says are very friendly and extremely helpful. [From Mark Langton, Letter from the Editor. *Toronto Computes* Feb. 1995, p. 2.]

Exercise 5

In groups of four to six, examine the sample introduction from *Toronto Computes*.

1. How does the writer attract the attention of the reader?

2. How has the writer stated his subject?

3. What ideas do you expect the whole essay to cover?

4. Based upon this paragraph, do *you* like Bob? Explain your answer.

Techniques for a Grabber. There are a number of techniques you can use to capture your reader's interest.

1. **Use a quotation and/or an unusual statistic or fact.** A quotation is an easy and effective device to use—if it is used sparingly. The daily newspapers are good sources of quotations that are suitable for current topics. If the subject is more general, *Bartlett's Familiar Quotations*, which you can find in the reference section of the library, may provide material.

2. **Employ a provocative, sensational, or extreme statement or image** that you then explain; your readers' initial interest can be stimulated by a shocking statement with which they may agree or disagree strongly.

3. **Ask a probing, disturbing, or pointed question.** Ask a question that does not have an easy answer. You will be forcing your readers to think right from

your opening statement. The balance of the essay should then explore possible answers to this question.

4. **Make connections to show how your topic has important implications** beyond the specifics of your essay; if possible, bring the essay into the life of your reader. Suddenly, you will be doing more than generating 300 words on an assigned topic. You will be talking about something that has meaning to your reader.

5. **Question common wisdom or accepted ideas** regarding your topic, or provide a definition with a twist. To do this, you must begin with a clear definition of your terms and use this as the "launching pad" for your ideas; if executed successfully, this strategy intrigues readers, who want to see how you develop your unique viewpoint.

See Module 5: Description and Narration.

6. **Incorporate personal events or life experiences in the form of narratives, descriptions, or anecdotes.** Using an interesting incident or anecdote can lure the reader into the remainder of the essay. But be careful—make certain that the situation you choose to describe is appropriate for the subject and focus of what is to follow.

GETTING THE WRONG KIND OF ATTENTION

Be careful not to attract attention in cheap, obvious, or misleading ways. Your attention-getting device should lead smoothly and logically into the content of the rest of the introductory paragraph. If you get your reader's attention by telling a lurid story of sex or violence, and then introduce your subject as the proper way to mow the lawn, your reader will feel manipulated. You will end up losing the reader's trust and interest.

Exercise 6

Here are five introductory paragraphs on drug addiction. In groups of four to six, identify the type of grabber being used in each, and speculate on the purpose and the content of the essay.

1. Happy to be released after serving a three-month sentence for prostitution, Kim hurried toward the drug pusher waiting for her in the lobby of the jail. According to a prearranged plan, she gave him $25 in exchange for a few lumps of crack cocaine. Because she was desperate for a high, she left the building, walked into an alley, and smoked her stash. Unfortunately, this incident was seen by a plainclothes policewoman. Kim is just one of thousands who have wasted their lives in order to finance their own physical destruction. They, better than most people, know the horrifying results of drug dependence.

2. Every day, the newspapers and television and radio news programs are flooded with stories about the tragic results of drug addiction. Indeed, in the past year,

over 2000 people died from drug addiction in this country alone. About 200 of these victims were teenagers who were probably just satisfying their natural curiosity or were searching for a thrill—and got more than they bargained for. Their deaths are the most potent evidence in the case against experimenting with drugs.

3. "Heroin is a death trip. I really enjoyed it. But once you get the habit, you're in trouble. One good friend is in the hospital with an $80 per day habit. Another is dead from hepatitis. Two others I know died from overdoses after buying better speed than they expected. Every time you stick that needle in your arm, you're playing with your life." These statements were made by a twenty-year-old boy who, like many of his friends, tried drugs out of curiosity and soon discovered that he was experimenting with danger.

4. Should people be encouraged to try new things? Of course! But what if crack is the new thing? Why is it all right to taste new foods and to visit new places, but not to try a toot? It is precisely this dichotomy that is confusing people who have been encouraged by their parents to experience all that life has to offer. To end this confusion, society must build a convincing argument against experimenting with drugs.

5. Taxes are hurting everybody, and drug abuse is hurting individuals and society as a whole. The answer is obvious: regulate marijuana use through legalization and government control. There is a precedent for this. Following prohibition, the sale of controlled levels of alcohol came under government control through licensed retailers who collected taxes on the consumption of the beverages. The same system could apply to soft drugs.

Establishing Background in Introductions

After you have the reader's attention, your introduction must provide some kind of context for the essay to come. This may include historical or factual background, definitions, or other explanations that your reader needs in order to make sense of the essay. Once again, think about a funnel: when you pour a liquid into a funnel, it must swirl around the wider top portion before it can pass through the narrow bottom opening. Similarly, the introduction funnels your reader through necessary background to the essay's narrow focus, which is the thesis.

 ## OMITTING THE BACKGROUND

Be careful not to overlook the context component; in such a case, your introduction will consist of a grabber followed by a thesis, with no apparent connection between them. No matter how good the grabber and thesis are, without the glue provided by necessary background explanation, they will seem confusing and illogical.

✓ RHETORICAL TRIANGLE

When considering how to establish context, keep your rhetorical triangle at hand to remind you of how much background your given audience is likely to need. If you have been picturing a specific reader, continue to do so.

The Thesis Statement

The third major goal of the introduction is to establish the thesis. In its most basic form, the thesis statement has three distinct functions:

See Modules 5–11 for rhetorical modes.

1. It tells the reader what your main point is.

2. It alerts the reader to the rhetorical mode you are using.

3. It indicates the order in which your essay will present its key information or subtopics.

The grabber and background sections of the introduction lead up to and flow into the thesis statement. Usually one or two sentences in length and appearing at the end of the introductory paragraph, the thesis statement has a crucial role to play in any essay because it makes the basic argument of the essay. Without a thesis, an essay lacks the structuring principle necessary to give it shape and form. Moreover, the reader who cannot easily identify a thesis statement becomes confused and asks, "What is the point of this?"

Thus, a typical thesis statement reads something like this: "By considering the influence of demographics, information technology, and the expectations for the global economy over the next ten years, it is possible to chart a route to success in the fashion industry." From this thesis, we learn that

1. The main point of this essay is that an ideal career path in the fashion industry in the 1990s can be plotted.

See Module 11: Analysis.

2. The rhetorical mode is analysis: the career path is being broken down into its component parts.

3. The discussion will examine subtopics such as demographics, information technology, and, finally, the global economy.

This type of thesis statement creates a very clear and precise plan for the essay: it tells the reader what to expect and in what order. In fact, the thesis statement acts in *some ways as a* **contract** between you (the writer) and your reader. You promise to deliver certain ideas in a certain mode and order, and the reader, based on what you are promising, either stops or continues reading.

Thesis as contract with the reader

As a second example, the thesis in the sample television essay reproduced at the end of this module is as follows: "Television viewing undermines the viewer's physical, mental, and emotional capabilities, and is considered such a negative influence upon the behaviour of younger viewers that it has provoked government intervention."

See Module 9: The Cause and Effect Essay.

1. The main point of the essay is that television viewing has many negative effects on viewers.

2. The rhetorical mode is cause and effect.

3. The subtopics that will be discussed are television's physical, mental, and emotional effects, and government legislation to protect children from these.

MY POINT IS ...

After you read a good thesis statement, you know *exactly* what the essay is about and what its main point is. In order to test whether your own thesis is specific enough, imagine a situation in which someone throws your finished essay onto the table in front of you and says, "I can't be bothered reading it—just tell me what your point is." In the case of the television essay, your answer will be, "My point is that television viewing has such negative physical, mental, and emotional effects that it has provoked government legislation to protect our children." Your response (once you remove the words "My point is that ... ") is the thesis. Ask of your thesis, "What's the point?" If it answers the question clearly, you have a good thesis.

Exercise 7

Return to the series of introductory paragraphs on drug addiction in Exercise 6. Your group has already identified the type of grabber being used in each, and speculated on the purpose and the content of the essay.

1. Underline the thesis statement in each of the paragraphs.

2. Place brackets around the background or context material that links the grabber to the thesis.

3. Evaluate the thesis statements. Do they each clearly identify the writer's

   a. main point;

   b. rhetorical mode; and

   c. subtopics?

   Of those that do not, exactly what needs clarification? Rewrite them, solving the problems.

Thesis Statement and "Topic Announcement" Are Not the Same. Sometimes an announcement of the general topic masquerades as a thesis statement. In such a case, the reader learns the essay's general subject, but has no idea of the point being made. For example, consider carefully the following thesis:

> This essay will consider the importance of sanitation in food preparation.

This may initially seem acceptable; however, ask yourself the question, "What is this essay's main point?" What does "sanitation" refer to? Is this essay about washing pans, washing hands, washing pants, or not about washing at all? What is the "importance of sanitation"? Is it unimportant or extremely important? This thesis does indicate to the reader a general topic (sanitation), but offers no main point; it is, therefore, inadequate.

See Step 3: The Outline, p. 36.

   Most often, an inadequate thesis occurs as a direct result of not fully completing step 3: the outline. When you find yourself making a "topic announcement" instead of a thesis statement, it probably means you did not spend sufficient time figuring out exactly *what* you wanted to say before you started deciding *how* to say it. As a result, you are writing a thesis before you know what your main point is.

The Mechanical Thesis. Beware of the boring or mechanical thesis statement. It may be a topic announcement: "In this essay I will examine common misconceptions about office administrators." It may also be technically complete: "This essay will show how, despite misconceptions that they are simply typists, office administrators must demonstrate several practical skills, polished communication abilities, and human relations expertise." Key elements of a mechanical thesis are the following:

1. References to "this essay" or "my essay." Your reader knows this is an essay; this information is therefore unnecessary and uninteresting.

2. References to what "I will examine" or "I will consider." This states that you, as the writer, will examine a topic or did consider a subject; once again, this does not tell your readers anything they do not already know. The thesis is not supposed to give an account of what you did or what your process was; it is supposed to articulate your main point. Your essay has your name on it; the reader knows that you are exploring an issue here.

 ## THE WRITER OF THIS ESSAY

By referring in your thesis to "the writer of this essay," you are only disguising, not solving, the problem of the mechanical thesis. Further, it seems quite unnatural to refer to yourself as though you are someone else.

THE MECHANICAL THESIS AND THE ROUGH DRAFT

There is nothing wrong with doing a complete but mechanical thesis on your first draft. When you revise it, however, be certain to eliminate unnecessary, unhelpful, and mechanical references. When you find these mechanical phrases, simply cross them out, and revise what remains of your thesis so that it becomes a *statement* of your main point.

 ### Exercise 8

In groups of four to six, evaluate the five thesis statements that follow. Be alert for topic announcements and mechanical thesis statements.

1. In each case, write down in your own words the following:
    - the writer's main point;
    - the mode (description/narration, process, comparison/contrast, definition, classification, cause and effect, persuasion, or analysis); and
    - the subtopics.
2. Where any of these elements is not present, or where you discover mechanical phrasing, rewrite the thesis statement to correct it.
    A. In this essay, the writer will distinguish between personal and professional goals in education.
    B. Computing has caused tremendous advancement in manufacturing, business practices, and leisure activities.
    C. I will talk about the attitude of Generation X people toward the world.
    D. The process of designing and integrating heating and cooling systems leads to a human-friendly building.
    E. This essay analyzes how awful our prisons are. Should we change them?

 Establishing Your Credentials. Another aspect of convincing your reader to continue reading is establishing your credentials as a writer in the specific writing situation you have chosen. The first question your reader unconsciously asks is something like, "Why should I spend my time and energy reading this?" When you think about credentials, it is necessary to understand that these qualifications are not concerned with you personally, but with you as a writer dealing with this specific topic. Often, the act of defining the limits and scope of the essay can establish your credentials as a writer. One good strategy for this is to recognize and acknowledge the complex nature and range of what you are writing about, and then to indicate how you have purposefully cut the issue down to a manageable size (the funnel model again).

Notice how the introduction to the sample television essay (p. 64), in its grabber and background, discusses the general significance and complexity of the television viewing phenomenon before focusing on the specific issue of negative effects. It also cites a statistic about average hours of television viewing. Through such strategies, an introduction can establish that the writer understands the intricacy of the subject, has done research, and therefore has the "qualifications" to present a valid argument.

Tone. The tone you choose to employ in your essay also factors into how your reader perceives your credentials. By establishing a definite tone (for example, serious, sarcastic, light-hearted, or even-tempered) at the outset, you can influence how your reader reacts to the information you provide. The sample television essay establishes a neutral, serious tone; this is clearly not a frivolous or humorous essay. In future modules, you will be reading essays written in a wide variety of tones.

Dialogue with Your Reader. Unlike in a conversation, the audience for your essay is not there in front of you; nonetheless, you need to try to make your essay feel as though you are engaging your audience in a discussion. Your readers should feel like active participants in the thought process, not just passive recipients of ideas or information in a sermon or monologue. You need to find ways to convince readers you are not simply telling them what to do, think, or believe, but rather engaging them in a process by which your essay can assist them in deciding for themselves.

Exercise 9

In groups of four to six, exchange your essays from Exercise 4, and evaluate and discuss their strategies for establishing credentials. In each case, is it clear why the intended reader should pay attention to the author? Evaluate the tone of the essay: is it established in the introduction and maintained throughout?

Exercise 10

In Exercise 6, you examined five introductory paragraphs in your groups. Examine those introductions again.

1. Does the writer in each case establish her or his credentials? If so, in what way?

2. What is the tone of each introduction? What kind of essay do you expect as a result?

3. What strategies are used so that the writer can enter into a dialogue with the reader, rather than seem to be preaching?

Exercise 11

Return to your finished essay from Exercise 4 and evaluate its introductory paragraph.

1. How effective is your grabber, and what techniques does it use to gain the reader's attention?

2. Find the thesis statement and evaluate it. Does it do the three things a thesis statement must do?

3. Is there sufficient background information to link the grabber and thesis, and to explain clearly the topic that will be discussed?

4. Do you establish your credentials?

5. Is the tone clear and appropriate?

6. Have you entered into a dialogue with your readers, rather than started preaching? Could the sense of dialogue be improved? If so, how?

7. In light of your thoughts and the suggestions of other readers, rewrite your introduction.

Body

As the term suggests, the body of your essay is the most substantial part, both in terms of its length and also in the sense that it provides most of the information and material you are presenting. Remember, in your thesis statement you promised

The body fulfils the contract laid out in the thesis.

your reader what the essay's main point would be, what mode it would take, and what subtopics you would address. The body, therefore, must deliver on all of those commitments.

The body of the essay also needs to have

1. a clear and logical organizing principle, with clear links back to the thesis statement;

2. coherence (that is, it must move smoothly from one paragraph to the next); and

3. enough variety of paragraph and sentence development to maintain the reader's attention.

ORGANIZING PRINCIPLE

See Step 3: The Outline, p. 36.

Crafting a good introduction obviously takes significant effort; similarly, when you are completing your outline, you need to structure carefully the body of your essay. There must be a reason why you present one subtopic before another. Several organizing principles are explained here; as you will discover in Modules 5–11, different methods are more appropriate or useful, depending upon which rhetorical mode you are using.

1. **Least to most:** This is one of the most common patterns. The body of an essay on immigration might begin with the least common reason for immigration to Canada, and then present more and more common reasons, and finally the most common reason. This organizing principle lets you end your essay with your strongest point. This least to most pattern can be adapted in numerous ways to fit the particular essay you are writing.

See Module 6: Process Analysis.

See Module 5: Description and Narration.

2. **Chronological:** Here, you present information according to the time sequence in which it occurred. This method of organizing essays works especially well for rhetorical modes such as process (where you discuss a series of steps to be followed in a specific order) or narration (the story of an event, or the step-by-step explanation of "what happened"). It is also suitable for particular topics such as examining the plot in a short story or the history of the growth of a company. It is, however, somewhat limited, because the majority of rhetorical modes and individual topics do not lend themselves to chronological development.

See Module 10: Persuasion, Refutation, p. 196.

See Module 9: The Cause and Effect Essay.

3. **Logical models:** Other principles for ordering the body of your text include logically oriented ones such as cause and effect, question and answer, and argument and counterargument. In all of these, the development of the essay is propelled by the momentum of the relationship between the two aspects. For example, asking a series of questions requires you to answer those questions. While providing a series of arguments, you will likely present (and disagree with) the counterarguments offered by opponents. Listing a number of effects makes your reader assume that you will provide the causes. Similarly, in the sample essay on television at the end of the module, the root cause (television viewing habits) is discussed in the introduction, and the body of the text moves in sequence through the various types of effects: physical, mental, emotional, and behavioural.

This type of organization can be very effective when handled in a controlled and careful manner, because it taps into one of the strongest and most dominant thought processes: our logical faculties.

Exercise 12

Evaluate again your essay from Exercise 4.

1. Look at the subtopics you address in each of your body paragraphs. Is there an organizing principle (least to most, chronological, or logical) determining their order? What is it?

2. Is the organizing principle clearly established, or could it be improved by adjusting the order of any of your points?

COHERENCE

Once the organizational principle has been determined, the next requirement is that your essay be coherent. Throughout the essay, each paragraph of the body should link back to, expand on, or in some other way be linked directly to the thesis statement of the essay. This is crucial, because it guarantees the structural unity and coherence of any type or length of essay. To ascertain the relevance of a specific paragraph to the overall development of the essay, take the topic sentence of the paragraph and match it back to the element of the thesis statement to which it relates. By doing so, you can quickly and accurately determine whether the paragraph has a proper place in the essay. Checking the links between your topic sentences and the thesis statement also has another beneficial aspect: you can follow exactly how your essay is unfolding, and make sure that it is following the progression you mapped out in your outline.

For example, in the sample essay on television at the end of this module, the essay's thesis and the topic sentences are very clearly linked:

> **THESIS:** Television viewing undermines the viewer's physical, mental, and emotional capabilities, and is considered such a negative influence upon the behaviour of younger viewers that it has provoked government intervention.
>
> **Topic sentence 1.** The physical effects of excessive television watching are obvious.
>
> **Topic sentence 2.** More alarming than the physical effects are the mental defects television creates.
>
> **Topic sentence 3.** In recent years, the effects of television on the behaviour of children and young adults have become a source of extreme concern to government officials in Canada.
>
> **Topic sentence 4.** As a result, a new Canadian broadcast code was introduced in 1994 in an attempt to control the effects of violence depicted on television.

Notice also how the topic sentences often include **transitional phrases** to link the new paragraph to the previous paragraph. For instance, topic sentence 2 reminds the reader of the topic of paragraph 1 ("More alarming than the *physical effects*") while it introduces the topic of paragraph 2 ("are the *mental defects* television creates.") Note also how topic sentence 4 begins with the brief transitional phrase "As a result," which shows the reader that the new paragraph discusses the results of what was discussed in paragraph 3. It is extremely important to include phrases like this to ensure that your argument is coherent. These are like signposts to your readers, telling them how to connect your various subtopics. In each of Modules 5–93, you will gain specific practice in using transitional phrasing that is appropriate to the different rhetorical modes.

See also Appendix A, Contract #10: The Paragraph.

NO CLEAR TRANSITIONS

Without careful attempts to connect each idea to the next one, each paragraph of your essay may sound like a different miniature essay unconnected to the paragraph before or after it. This creates confusion and can spoil a perfectly good argument. This is why having a clear organizational principle is so important: when you know why you have presented your ideas in a certain order, it is far easier to create logical, helpful transitional phrasing between those ideas.

Variety is the spice of life.

Finally, follow this general rule. Vary the length of paragraphs and sentences. Vary the organizational principle of paragraphs and sentences. This helps keep the interest of your reader. Sometimes every paragraph or sentence is the same length. They are constructed in the same fashion. This is uninteresting. The reader becomes bored. This should be avoided.

Exercise 13

1. Rewrite the paragraph you just finished reading. Try to create a sense of variety in the sentence structure by combining some sentences and using transitional phrases.

2. Examine again your essay from Exercise 4. Check the relevance of each specific paragraph by taking the topic sentence of the paragraph and matching it back to the element of the thesis statement to which it relates. Does each topic sentence clearly relate to the thesis? Should you adjust the thesis or topic sentences to increase the linkages?

3. Check the connections between the various paragraphs. Have you included transitional phrases or "signposts" to show your reader the connections between your ideas?

Conclusion

The conclusion is the last paragraph of an essay. A good conclusion is one that begins with an element of summary, but most importantly, forces your reader to think beyond the essay she or he has just read. A good conclusion leaves your reader pondering the significance or implications of your argument, and the personal impact or consequences of this subject.

THE MECHANICAL SUMMARY

See Module 4: Summary Skills.

There is no doubt that the conclusion should open with some form of summary; however, the summary should never begin with phrases like "As you have just read," "I have just shown," or "As I mentioned earlier." This is mechanical, clumsy, and boring writing—the readers know they have just read your essay. Like the mechanical thesis statement, such phrasing adds nothing to the readers' understanding or appreciation of the essay (in fact, it may be seen as insulting in its repetitiveness). Beware also of substituting for the summary a word-for-word repetition of the thesis statement from the introduction; this does nothing to encourage readers to reflect on or think further about the issues dealt with in your essay. Any kind of summary that you produce for the conclusion of the essay needs to be written in substantially different words, or from a new angle or perspective gained in the essay.

THE FINAL THOUGHT

Summary

Final Thought

Even the most effectively written summation, however, falls short of the mark if it is not combined with a way of pushing readers beyond the confines of the information and perspective you have just provided for them. You can think of the conclusion as the introduction-funnel in reverse, if you like. The summary (the narrow end) reminds the reader of what has been established in the essay, while the remainder of the conclusion (the wider end) opens up the broader implications of the topic.

A second way to imagine this is as follows. Think of a poor essay as a fully closed circle, where the conclusion simply brings your reader right back to where he or she started. The essay announces in the thesis that it will prove a certain point, and then ends with a summary showing how it has proven the point. The reader will likely say "So what?" and forget the essay because the writer has left nothing further for the reader to ponder. This essay is like a ball that the reader simply throws away.

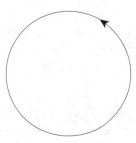

By contrast, a good essay is a circle with a tail heading off beyond the starting point of the essay. This essay's conclusion begins with a summary, but the tail, pointing at the world outside the essay, represents the reflections, ideas, and opinions the essay is leaving for the reader to consider. Your conclusion provokes such thought by leaving the reader with something bigger to think about. This essay ends with a "hook" that sticks in the reader's mind; he or she is not able to easily forget it.

Numerous techniques exist for accomplishing this, and often you can decide on the most effective method only in the context of your particular essay. Nonetheless, here are some methods for writing more thought-provoking conclusions:

1. End your essay with a question or series of questions.
2. Point to the broader implications and relevance of your topic beyond the essay's narrow focus.
3. Encourage your reader to take a particular action or to question a particular belief.
4. Examine possible future consequences or problems that may arise if this topic is not dealt with in a serious and timely manner.
5. Include a particularly startling fact, statistic, image, or quotation that you do not analyze, but leave for your reader to consider.

LIKE GRABBER, LIKE FINAL THOUGHT

Most of the techniques used for the grabber are equally applicable when you are thinking of a final thought. Think of the introduction and conclusion as inverted versions of the same basic funnel structure. ⊠

By doing any or all of these things, you will make your readers put down your essay not with a sense of smugness or relief ("Thank goodness that's over; it's time for dinner!"), but with the unavoidable feeling that they must give some serious consideration to the topic you have examined in your essay. This is certainly not an exhaustive list, but it does provide an idea of the methods a writer needs to use to capture the reader's attention.

Exercise 14

Here are five conclusion paragraphs for an essay on the topic of television. In groups of four to six, examine them carefully.

1. Underline the summary component, and write down a sentence explaining what you feel the essay's main point and subtopics were.

2. Identify the type of "final thought" being used in each, and evaluate its effectiveness. Would it leave you with something to think about? Why or why not?

A. By bringing entertainment and information into our homes in a massive and instantaneous manner, television has been a welcome influence on all of our lives. Back in 1948, the highly respected but suspicious American educator Mary Somerville proclaimed that "Television won't last. It's a flash in the pan." Thankfully, she herself was the "flash in the pan."

B. Television seeks to separate you from your money; kills you physically, mentally, and emotionally; and abuses your children's perceptions of reality. Think about it: a con man, contract killer, and child abuser are right now living in your house. Wait—do not rush home, and do not call the police. You know they are there; in fact, you have known about them for a long time. You invited them—you even pay for them to stay there each month. They live inside your television.

C. The next time your children get into trouble in the playground or the classroom, consider this question: who is the most responsible for taking care of our children and young people and shaping their attitudes about life? Is it we ourselves, who juggle the demands of work, school, parenting, and socializing? Is it our relatives, who step in to help us when we have no more time to give? Is it our loyal and helpful babysitters? Or is it the television set, which, after a hard day at work, we silently thank for keeping our children quiet for a couple of hours?

D. The effects of television and the process whereby it alters our perceptions deserve careful consideration. Over the last thirty years, television has become the single most important source of information and entertainment in North America. It is truly frightening—so significant and so essential has television become that reaching for the remote control has become as automatic a reflex as breathing, eating, or sleeping.

E. Ultimately, we are so accustomed to watching television—where no matter what horrors occur, they never have any effect on us in our cozy living rooms—that it has warped our perception of reality in ways we do not even realize. This was brought home to me best a couple of years ago when I was watching a program called *I Witness Video*, which aired amateur videotapes of (among other things) natural disasters. The program showed a video of a hurricane-swelled ocean coast taped by someone standing on a dike and filming with a camcorder. The waves became increasingly turbulent, when suddenly the person filming was swept off the dike by one of the waves. "What an idiot!" I thought; then I asked myself, "What could possess a person to keep filming despite such obvious peril?" My answer? Viewing the world through the lens of a camcorder, like viewing the world through a television screen, gave this person a sense of invulnerability and cut him off from reality. There is an important lesson here: we had all better snap out of our television-induced coma before life sweeps us into oblivion.

Exercise 15

The following essay is the final draft of the student essay whose development you have been watching since the start of Module 1. Read this carefully and actively, noting any elements of the essay structure or ideas that you find particularly interesting, effective, correct, or incorrect. You will be discussing this essay with your group.

Sample Essay

TELEVISION: STATE CONTROL OR SELF-CONTROL?

Over the last thirty years, television has become the single most important source of information and entertainment in North America. At the end of a hard day at work or school, a typical North American might head home to prepare a quick dinner, put up the feet, and reach for the remote control. In fact, the typical North American adult spends almost four hours per day in front of the television: this represents almost one-sixth of his or her life, and almost one-quarter of his or her waking life. Naturally, this has significant consequences. Television viewing undermines the viewer's physical, mental, and emotional capabilities, and is considered such a negative influence upon the behaviour of younger viewers that it has provoked government intervention. (1)

The physical effects of excessive television-watching are obvious. For instance, the sedentary lifestyle associated with television-watching is responsible for poor eating habits. Stereotypical "couch potatoes" fill their couches (and bellies) with potato chips or other fat-filled, nutrition-neglecting snack foods. A lack of physical fitness is the obvious result when viewers who sit at work or school during the day sit stupefied by the "idiot box" at night. It is no wonder, then, that viewers, their hands in the bag of chips, cheeks filled like those of a squirrel before hibernation, bodies sagging toward shapelessness, are mesmerized when "certified trainer" Tony Little's advertisements promise to "lock you in" and slim you down with his Ab-Isolator exercise gadget. Television has largely created the problem of the out-of-shape viewer; now here comes television claiming it will also solve the problem. In truth, buying Tony's Ab-Isolator reveals only that someone is "locked in" to the prison of television dependency. (2)

More alarming than the physical effects are the mental defects television creates. Researchers argue that watching television is like taking narcotic drugs: the viewer enters a kind of trance in which brain-wave activity is measurably reduced. In this trance, willpower is sapped: the viewer experiences a numbing, mindless pleasure. Think of *The Simpsons'* Homer Simpson, belly jiggling, beer in hand, drooling out of the corner of his mouth, literally stuck to his couch, eyes permanently vacant, glazed and glued to his TV. Further, whether we are watching the news, a sporting event, a comedy, or a drama, television presents us with moving images that give us the impression of "being there." As a result, many people do not think about what they are watching, and even mistake television for reality. Reading a book, by contrast, encourages mental activity by presenting us with words and ideas that we must interpret and imagine for ourselves. (3)

In recent years, the effects of television on the behaviour of children and young adults have become a source of extreme concern to government officials in Canada. They feel we have become desensitized to violence: we are so used to watching murders, rapes, and assaults on television that we accept these as normal events. Research supplements such contentions by showing that continued exposure to TV violence can make children act in a more aggressive, antisocial, or even cruel fashion, and can negatively affect responsibilities such as their schoolwork. (4)

As a result, a new Canadian broadcast code was introduced in 1994 in an attempt to control the effects of violence depicted on television. Gratuitous violence—that is, actions seeming simply to glamorize violence—was banned. Violent scenes suitable for adults can now be shown only after 9 p.m. Programs depicting any kind of violence against minorities and women are now very carefully evaluated before being shown. Finally, particular attention is being paid to programming for children. For instance, violence as a way of solving problems is theoretically no longer allowed in children's television. As a result, Canadian children can no longer see the kick-boxing, colourfully costumed, always violent *Mighty Morphin Power Rangers*. In addition, when violence is shown, the negative consequences and results are also supposed to be shown. In other words, when guns are fired, people are supposed to be seen getting hurt, because this is what happens in the "real world." (5)

Many have praised this legislation as a good idea that is long overdue. Others argue that people need to take responsibility for their own television viewing habits and those of their children. The real problem, they feel, is that many parents use television as a babysitter: as long as the TV keeps the kids quiet, parents are indifferent to what their children are watching. The same critics claim that even the most violent program could be an educational experience if parents monitored their children's viewing habits and watched and discussed the programs with them. (6)

Simply eliminating or toning down obvious physical violence betrays the same kind of weak thinking one might expect of the physically and mentally unfit couch potato. Physical violence—bloody gun battles, rapes, and murders—has in the wake of public concern simply disguised itself: now we have major medical dramas on American and Canadian television titillating us with the "violence" of major intrusive surgeries. Injuries occur, blood spurts, bones break—and in response scalpels slash, more blood spurts, doctors and nurses hack and sew—and we experience the same vicarious titillation. The cop shows have also relocated the violence—*NYPD Blue* presents us, like the detectives, with near-nude, bloody corpses after a crime—and then the events leading to the crime are graphically described. Courtroom dramas work the same way, presenting us with legal machinations after graphically described rapes or murders. In both cases, our brains are now enlisted to visualize the violence. The O.J. Simpson trial tantalized audiences with televised verbal violence in exactly the same way. (7)

Finally, the soap operas have relocated the violence to an emotional level: witness *Melrose Place,* where dim-witted protagonists climb indiscriminately into bed with one another without any lasting emotional, spiritual, or physical consequences. This is a world of rampant sex with no real worries over sexually transmitted disease, no low self-esteem, and no broken heart for longer than twenty minutes. Like mathematicians at work on a supercomputer, the writers seem bent on running through every single bedroom permutation and combination of the major male and female characters. Despite this, the government is apparently unconcerned about the emotional violence of such a distorted world view, although it is available at 8:00 p.m. once a week to those children who want it. (8)

It can be argued that television is destroying our physical, mental, and even emotional fitness, and providing dangerous role models and problem-solving strategies for our impressionable children. Undoubtedly, in numerous instances, some or even all of these effects can be clearly documented. But are these effects not all the result of our own decision to watch—or in the cases of our children, our decision to let them watch? Are we so incapable of self-control that we need television producers and the government to make these decisions for us? (9)

Like any other "narcotic" and mind-altering substance, television in excess can have these and other very serious consequences. Also like use of these substances, television viewing requires moderation, selectivity, self-control, and, in the case of children, parental involvement. Ultimately, only you can press the "off" button on the remote control and peel yourself off the couch. (10)

Hey, couch potato—it's time to uproot yourself. (11)

THE GENERAL CHECKLIST

Whenever you finish writing an essay, answer the series of questions on the inside covers of this book as a final check before you submit your essay to your instructor or share it with your collaborative group. While referring to your essay as needed, think carefully about your answer to each question. This way, you can clearly determine any areas needing further attention. At first this will be a slow process; over time, however, you will become familiar with the checklist and adept at using it to identify and correct potential shortcomings in your writing.

Exercise 16

In groups of four to six, pretend that you are the writers of "Television: State Control or Self-Control?" and, in writing, answer each of the revising/editing questions on the inside front and back cover of this book. Based on your answers, what is your evaluation of this essay? What improvements might you suggest?

SUMMARY

You may now sit back and enjoy your essay with the same satisfaction that a television executive feels upon watching the first episode of a new program that has been overseen from its earliest planning stages. You know the basic programming decisions needed to create an essay: *the rhetorical triangle, content generation, outlining, drafting, revising,* and *editing.* You also know all of the basic ingredients of an essay's *introduction, body,* and *conclusion,* and how they fit together. Of course, different kinds of essays, like different kinds of television programs, require certain modifications to this basic process and structure. In Modules 5–12, you will learn the purpose, structure, and process modifications appropriate for these different types of essays.

Summary Skills

LEARNING OUTCOMES

By completing a series of oral and written exercises and writing a summary using the six-step method, students will

1. *distinguish when summary writing is appropriate;*
2. *use note-taking to uncover main ideas and reduce an essay to its original outline;*
3. *correctly paraphrase an author's ideas, rather than reiterate an author's words;*
4. *synthesize an author's main ideas and implicit themes.*

OVERVIEW

Emerging from an important meeting, you bump into Josef, a co-worker. He is out of breath, and explains that he had car trouble on the way to work. "So what did I miss at the meeting?" he asks. Later that day, your boss, Theresa, calls you into her office. Worried about a major deadline, she says, "Look, I can tell that you did a really thorough report on the new software package, but I really don't have time to read it all now. Tell me what I need to know so I can make my decision."

Josef and Theresa are each asking you for a **summary**. Josef wants you to provide a rapid overview of the key issues raised and decisions made at the meeting. Theresa wants to know the recommendations made in your report, and the most important reasons for these particular suggestions. Neither of them wants you to recount every detail; instead, each relies on you to select and recount only the most relevant ideas.

Summary skills are thus a part of daily life. You might summarize the plot of a movie or the key points of a lecture for a friend. When you read the sports section of the newspaper, the articles and box scores present game summaries. Almost every significant report you write on the job will begin with a summary; this way, a busy reader like Theresa can get an overview of the main information, and then read only those sections that she needs in order to verify information in the summary. At the end of every module in this book is a summary. After first reading the module in full, you can read the summary to remind yourself of the main ideas and to determine which specific sections you should read again.

PURPOSE AND FUNCTION

The *Gage Canadian Dictionary* defines the word *summary* as follows:

> *n.* a brief statement giving the main points: *The history book had a summary at the end of each chapter.*

When you write a summary of a piece of writing, you try to provide only "the main points." The sheer quantity of information you are presented with in all your classes and textbooks (and later in journals and reports at work) makes it absolutely essential that you be able to reduce information to its **gist**—that is, to its most important components.

Gist is the substance, the core, the key points.

When you write a summary, you are distilling the most crucial information. Because your reader may read your summary *instead of* reading the entire original report or essay, it is extremely important that your summary be faithful—that is, it must preserve the proportions and emphasis of the original; you cannot add anything or stress anything that is not emphasized in the original. You are like a reporter: you must be as **objective** and unbiased as possible. Similarly, you must remember that your goal is to compress the text: you must communicate the broad ideas, not the intricacies and minor details. The reader who wants all of those details will read the original.

Thus, in a trip report, you might summarize for your co-workers a number of presentations on new technology at a convention. After advice from a lawyer, a restaurant owner might write a memo reminding employees of hospitality laws about serving liquor. The finance student might summarize relevant, recent tax law changes for a client. In order to provide support for the paroled inmate or for other corrections staff, the correctional worker might research and write a summary of available community resources.

Exercise 1

Without again examining the previous three modules, summarize the six-step process of essay writing in two paragraphs: one on "What to Say," the other on "How to Say It." This is a good test of whether you have understood and absorbed the ideas. Remember: every single detail is not important; the question is, can you summarize the main principles for someone who has not read the first three modules?

Exercise 2

1. In groups of four to six, try to find a movie you have all seen, a book you have all read (even for a course), or a subject you have all taken.

2. Once you have arrived at your common topic, spend five minutes each (no discussion) writing a one-paragraph summary.

3. Compare your summaries in terms of length, details, and focus. What is the most important idea emphasized in each? What differences do you notice?

4. Which summary is right, or which is better? How do you know?

SUMMARY SKILLS

Summary skills depend upon three related skills: **reading and note-taking, paraphrasing,** and **synthesis** of what you read.

Reading and Note-Taking

Note-taking is certainly not a new skill to you, but it is important to see this skill in a new way, as the foundation of the larger skill of summary writing. Office administrators learn fast transcription methods such as shorthand so they can write down virtually every detail of what someone is saying. As a student, you probably do not know shorthand, which means you cannot write down everything that the instructor says. In any case, whether in class or at the library, this is not your purpose in note-taking. Instead, note-taking is an exercise in **critical thinking:** you carefully look for the main ideas, and you leave out the smaller details, facts, and less important examples.

THE SIX-STEP PROCESS IN REVERSE

See Step 6: Editing, p. 47.

See Step 3: The Outline, p. 36.

In Module 3, you learned how to fit the parts of an essay together. Good note-taking and summary writing essentially involve taking the essay apart. In a sense, you work through the six-step process in reverse. You start with the finished product—the **edited, revised essay.** When you take point-form notes from it, you are in a sense returning the essay to the **outline** of the main ideas. You need to strip out all of the details of *how* the writer says it: all you are concerned with is getting down to the core of *what* the writer says. This means you must not be distracted by the sentence structure, the interesting images, or the fully developed examples; you must remain focused on the key ideas.

THE WRITER'S RHETORICAL TRIANGLE

See Step 1: Imaging the Essay, p. 17.

When you take notes on something you have read, whether to write a summary or not, you should be able to imagine the very first step that the writer took. This means that you should be able to draw the rhetorical triangle used by the writer. The best way to ensure you produce an accurate summary is by briefly imaging the essay as the original writer likely did. This means clearly identifying

1. what the writer's specific topic is;

2. who the writer's intended audience is;

3. what the writer's point of view and specific purpose are.

When you are reading something, you evaluate these issues without thinking; writing out the rhetorical triangle after reading simply provides you with a visible guideline for organizing your summary. This will help you to distinguish carefully between main ideas and the less relevant ones. This way, your note-taking, and ultimately your summary, will be motivated by a clear purpose—the purpose of the original author.

But what if your purpose for reading is intentionally different from the author's purpose for writing? You still need a clear picture of why the author wrote, but now you want to interpret this in the light of your own purpose. You should consider creating a second rhetorical triangle in which you specify *your own purpose* and the relationship of the author's rhetorical triangle to your purpose. For example, when you are creating a research essay, you will know your own purpose and will be reading and summarizing external sources in order to fit your purpose.

See Module 12: The Research Essay.

CUES AS TO WHAT IS IMPORTANT

When you listen in class, you have the help of the instructors' verbal and nonverbal cues: through emphasis or repetition, the instructors may draw your attention to their most important points. Similarly, when you read an essay or article, a variety of cues will help you determine what is important.

Title

The title is often a miniature summary of its own. It often distils the main point or, at least, suggests a focused topic. Think about the title before you read an article. If you do not understand it before you read, consider it when you have finished the essay; now, do you understand?

Exercise 3

The essay at the end of Module 3 is called "Television: State Control or Self-Control?" What is the significance of the title? How does it relate to the writer's main point?

Subtitles

Often an essay will have a longer, more descriptive subtitle or caption. This can offer significant insight into the essay's particular focus. Similarly, a longer essay may be divided into numerous smaller sections, each with a descriptive subtitle. For instance, as part of Module 11: Analysis, you will read the first section of an essay by Ruth Morris called "A Practical Path to Transformative Justice." If you strip out all of the text from this article, the following subtitle headings remain:

INTRODUCTION
1. Why should we change our justice system?
   A. expensive
   B. unjust
   C. immoral
   D. failure

Exercise 4

Examine carefully the title and subtitles of Ruth Morris's essay. Knowing that you have not read the article, discuss your expectations of the essay and anticipate what her rhetorical triangle might look like.

Thesis

As you know from Modules 2 and 3, an essay must have a thesis statement that articulates its main argument. If you can identify the thesis statement, you can correctly identify the author's main point. Often, the thesis will appear at the end of the introduction (for instance, in the sample essay, "Television: State Control or Self-Control?"). But the more experienced the writer, the less likely that the thesis will always appear at the end of the first paragraph. When you read, you should always be looking for the thesis, which, once identified, you should underline and note.

Topic Sentences

See Appendix A, Contract #10: The Paragraph.

Every paragraph, by definition, contains a topic sentence that sums up the contents of the paragraph. Topic sentences will be directly related to the thesis, as well as to previous paragraphs. Scanning these before reading can help to highlight the general subtopics and, thus, reveal a skeleton outline.

Introductions and Conclusions

See Module 3, Conclusion, p. 60.

As you know, the introduction generally provides background material, an overview of the topic, and a thesis. The conclusion generally summarizes the article and suggests the subject's wider implications. Scrutinizing these together can yield a clear sense of what the writer views as important.

READ THE WHOLE ARTICLE

If you are going to write a summary, do not pay attention only to the title, subtitles, thesis, and topic sentences *instead of* reading the article. Experienced writers do not rigidly follow the standard "recipe" of essay organization; you therefore cannot count on everything you need being so readily available. If you do depend on this, you may end up missing the point of the article entirely. These are not tricks to save you the trouble of reading the whole essay; these are ways to help you make good decisions about what you read.

WHAT TO LEAVE OUT

Along with the cues to what is important, you are also looking carefully for what is less important or unimportant; you will not be concerned with this material.

Following is the introductory paragraph of the sample essay at the end of Module 3, plus some sample note-taking done by a reader of the essay. Some of these notes represent the thoughts of the reader when first reading this paragraph. Others represent a **synthesis** of what the reader understands of the overall essay. Notice the radical reduction of the text taking place here. Specific examples and details are not commented on; instead, the main ideas are extracted.

people's needs: information, recreation, relaxation

time-consuming

"Thesis: negative effects provoking legislation."

> Over the last thirty years, television has become the single most important source of information and entertainment in North America. At the end of a hard day at work or school, a typical North American might head home to prepare a quick dinner, put up the feet, and reach for the remote control. In fact, the typical North American adult spends almost four hours per day in front of the television: this represents almost one-sixth of his or her life, and almost one-quarter of his or her waking life. Naturally, this has significant consequences. <u>Television viewing undermines the viewer's physical, mental, and emotional capabilities, and is considered such a negative influence upon the behaviour of younger viewers that it has provoked government intervention.</u>

Exercise 5

Read very carefully the following paragraph (paragraph 2 from the sample essay at the end of Module 3). Use your note-taking skills.

1. Underline the topic sentence.

2. Underline the important or key words.

3. In the margin, "translate" important ideas into your own language.

4. Are there any detailed examples or lists that you can condense radically to a main idea of a few words, or eliminate?

5. Having read the entire essay, draw up the writer's rhetorical triangle.

> The physical effects of excessive television-watching are obvious. For instance, the sedentary lifestyle associated with television-watching is responsible for poor eating habits. Stereotypical "couch potatoes" fill their couches (and bellies) with potato chips or other fat-filled, nutrition-neglecting snack foods. A lack of physical fitness is the obvious result when viewers who sit at work or school during the day sit stupefied by the "idiot box" at night. It is no wonder, then, that viewers, their hands in the bag of chips, cheeks filled like those of a squirrel before hibernation, bodies sagging toward shapelessness, are mesmerized when "certified trainer" Tony Little's advertisements promise to "lock you in" and slim you down with his Ab-Isolator exercise gadget. Television has largely created the problem of the out-of-shape viewer; now here comes television claiming it will also solve the problem. In truth, buying Tony's Ab-Isolator reveals only that someone is "locked in" to the prison of television dependency.

Paraphrasing

Once you have used your marginal point-form notes and created your stripped-down outline, you need to do something with them. This is where paraphrasing comes in. The *Gage Canadian Dictionary* defines *paraphrase* in the following manner:

v. state the meaning of (a passage) in other and different words.

For your notes to be genuinely useful, they should represent a "translation" of the writer's ideas into your own "different words." Once you have identified the key points and ideas, paraphrasing them is the best way to demonstrate that you have understood and have firm control of the writer's ideas, some of which are clearly stated and some of which may not be fully stated.

PARAPHRASING IDEAS

See Module 12, Plagiarism, p. 248.

Paraphrasing has its potential problems. First, it is very important not to be guilty of **plagiarism** by stealing phrases from the original: if you use phrases or ideas from your original source without acknowledging these through quotation marks and clear citations, you are guilty of plagiarism, or the theft of ideas. At the very least, the normal consequence of this is a zero on an assignment.

Synonym: a word having the same or nearly the same meaning.

Similarly, paraphrasing does not mean using the **thesaurus approach**, in which you look up each word in the thesaurus and replace it with a synonym. Instead, it is important to read attentively and to synthesize, using your own words, the main ideas that the author states or implies.

An easy way to think of it is like this. When you are having a conversation with someone else, paraphrasing is often a valuable tool. Perhaps someone makes a statement that does not clearly express a thought or emotion; as a result, you seek clarification. You essentially restate what you have heard, and if you do this successfully, you often "read between the lines" and uncover an unstated thought. For instance, imagine your friend Hanh saying to you

Come on! You've *got* to get your part of the class project in on time, or it looks bad for the whole group!

Now imagine yourself responding with one of the following three responses:

1. "So you're saying I've got to get my part of the class project in on time, or it looks bad for the whole group?"
2. "So I must complete my portion of our class assignment, or it will appear poorly for our band?"
3. "Sounds like you're stressed out and you're really worried I'll get the whole group in trouble if I can't get my work done. Is that it?"

The first response is the equivalent of plagiarism. By using the exact same words, you are not demonstrating that you have understood what Hanh is saying. Instead, it sounds like you are making fun of Hanh by repeating her words; if you are lucky, all she will do is give you a dirty look. An author from whom you stole written ideas or phrases would be considerably more irritated. If you are caught plagiarizing by your school, severe penalties can be expected, including failure or even expulsion.

The second response has used the thesaurus approach by translating what Hanh has said word-for-word into other "equivalent" terms. This sounds extremely mechanical and awkward and, inevitably, some of the equivalents do not quite work (for instance, *band*). Again, it sounds like you may be making fun of Hanh. You may have understood what her individual words mean, but you have certainly given no evidence that you have understood her overall meaning.

The third response has tried to synthesize what Hanh has said and what she has implied. Hanh never came out and said, "I am feeling a lot of stress, and I am anxious because of this," but the good listener, like the good reader, focuses on the key ideas and the unspoken thoughts or emotions. This is the most useful kind of paraphrasing; it demonstrates clearly your attempt to understand not just her words, but her overall meaning.

Exercise 6

Create paraphrasing responses designed to clarify what the speaker means. Try to "read between the lines" to disentangle the main idea and any unspoken emotions or thoughts. Like the third response in the list, start with the phrase "It sounds like ..." and then try to state the unspoken feeling or thought.

1. "Kim needs my help at home with the kids, but I'm so busy between my work and my physiotherapy after my back operation that I can hardly catch my breath."

2. "It's ridiculous! I can't take it anymore! Every time I go out to a movie or dinner with Sandy, we run into someone Sandy used to date!"

3. "The assistant manager keeps making jokes about how we should have an affair. I don't know what to do. He knows I'm married, but sometimes I think he's serious."

4. "When will you learn how to use a dictionary? You make the exact same spelling errors on every essay! Why should I correct them for you week after week?"

MASTER THE IDEAS; DO NOT BE A SLAVE TO THE WORDS

When you paraphrase written statements, the same concepts apply. You must not plagiarize—for obvious reasons. If you use the thesaurus approach of word-for-word translation, you will end up with awkward or incorrect phrasing; hence, this is not acceptable either. To paraphrase a writer's written thoughts successfully requires that, as in the conversational examples, you work with ideas rather than words.

Read attentively. Write your notes carefully beside the original text or in a separate notebook. This is returning the full essay to step 3: the outline. Write out a rhetorical triangle. After reading the text, close the book and write down the gist of what you remember. This way, you are not focused on imitating a series of words in the exact order in which they appear in the original text. You are focused upon producing, in your own idiom, an idea that you have mastered.

Idiom: your own particular phrase or expression for an idea.

☀ INTERESTING DETAILS VS. IMPORTANT IDEAS

What you remember is not always important. Sometimes you will remember interesting details rather than main ideas. Think about a famous movie like *ET*. Do you remember the plot, or do you remember pictures of the flying bicycle in front of the full moon? You need to differentiate what is truly important from what is simply interesting.

HIGHLIGHTER HINTS

If you use a highlighter in your note-taking, remember to review your highlighting and note-taking once you have finished reading an essay. If you notice a much greater amount of highlighting on certain pages, there are two possibilities. Either this is an unusually important portion of the text (which is possible), or you have not understood this section and therefore have highlighted too much.

This is exactly what you do when you tell a joke. You do not remember the exact wording of the joke; you remember the key idea and the punch line. You know "the point," but when you tell the joke each time, you will inevitably take a different route to get there.

☀ PLAGIARISM OF IDEAS

See Module 12: The Research Essay.

Paraphrasing with an element of summary is a crucial skill for a research essay, but you must remember that issues of plagiarism revolve around ownership of ideas as well as of words. If you take a key phrase or sentence or paragraph and do not acknowledge it, that is plagiarism. If you summarize and paraphrase this phrase or sentence or idea, and use the paraphrase without clearly acknowledging its source in the text, this is still plagiarism. Summary and paraphrasing skills are meant to help you synthesize materials, not to help you steal them!

Synthesis: What the Writer Said

The skilled summary writer processes and collapses text until only important ideas remain. This happens through a combination of simultaneous actions. When you are reading, note-taking, and paraphrasing, you pursue the following strategies, more or less simultaneously.

Proposition: statement affirming or denying something. See Module 10, Primary Proposition, p. 192.

1. Focus on main ideas or **propositions**, both from organizational cues and from the content of the essay.

2. Delete unimportant or trivial ideas. Leave out most specific facts and examples. With a particularly detailed example, strip out the details and reduce it to the main reason why it was mentioned.

3. Collapse lists into single general propositions; exclude specific examples in order to focus on the general truth they illustrate.

4. Invent more general propositions where they are not explicit. Think about the paraphrasing exercise in which the key thought or emotion was not explicitly stated; if necessary, a good summary similarly will synthesize information in the text to expand upon unspoken ideas.

Exercise 7

In groups of three, do the following exercise. One person will be the storyteller, one person will be the listener and note-taker, and the third person, who will also listen, will be the timekeeper.

1. Find a fairy tale or myth (for example, "Little Red Riding Hood" or "Beauty and the Beast") that all three group members know. Note: do not choose a nursery rhyme or other poem that can be recited.

2. Once the story has been agreed upon, the storyteller has thirty seconds to prepare to tell the story.

3. After this preparation, the storyteller will tell the complete story in no more than one minute.

4. While the storyteller speaks, the listener carefully takes notes. What did the speaker include? What did the speaker decide not to include in the summary version of the story? The timekeeper makes note of when time has elapsed, and encourages the storyteller to wrap it up.

5. Beginning with the listener, discuss and classify the excluded material into the following categories:

   a. material that should have been left in: why should it have been there?

   b. material that the person was right to leave out: why was it right to leave it out?

   c. any general rules about what to leave in and what to exclude from a story summary.

6. Now discuss the theme, or "point," of the story; that is, do *not* discuss what happened, or the plot. Discuss what the story meant or what the point was. As an example, think of the fairy tale *Beauty and the Beast*. To put it loosely, the point of this story is a lesson like "Beauty is more than skin deep," or "You cannot judge a book by its cover."

Plot: sequence of interrelated events that make up a story.

7. Re-evaluate the material that you left out and/or included in light of your sense of the theme.

CATEGORIES OF SUMMARY

As discussed, the first things to be disposed of in a good summary are the specific words and sentence structure used by the writer. The poorer the summary is and the less mastery you have of the material, the closer you will stay to the original wording and sentence structure. Generally, when you write a summary there are four possible outcomes based upon how well you have mastered the ideas of the text.

Misrepresentation

At this level, you have identified incorrectly what is important. You may be omitting key information, overemphasizing something that you found personally interesting, or simply inaccurately representing what is in the essay. This is the worst kind of summary because it misleads the reader, who is depending on your accuracy. This gets you an "F" on an assignment, and might get you fired from your job.

Word/Sentence Level Accuracy

At this level, you understand only the words you are reading. You are not understanding the way the words and sentences fit together; therefore, you are not distinguishing irrelevant from relevant details. Not having determined the clear focus of the passage, you may be omitting crucial elements. You may include important details, but you are not necessarily emphasizing them as important. There is a reasonable possibility that you are plagiarizing important phrases; if you are not plagiarizing, you are likely using the thesaurus method to translate literally and awkwardly. This gets you an "F," or, at best, a "D" on an assignment, and provokes complaints from co-workers such as "This is too long; can't you cut it down?" and "Exactly what's important here?"

Paragraph Level Accuracy

At this level, your summary correctly identifies the main ideas. There is probably no integration of ideas from different paragraphs in the original: the structure and order of the summary is based almost exclusively on the order of main ideas in passage. If you do this well, this gets you a "B" on the assignment and some compliments from co-workers for a "solid job" of explaining the text.

Theme Level Accuracy

At this level, you have truly mastered what you have read. Your summary not only correctly identifies the main ideas of the essay, but generalizes beyond the basic information presented in the text to articulate the passage's implied themes. You blend these together in a structure that is not simply an echo of the text's structure. There may be no overlap between the words used in the original text and the words used in your summary. This gets you an "A" on the assignment and high praise from your fellow employees, who admire how succinct you are and make comments like "This is crystal-clear; I understand completely."

 ### Exercise 8

Following are five summaries of the paragraph for which you made notes in Exercise 5. Read the five summaries carefully.

1. Which ones are best? Which ones are worst? Why?

2. Decide in which of the four categories of summary each of these five summaries belongs. Provide at least three very specific reasons for choosing that category. Assign a grade based on the category.

3. If you were doing a summary of the whole essay from which the paragraph is taken, which summary would be the most appropriate to use as part of it? Why?

   A. There are important physical effects of excessive television watching. For example, television-watchers are used to sitting and eating poorly. Couch potatoes eat potato chips, or other fat-filled snack foods. People lack physical fitness who sit at work and come home to sit watching television. They are mesmerized by advertisements like Tony Little's Ab-Isolator, which promises to slim them down. Television started the problem, and now it claims it will solve the problem. If you buy the Ab-Isolator, it just shows you are in the prison of television dependency.

   B. Unlike people who are fit and eat healthily, people who do not eat nutritious food are susceptible to television's seductive lure. If you eat a lot of potato chips, spend a lot of time sitting at work, and do not exercise, you will fall victim to television.

   C. Television viewing creates a vicious circle of lack of exercise and poor nutrition in the addicted viewer.

   D. Tony Little's "Ab Isolator" is the best solution for a very common problem: a lack of fitness caused by people watching too much television and not eating well. Tony will "lock you in" on your target of fitness, and help you shape up while you watch television.

   E. Watching too much television has a significant health impact. "Couch potatoes" tend to eat fatty snack foods and compound this problem through lots of sitting and little exercise. Ironically, they are as a result particularly susceptible to advertisements for products that will supposedly help them shape up.

OCCASIONS FOR SUMMARY WRITING

When faced with a writing task, you need to be able to identify occasions when a summary is appropriate to your purpose.

If you are asked to produce a summary of a piece of writing, your task is obvious. But you will not always be so clearly told to write a summary. Other occasions for summary writing are as follows:

See Module 3, Conclusion, p. 60.

1. In every essay, you must begin your conclusion with a summary.

2. Any business report will start with a summary, or **executive summary**; this is the first (and sometimes only) thing a reader reads and the last thing the writer writes.

3. If you are asked to produce an **annotated bibliography**, you are being asked to produce an alphabetical listing of a series of works with a **capsule summary** of each work's main point and approach to the subject.

4. If you are asked for a **synopsis** or **plot synopsis**, this is in general a summary of a literary story (fiction or drama).

5. An **abstract**, or **précis**, is a summary of a written document.

6. If you are asked to provide an **overview**, **the big picture**, or **briefing statements**, you are being asked to distil key information in summary form.

7. If you are asked to **condense** large readings for your studies or for a research paper, you are being asked to summarize.

8. Finally, if you are asked to take the **minutes of a meeting**, you are being asked to produce a point-form summary of the important issues raised and discussed, and their outcomes.

Exercise 9

Fill in the Top Ten List that follows with situations in your field where the summary technique might usefully be employed in a writing task. Use the cue words listed above to describe these topics. For instance, the radio or television broadcasting student examining the CBC's charter might select the following topic:

1. Overview of the CBC mandate

Fill in as many as you can, and then continue reading the module. As other possible applications occur to you, return to this list and finish it.

TOP TEN APPLICATIONS FOR SUMMARY WRITING IN MY FIELD

1.
2.
3.
4.
5.
6.
7.
8.
9.
10.

APPLYING THE SIX-STEP METHOD TO SUMMARY WRITING

 PRELIMINARY STEPS

Unlike other kinds of writing, you must have read carefully and *completely* the piece you are summarizing before you can even begin this process.

Step 1: Imaging the Essay with the Rhetorical Triangle

 Draw up your rhetorical triangle as usual, paying close attention to all corners. Ensure that you are taking into account the fact that your audience has likely not read the piece you are summarizing. What is your audience's level of knowledge and interest—are you attempting to produce a straightforward summary, or are you seeking to simplify or clarify the language as well? Remember that you must also understand clearly the rhetorical triangle of the writer of the piece you are summarizing. Your summary must reflect the same focused topic and purpose as the original. By nature, your summary must be *objective*.

Step 2: Content Generation

Because it is not a creative act, generating content is different when you are writing a summary. Summary does involve using more than one method—it is a combination of note-taking, paraphrasing, and synthesis. In general, remember to begin with careful point-form note-taking. Use titles, subtitles, the thesis statement, topic sentences, the introduction, and the conclusion to help you identify the key points. In general,

a. Identify the main ideas or propositions stated explicitly in the passage.

b. Construct main ideas and themes for the passage if they are not explicitly stated.

c. Assess the importance of all sentences and ideas relative to the main idea.

d. Delete unimportant sentences from the passage, such as those that are trivial, redundant, or contain unnecessary information. Judge importance relative to the main idea.

Step 3: The Outline

Your summary's length will depend upon the length of the original document, but a summary rarely has sufficient content to be structured as a full essay: assume an average summary will be a paragraph, or two or three paragraphs. An abstract will sometimes be longer. After your content generation, your point-form notes should represent a bare-bones outline. Outline your summary in the following fashion:

OPENING STATEMENT

You must clearly inform readers right away that they are reading a summary; do this by immediately revealing the title and author of the piece you are summarizing in one of two ways. First, you can use a title or heading: "Summary of 'Achieving Electronic Privacy' by David Chaum." Second, your first sentence can clearly state the title and author, and state the essay's thesis or main point: "David Chaum's 'Achieving Electronic Privacy' is a practical analysis suggesting that an encryption system is needed to better protect the privacy of people using computer billing systems." Incorporating a quick statement about tone (It is a "*serious* look at," a "*humorous* analysis of," and so on) and/or complexity ("It is a *simplified* look at," "It is a *detailed* exploration of," and so on) helps to give your reader a useful sense of the essay's flavour if you are doing an annotated bibliography.

See The Mechanical Thesis, p. 55.

✳ THE MECHANICAL OPENING STATEMENT

Never begin a summary with a statement like "David Chaum wrote 'Achieving Electronic Privacy.'" Like the mechanical thesis statement, this is boring. Incorporate the author and title into a larger statement with components such as the thesis, tone, and complexity, as in the example above.

BODY

Do not slavishly replicate the order of the original. Present only the most significant arguments and themes that you have extrapolated in your own order.

FINAL STATEMENT

There is no need for a summary within a summary; simply conclude with an accurate reflection of where the original argument finished. You may include a suggestion of the implications of the argument suggested by the writer, tying together implicit themes, or bringing forth the not fully articulated significance of the title.

Step 4: Writing the Rough Draft

When writing your first draft, remember that writing a good summary depends on a number of key factors: clear organization, effective transitional devices, and clear, exact language. Be certain you have stripped out all of the distracting "how"—that is, all of the particularly complex or extremely detailed images and examples. If you need, or want, to use a particularly good phrase from the original, simply put it in quotation marks. In general, keep combining and recombining propositions and ideas into more and more general ones.

Step 5: Revising

When revising your summary, match up the elements of your first draft with your notes on the original. Have you missed any important points? Have you overelaborated any points? Check for logical ordering of events or details and completeness of explanation. Make sure you have placed emphasis where the author of the original did. In general, future drafts will be shorter; remember, you are working backwards through the process, absorbing details in more and more general propositions and reducing, reducing, reducing. Summaries are good places for using those "big words" that collapse many words into a single statement.

"AND THEN ... "

A bad summary is a list of items introduced in a series of statements that sound alike and are joined by words like "and then." "First, the author says this ... And then the author says this ... She also says this ... And then she says that ..." A good summary must very clearly show how ideas are connected to one another with the use of appropriate, specific transitional words. Whenever you notice that your draft has used this kind of organization, simply cross out the sound-alike phrases and the "and thens," and paraphrase these with more specific terms. Never include the statement, "The author says ... "

Step 6: Editing

Looking for your most common errors, carefully edit your summary. In particular, be certain that you are consistent in using only one of the past or present tense.

Exercise 10

Part A: Here is a first draft of a sample summary of the television essay from the end of Module 3. Read it carefully, with an eye on its accuracy as a summary and on any revision it needs.

Sample Summary

The essay "Television: State Control or Self-Control?" argues that television, one of our most important vehicles of information, recreation, and relaxation, has such significant negative effects that government legislation was an inevitability. Television viewing creates a vicious circle of lack of exercise and poor nutrition in addicted viewers. It lulls them into a stupor, and blunts their critical-thinking skills in a barrage of alternately seductive and "realistic" images. As a result, in January 1994, the Canadian government, particularly alarmed by the effects of violent programming on children, legislated a new broadcast code aimed at reducing and controlling the depiction of television violence. Yet this initiative may be wrongheaded: the overt gunplay and acts of assault may have disappeared, but this explicit violence has simply migrated. It lurks now in the implicit savagery of the medical dramas' bloody acts of surgery, in the brutality of the cop and court shows' forensic reconstruction of bloody criminal acts, and in the emotional aggression of the soap operas' bed-hopping sexual automatons. Ultimately, your view of this legislation depends on whether you believe in blanket state control, or in the individual's responsibility to guide his or her family, and control him or herself.

1. Where has the thesis of the original essay been summarized?
2. Match up details to the original paragraphs: are the items presented in the same order and proportion as the original?
3. Has anything necessary been omitted?
4. Where does the original article say government legislation was an "inevitability?"
5. Where does the original article say "this initiative may be wrongheaded?"
6. How has the author of the summary responded to the title?
7. What do you think of the summary's final statement? Where does the original state this?
8. Check the summary for coherence: transitional devices, level of language, and variety of sentence structure. What would you improve?
9. Which of the four styles of summary is this? Why? What mark would you give it?

Part B: Here is a revision of the summary:

Summary of "Television: State Control or Self-Control?"

State control of television viewing was inevitable because of potential harmful effects, including the following:

- the vicious circle of lack of exercise and poor nutrition in addicted viewers;
- the blunting of critical-thinking skills through a barrage of alternately seductive and "realistic" images; and
- negative role models for children.

Legislation was enacted by the Canadian government in January 1994 to reduce and control the depiction of explicit violence on television; nonetheless, the legislation does not control implicit violence, such as the following:

- surgery in medical dramas;
- forensic reconstruction of criminal acts in police and court shows; and
- emotional aggression such as that seen in soap operas.

Television is such an important and complex vehicle for information, relaxation, and recreation that legislation is ultimately problematic. In the end, the control of television may need to come from the individual, and not from the state.

Look at the questions from Part A of this exercise and answer them again for this summary. How do the two summaries compare? Why is the second summary more successful than the first?

Exercise 11

Using the modified six-step method, write a summary of the essay that follows.

1. Some of the vocabulary and ideas in the essay are complex, so the first time you read this, make certain you understand all of the words. Underline and look up in your dictionary any you do not understand. Then reread the sentence to make certain you understand it.

2. As you read, underline any sentences or ideas that seem to be particularly important.

3. Try to identify topic sentences and the thesis, and "translate" key points into your own brief notes in the margin or elsewhere.

Sample Essay

CAMPFIRES, IDEALISM AND PIECES OF SKY

THE GLOBE AND MAIL, MAY 27, 1995, P. D2

BY NEIL BISSOONDATH

An excerpt from "Pieces of Sky" in If You Love This Country *(1995), Penguin Books Canada Ltd.*

Five years ago, my companion and I were on vacation in France. Wandering around Nice one morning, we spotted on a deserted street two 500-franc notes (about $250 in all), one lying on the sidewalk, the other under a parked car. With visions of some frantic pensioner in our heads, we entered a nearby bank in the hopes that a customer may have reported their loss. (1)

We were met with utter incredulity. As we stood there, the bills held uneasily in our hands, they asked where we were from, and on being told, mumbled, *"Ahh, les gentils Canadiens ..."* in a way that you knew stories would be told of the innocent Canadians, that we would be objects of mirth. And yet, for once, condescension did not rankle. After all, in the larger scheme of things it was not a bad image to leave behind. (2)

We took our leave, feeling a little silly, a little guilty—and as far as I was concerned, glad to be simple Canadians in a world that saw naiveté in simple honesty. (3)

Innocence, naiveté: Call it what you will. But to give up on it is to surrender our essential idealism. We seem at times to be in danger of doing just that. The signs are there: in those, for instance, who would break Quebec away from Canada as well as in those who, through weariness or short-sightedness, would allow Quebec to break away; in a willingness to sacrifice the unfortunate of our society in the name of fiscal responsibility; and in the marvelling at the multiplicity of languages on European cereal boxes while raging at the other official language printed on our own. (4)

Principles, values, and beliefs are big words easily tossed around. Politicians and philosophers believe they give them weight, but they rarely ever do; they merely make evident the weight with which they have already been invested by the public. And it is our little actions which give them weight, lend them meaning; that give us as a people, anglophone and francophone, a specific personality that is not always easily perceived, but that is there nonetheless, shaping us and being shaped by us in an act of mutual and ongoing creation. (5)

Canada has always been an act of faith—and acts of faith depend on idealism. To give up on our innocence is to give up on our idealism, is to give up on ourselves. It is to astigmatize our eyes, so that what we see is not the whole sky but just pieces of it. (6)

4. Reread the essay one paragraph at a time. Bearing in mind your underlining for emphasis, after you read each paragraph, write in the margin a point-form note of what the main idea is. Have you simply copied some words from the text, or are these words your own translation of the main idea? Does each paragraph contribute something important to the main idea?

5. Can you spot the thesis? When you do your summary, you will want to begin with that in your opening statement. Match up sentences to original paragraphs where possible: which level of summary have you done?

6. Beginning with your rhetorical triangles, follow the modified six-step process and produce a summary.

Exercise 12

Using the modified six-step method, write a summary of one of the items listed in your Top Ten List.

SUMMARY

Summarization is the process of condensing a written work down to its most important ideas and/or unspoken themes. In order to write the summary of a piece of writing, you must accurately and objectively present an author's ideas with the emphasis and proportion of the original. In order to do this, you need first to strip away all of the writer's *how* in order to reduce the essay to a skeleton outline of *what* the author says. To accomplish this, use three processes:

1. careful, critical note-taking;
2. paraphrasing of the writer's ideas into your own words; and
3. synthesis of the writer's ideas by deleting less important examples or facts, and generating increasingly general propositions and themes that account for and subsume these details.

CHECKLIST

- Have you clearly mentioned the title and the author in either your heading or your opening sentence?
- Have you carefully considered title, subtitles, topic sentences, and the introduction and conclusion in assessing the relative importance of various ideas?
- Have you identified the thesis and made certain to paraphrase it in your opening statement?
- Have you paraphrased or plagiarized?
- Are your paraphrases based on ideas or words?
- Have you included all of the main ideas?
- Have you elaborated any themes or implicit ideas in the work?
- Have you followed the writer's organizational pattern too closely? Is there a better way to integrate these materials?
- Are there any details that can be eliminated from your summary without affecting the reader's understanding of the general propositions?
- Do you conclude where the writer concludes or with an elaboration of the thematic consequences of the writer's argument?
- Which of the four kinds of summary have you produced? Why? Is this good enough?

Description and Narration

By completing a series of oral and written exercises and writing an essay of description/narration using the six-step method, students will

1. *distinguish when the rhetorical modes of description and narration are appropriate;*
2. *distinguish between a subjective and an objective point of view;*
3. *use chronological or spatial organization as needed;*
4. *use the transitional devices that most effectively unify a descriptive/narrative essay.*

OVERVIEW

You have just returned from two weeks in Venezuela. Ravi, a co-worker walking by your work station, comments that you look flushed and tired, and asks, "How are you feeling?" You later attend your night school class, where you are given an instructor evaluation form. Question 1 asks you briefly to "describe your instructor's teaching methods." Question 2 asks you briefly to "describe the instructor's attitude toward the students."

DESCRIPTION

In both of these situations, you are being asked for **description.** In the first scenario, you are being asked to describe or explain how you feel. In the second scenario, you are being asked to provide an account of the nature of your instructor's teaching. Description involves communicating your sense of an object or experience—something seen, heard, smelt, tasted, touched, or felt—through words. As such, description is an everyday activity: you might describe to a friend a gorgeous dress or sharp suit you saw in the store window, or the flavour of an exotic spicy dish you had at a new restaurant, or the sounds of an apparent domestic dispute next door.

NARRATION

Now imagine that while you are at your work station, Ravi trips over a nearby electrical cord and tumbles down a small flight of stairs, spraining his ankle, and knocking the computer attached to the cord to the floor. Your boss, hearing the noise, comes running out of her office to ask what happened. You explain as best you can how the accident occurred. Later that day, you meet some friends for dinner and regale them with stories of your adventures in Venezuela.

In both of these situations, you are engaged in **narration.** In each case, you are telling a story or recounting a series of events that you experienced. In each case, you organize your story in a logical sequence so that it will make the most sense to your listener.

Narration is the description of a sequence of events—or the telling of a true story—to communicate a particular point. You use narration every day: you might discuss the funny thing that happened to you on the way to work, the way your girlfriend/boyfriend/spouse acted strangely this morning, or the way you hit a tremendous home run in Saturday's softball game. Similarly, the media surrounds you with narration: every day the television and print news report stories of families on welfare and their daily struggles; tales of terrorist attacks, traffic accidents, and thefts; and accounts of mundane events like a trip to the zoo or a child's first visit to the dentist.

Relationship of Description and Narration

Description and narration are related processes. When you are telling the story of your adventures in Venezuela, the success or failure of your narration will largely depend upon how vividly you describe the countryside, the people, and the various sights and sounds—in other words, how well you can evoke in your audience a sense of "being there." Narration without a certain amount of detail is like a skeleton story: the basic details are there, but they need to be fleshed out with description. Similarly, description most often is linked to some amount of narration. When you describe the dress, spicy dish, or noise, you most likely place it in the context of a narrative, however brief, that explains how you came to discover each of these items.

RELATION TO OTHER MODES

You will find both of these modes extremely important when you write other kinds of essays. Often, when you need examples to support other kinds of arguments, these examples will be either descriptions or brief narratives.

ESSAY OF DESCRIPTION: PURPOSE AND FUNCTION

The *Gage Canadian Dictionary* defines the word *description* as follows:

> *n.* **1** the act of describing; the act of giving a picture or account in words.

In a descriptive essay, you try to furnish a picture of something: an object, a place, a person, an activity, an event, or a feeling. You are like a painter, but where the painter works with canvas, paints, and brushes, you work with a virtually limitless palette of words. Since we all experience the world through the five senses and our emotions, your word choices should aim to appeal directly to your reader's emotions and senses of sight, hearing, touch, smell, and taste.

Empathy: the process of imaginatively experiencing what someone else has undergone.

In descriptive writing, it is as if you are the eyewitness (and earwitness, and nose-witness) who has found the body in a murder case. Your readers are the police officers or jury members to whom you are explaining exactly what you saw. Thus, you are seeking to create understanding, or even **empathy**, in readers who likely have no first-hand experience of what you are describing. To accomplish this, therefore, you want to convey your description as accurately and precisely as possible. By the time you are done, your readers should be able to visualize and discuss intelligently the object of your description.

Thus, the travel agent who has just returned from Amsterdam and is preparing an Amsterdam promotion for a newsletter needs to communicate a lively sense of the places she saw there. Computer programmers must describe coherently to clients the kinds of programs and devices that can be used in developing computer systems. The early childhood teacher needs to be able to describe a theme and project (for instance: autumn, and what we see outside in autumn) in a clear way that children can understand.

ADJECTIVES AND ADVERBS

Adjectives and adverbs are the keys to concrete writing. Remember that, as a general rule, adjectives come before the noun they modify or after certain verbs such as *be* or *feel.* (The *cool, blue-green* ocean beckoned to them. My friend is *confused.*) Adverbs can be placed before or after the verb, but often change meaning when placed in a different position. (I am the *only* person who speaks Hungarian. I am the person who speaks *only* Hungarian.)

ESSAY OF NARRATION: PURPOSE AND FUNCTION

The *Gage Canadian Dictionary* defines the words *narrative* and *narration* in the following fashion:

> *Syn. n.* **1** Narrative, narration = something told as a story. Narrative chiefly applies to what is told, a story or an account of real events or

experiences told like a story in connected and interesting form: *The account of her trip through the Near East made an interesting narrative.*

In a narrative essay, you are telling the story of a series of events. As the definition indicates, these are generally "real events or experiences" from your life. Life, however, is an endless series of overlapping events; therefore, when you decide to write a narrative essay, you must select specific experiences or particular occurrences and connect them so that they read like a story with a beginning, a middle, and an end. You do not include every single detail, only the details that are relevant to your purpose.

Selection of details.

In narration, it is as if you are the eyewitness to the murder itself, and your readers are the police officers or jury members to whom you are explaining exactly what you saw. Thus, as in the case of description, you want to create understanding and empathy in readers who did not see, hear, and otherwise experience what you did. To accomplish this, therefore, you describe the events in a logical order and as accurately and precisely as possible. By the time you are done, your readers should be able to understand exactly what occurred and draw logical conclusions based on this understanding.

Thus, law enforcement officers who discharge their weapons must fill out reports that provide a complete, coherent narrative of the events leading up to that decision and action. An early childhood educator may write a narrative based on his or her observations of a withdrawn child's difficulties interacting with other children.

VERB TENSES

Verb tenses must be kept consistent. Remember that there are three main tenses in English: past, present, and future. These three tenses are subdivided into four more categories: simple, progressive (continuous), perfect, and perfect progressive (continuous). Watch for adverbs and adverbial expressions (such as *before*, *previously*, *after*, *next*, *later on*, *afterwards*, and *then*) that indicate changes in tense. By maintaining consistency within the three main groups, and switching from one main group to another only when there is a definite shift in time within the narrative, you will maintain verb tense consistency.

DESCRIPTION AND NARRATION MUST HAVE A POINT

Description and narration are the means to an end—that is, you use them to get across a message—not the end in themselves. The end may be entertainment (describing a humorous scene or telling a funny story), information (explaining to someone what a new building will look like, or revealing what happened to a friend last week), or instruction (describing what poison ivy looks like, or telling a cautionary story with a "moral" or lesson).

You have probably had the experience of listening to someone who likes to tell stories, but is not terribly good at it. A bad story has no beginning or end; instead, it is all middle, and simply meanders from one detail to another, prompting you to ask, "What's the point?" You write a descriptive or narrative essay only when you have a specific point to make that emerges clearly from the events described in your essay.

Exercise 1

In groups of four to six, create a description and a narration. One person should write down at the top of a page the sentence "Kim was an honour student." Now take turns, without any discussion, passing the description from person to person so that each person can add a sentence to flesh out the description. Do not take more than one minute per person.

A second group member should write down the sentence "Andariyos thought it was going to be just another day at work; was Andariyos ever wrong!" Now take turns finishing the narrative. Have each person add a sentence to the story without consulting with the others.

After ten to fifteen minutes, stop and have someone read aloud each of the two pieces. Answer the following questions:

1. How vivid or "real" is the description/narration? What are some particularly successful moments? What makes these so good?

2. How well-organized or coherent is each? Are there problems that you detect when reading them over?

3. What is the "point" of each description/narration? Is there one?

Now try the exercise again with the following opening lines. This time, however, begin by spending a few minutes as a group deciding upon a point or dominant idea that your description or narration will illustrate.

Description: The building looked dark and empty.

Narration: Olga knew something was about to happen.

After ten to fifteen minutes, stop and have someone read aloud each of the two pieces. Answer the questions above once more. Is there any significant difference between the quality of the two attempts?

WHERE TO PUT THE THESIS

See Module 3: How to Say It, The Thesis Statement, p. 53.

See Module 10: Persuasion, Deductive or Inductive Organization, p. 205.

As you know, the thesis statement makes the main point of an essay. Most essays use **deductive** organization; this means that the thesis comes at the start of the essay, generally at the end of the introduction. In description and narration, however, writers often choose **inductive** organization. To create suspense or another mood, they gradually fill in the details of the description or tell their story, and only present their main point or thesis in the conclusion of the essay.

Still other essays do not precisely provide a thesis. The overall essay creates a central impression or main point, but this remains implicit rather than explicit.

SUBJECTIVE/OBJECTIVE

In description and narration, the question of your point of view is particularly important because a unified, specific point of view is essential to helping your reader. You must determine whether your description or narration is **objective** or **subjective,** or a combination of the two.

In television courtrooms, when witnesses swear to tell "the whole truth and nothing but the truth," they are promising an *objective,* impartial account of events. This is easier to provide in some situations than others: if you happened to be walking by when a traffic accident occurred, you might be able to provide a reasonably unbiased, objective account. If you were involved in the accident, however, your account would likely be more *subjective:* it might be coloured by your desire to blame someone else, and would certainly be affected by the fact that an inside participant can never see the "whole picture" the same way an outside observer can.

In objective description and narration, you describe something factually and dispassionately in terms of what would be evident to anyone's senses: "It was a very sour taste," "She had green eyes and shoulder-length dark hair," "The band played six up-tempo, high-volume tunes." By contrast, when you are interpreting, evaluating, or reacting to what you are describing or narrating, you are providing a subjective account: "It was an awful taste," "She was gorgeous," "The band belted out six tuneless thrash metal offerings at eardrum-splitting volumes."

True objective description is rare, and most likely to be found in such writing as technical manuals. Most writing is objective–subjective: a combination of external, verifiable, objective details and a narrator's subjective interpretations of them. This is natural, since we are usually somehow involved in whatever we are describing or narrating, and are therefore likely to make certain judgments about our subject. The verb *seem* is a cue that the narrator is subjectively interpreting objective details. For instance, "Mr. Maurice seems dejected" is a subjective conclusion based on (for example) how Mr. Maurice is sitting and what he is doing.

Exercise 2

Evaluate the details from Exercise 1: which are objective, and which are coloured by the interpretation of the person from whose viewpoint the narration or description is being seen? Overall, assign a label to each: objective, subjective, or objective–subjective.

SPATIAL/CHRONOLOGICAL ORGANIZATION

A bad description is a random series of disorganized details, something like a list without much shape. For example, read the following eyewitness description:

> The thief wore a black shirt and white tennis shoes, had green eyes, walked with a limp, was about 2 m tall, wore red track pants, and had blond hair.

It is very difficult to visualize this thief because the details are presented in a completely random order.

Compare this version:

> The thief was about 2 m tall, and had blond hair and green eyes. He wore a
> black shirt, red track pants, and white tennis shoes, and walked with a limp.

The details are exactly the same, but here they are presented much more effectively, in order from top to bottom, in the same way that a person's eyes might notice them.

Your point of view is crucial not just in determining the type of description or narration, but also in deciding upon an organizational principle. Suppose you were asked to describe the structural damage done by a fire to your workplace. You might start at the front door and work your way from room to room the same way a person would actually do it on a "guided tour." This is **spatial organization**, and is an excellent, reader-friendly means of description. Spatial organization includes top to bottom, left to right, and west to east—generally any steady movement from one direction to another.

Often the method you choose will depend upon a physically specific point of view. For instance, if you are looking through a hole in the wall or sitting on a subway train, everything you describe will be determined by the limitations placed on you by your perspective.

DESCRIBING TOP TO BOTTOM

When describing people or buildings, choose top to bottom over bottom to top; it is much easier for your readers to grasp since this is the way they typically look at things.

Despite their very real differences, there are some similarities between writing a nonfictional narration essay and a fictional short story. For example, like the short story, the nonfictional narration also has elements such as setting, characters, style, tone, and theme. The main difference here is that you are not inventing these elements; rather, you are drawing these from your experiences.

One point of difference between the two types is that nonfictional narrative essays are almost always presented in **chronological** order: they present the events in the order that they happened, from start to finish. This is not always the case in fictional narratives, which frequently employ such strategies as flash-forwards and flashbacks, and mix the order of events to create different impacts and impressions on readers.

Exercise 3

In your groups, examine your collaborative works. What principles of organization are evident? Having identified these, would you want to tighten them up?

SPECIFIC VIVID LANGUAGE

As discussed, successful description and narration depend upon the use of **specific, evocative language** as opposed to vague generalities. In most description and narration, your purpose is to conjure up a complete image in your reader's mind. As such, the enemy of good description or narration is vague, generalizing words like *good*, *bad*, *big*, *small*, *easy*, and *hard*. It is important not to rely upon lazy language that vaguely tells the reader something; instead, try to use specific words that *show* the reader. Describing a building as "big and impersonal," or a person as "seeming happy" does not allow the reader to visualize these items. On the other hand, describing a building as "ten stories of cold concrete and burnished steel," or the person as "winking, smiling, then chuckling in delight, and finally doubling over in bellyfuls of laughter" conjures vivid images in the reader's mind.

Specific descriptive detail almost inevitably involves an appeal to one or more of the **five senses:** sight, hearing, touch, taste, and smell. When you are elaborating for the sake of greater precision, use language designed to appeal to specific senses. Also, appeal to **emotions or mood;** try to convey a sense of the emotional flavour of the moment: happiness, sadness, fear, ambivalence, and so on.

MODIFIERS

Be very careful when using modifiers that end in *-ed* and *-ing*. When using a modifier ending in *-ed*, it is always someone who is affected by something. (Friedrich is *entranced* by organic chemistry. Andrea is *interested* in Internet applications in nursing.) When the modifier ends in *-ing*, something is affecting someone. (The snow is *entrancing* the exchange students. Some jobs are *interesting* for some personality types.)

Narration often uses **dialogue** as another kind of vivid language. Rather than simply reporting the general topic and outcome of a conversation or decision, you may choose to include the exact words of the dialogue in order to create a sense of immediacy, reality, and, perhaps, suspense.

Exercise 4

1. In each of the four following samples of narration/description, examine the first version and circle any vague or overly general terms.

2. Then examine the second version's expanded details. Make note of more precise vocabulary and which senses are being appealed to.

3. Identify whether the details are objective or subjective, and why.

   I. A. Patient is unresponsive.

        B. Mrs. Lam is very sluggish in waking up, and, after waking, is disoriented and unable to answer basic queries for several minutes. She has an unfocused gaze, slurred speech, and a general apathy toward visitors. She seems to have given up on becoming healthy.

II. A. Carrie has a nice car, but it's hardly appropriate for work.

B. Carrie's sleek, sporty, cherry-red 1996 Corvette convertible is a very sexy automobile, but it hardly suggests the stability and dependability that we'd like her to project when she is out on sales calls for our company.

III. A. Gros Morne is a neat place to visit.

B. Though a well-kept secret compared to, say, Banff or Cape Breton, the tablelands and fjords of Gros Morne National Park are no less inspiring. Flat-top hills loom over the sea; steep-walled cliffs rise from untouched river valleys; Arctic alpine plants and wind-dwarfed trees dot the tundra landscape. There's a vastness to Gros Morne that is more severe than serene, more primeval than pastoral.[From "You Can See Forever." *Centuryhome* March 1995: 18.]

IV. A. After ringing up the purchase, the clerk pockets money from the cash register.

B. The customer has left the counter with his merchandise and change but the clerk lingers over the open drawer of the cash register, her heavily ringed fingers appearing to straighten the bills and coins inside.

As she stares vacantly out into the store, one hand casually pulls a couple of bills from the $10 slot. Then, in a swift movement, she crumples the notes into a wad, shoves them in her pocket and closes the drawer to await the next customer. [From Mary Gooderham. "Stores Profit from Video Security." *Globe and Mail* 10 June 1995: A10.]

OCCASIONS FOR DESCRIPTION AND NARRATION

When faced with a writing task, you need to be able to identify occasions when description or narration is appropriate to your purpose. Obviously, if you are asked to describe a person, place, thing, event, or feeling, you will write a descriptive essay. You will not always, however, be so clearly told to write a descriptive essay. The following word cues clearly call for a descriptive essay:

1. If you are asked to **talk about** something, or **"tell me about"** yourself or, for example, your former job, you are being asked for a description.

2. If you are asked to list or explain the **nature, characteristics, features, qualities, traits, attributes, or properties** of something, you are being asked for a description.

3. If you are asked **"What is/was it like?"** you are being asked to describe an experience. Likewise, questions involving sensory details call for description: **What did it look/sound/feel/taste/smell like?** Similarly, questions about the sensory categories of **size, shape, speed, sound, flavour, odour, feeling, or mood** generally call for description.

4. If asked to **depict, present, represent,** or **portray** something or someone, you are being asked to describe.

PORTRAY

One of the most commonly misused descriptive cue words is *portray*. "Portray" means to describe in words: "His story portrays life as a homeless person." It can also mean to represent something or someone artistically: for instance, "Tom Hanks portrayed Forrest Gump in the movie of the same name." It cannot be used in this fashion, however: "She portrays happiness with her job," or "He portrays a love of life." In these cases, it is being used mistakenly in place of the word *display* or *embody*.

You will rarely be asked explicitly to **narrate** a story or event; more often you will be asked to **tell/explain/recite/recount/relate** a certain story. You may simply be asked to describe or explain what happened or what took place in a certain situation; you are being asked to narrate these events.

You may also be asked to present a **case study.** Whether this is a case study of a victim of domestic violence or of a patient's reactions to a new drug, it is essentially a narrative account of what happened to this person.

COMBINING DESCRIPTION AND NARRATION

Remember, narration and description are similar processes; many times what you will end up writing is a combination of the two. Remember also that, most often, you will not write pure descriptive or narrative essays, but rather use brief descriptions and narratives as parts of longer pieces serving other purposes.

Exercise 5

Fill in the Top Ten List that follows with situations in your field where the descriptive or narrative modes—or a combination thereof—might usefully be employed in a writing task. Indicate whether the topic would call for description or narration, and whether this would be subjective, objective, or subjective–objective. Use the cue words listed earlier to describe these topics. For instance, the recreation leadership student might choose the topic.

1. **The qualities of a good leader (description—objective)**

Fill in as many as you can, and then continue reading the module. As other possible applications occur to you, return to this list and finish it.

TOP TEN APPLICATIONS FOR DESCRIPTIVE/NARRATIVE WRITING IN MY FIELD

1.

2.

3.

4.

5.

6.

7.

8.

9.

10.

APPLYING THE SIX-STEP METHOD TO DESCRIPTION/ NARRATION WRITING

Step 1: Imaging the Essay with the Rhetorical Triangle

Draw up your rhetorical triangle as usual, paying close attention to all corners. Ensure that you are taking into account your audience's familiarity with the subject, the purpose that you want your description or narration to achieve, and the coherent point of view that you will be adopting on your subject. Is this an objective, subjective, or objective–subjective essay?

Exercise 6

Here is a brief description from a business memorandum:

> Computers are remarkably stupid machines, completely incapable of doing anything unless someone explains it first. To put this into perspective, computers possess the same basic intelligence level of sheep (which are remarkably stupid animals). Unlike sheep, however, computers are clean, although they have been known to spit up garbage.

Fill in the rhetorical triangle for this description. Who is the audience? What level of familiarity has the author assumed? What is the purpose of this description? How can you tell?

NO FOCUS

Just because some descriptive or narrative writing does not explicitly announce its main point in a thesis statement does not mean that you do not need to have one. It is crucial to your essay's focus that you establish what point you intend to make; you may choose to imply it rather than state it explicitly, but you must know what it is at this stage of the writing.

Step 2: Content Generation

The next thing to consider is the amount of detail you will need to provide in order for the reader to understand completely or empathize with your description or narration and its main point. Generate content using more than one method; focus on

Five "Ws" and one "H"

starting with the skeleton sequence of events or list of characteristics the reader will need to understand. For description and narration, the reporter's questions (who, what, when, where, why, how) are a particularly useful place to start. Then think about fleshing these out with sufficient detail and information—specific sensory inputs so that the events become real for the reader, and your point is made. You can even use the five senses as a method of generating content. Ask yourself the questions, "What would I see/hear/touch/smell/taste? What emotion or mood would I feel?"

Try not to tell everything, but rather to show the reader. For instance, rather than explaining "he was sad" or "she was angry," it is often more effective to describe what these people were doing and allow readers to conclude these things: "His head bowed and his body intermittently shuddering, he sat softly sobbing," "Muttering and scowling, she stomped around the office."

Show; don't just tell.

Exercise 7

Here is a paragraph from the novel *Jane Eyre* by Charlotte Brontë:

> Folds of scarlet drapery shut in my view to the right hand; to the left were the clear panes of glass, protecting, but not separating me from the dreary November day. At intervals, while turning over the leaves of my book, I studied the aspect of that winter afternoon. Afar, it offered a pale blank of mist and cloud; near, a scene of wet lawn and storm-beat shrub, with ceaseless rain sweeping away wildly before a long and lamentable blast.

To what senses does Brontë appeal? What details has she used in order to do this? What is the mood created? How has she used detail to create her mood?

Descriptive or narrative nonfictional essays that focus on real events and real people are generally taken directly from your life experiences. Thus, they are in some ways very easy to plan out. However, nonfictional narration can sometimes be tricky in the execution. If your narration deals with an unpleasant event or requires you to say things that might hurt or offend someone, you may have to think carefully about exactly how you present the facts, or even make decisions as to whether or not you want to alter names to protect the guilty (the innocent rarely need protection). Your purpose, audience, and point of view will guide you in such considerations.

Step 3: The Outline

Outline your essay in the following fashion.

See Introduction, p. 49.

INTRODUCTION

Begin with your grabber as usual. Be certain to explain the topic adequately—that is, describe the nature, the importance, and the result of what you are describing or narrating. In a deductive essay, your thesis statement should clearly indicate the narration's or description's general point and mode: "Last fall, when I began classes, I entered an exciting new world of increased challenge, expectation, and responsibility," "A Silicon Graphics computer can generate such realistic 3-D images with sound and video that it will transform the way we think about art."

See Body, p. 57.

BODY

The body should consist of detailed explanations of the (most often) spatially organized details in the description, or the (most often) chronologically organized events in the narrative. Be certain you have defined, explained, and simplified all terms and concepts that may be unfamiliar to your audience. Be certain to provide specific sensory detail and dialogue where useful.

See Conclusion, p. 60.

CONCLUSION

Summarize and consider the results of the description or narration. In an inductive essay, state your thesis for the first time. Give a sense of the worth, outcome, or effects of the object of description or story told.

Step 4: Writing the Rough Draft

When writing your first draft, remember that writing a good descriptive/narrative essay hinges on a number of key factors: clear organization, sufficient detail, and clear, exact language. Check for these.

Step 5: Revising

When revising your essay, check for logical ordering of events or details, completeness of explanation, adequate sensory detail, and a sufficiently specific vocabulary.

 VERB TENSE

Verb tense inconsistency is a common problem in a narrative essay: be certain that you are consistent in using the past or present tense and that, when you change tenses, it is because of a change in the time frame of the essay.

Sharpen the focus of your descriptive or narrative essay by using transitional phrases and rhetorical techniques that highlight your linkage of events or details to one another. Consult the list of transition techniques that follows.

Step 6: Editing

Looking for your most common errors, edit carefully your descriptive/narrative essay. In particular, double-check the consistency of your tenses.

TRANSITION TECHNIQUES FOR DESCRIPTION/NARRATION

Alliteration is word-bonding, which glues phrases or groups of words together. In alliteration, you use in succession two or more words that start with the same letter or sound: for instance, "Juanita's fork poised briefly above the chocolate cake, and then descended, detaching a dark, decadent morsel. Feeling not the slightest bit guilty, she devoured it with delight." Alliteration can be extremely effective in focusing the reader's attention on the action or item being described. However, be careful: when alliteration is overused, it can sound cloying, silly, or even condescending.

Repetition not only of initial sounds of words but of whole words or phrases can also tie different items together: "Hundreds upon hundreds of homes were destroyed in the earthquake." The repetition of the word "hundreds" creates a better sense of the vast quantity under discussion.

In description and narration, **the length of words and sentences** can have a profound impact on the effect of your writing. Compare these two sentences, which have the same meaning. Which one is more effective?

> Be brief and to the point.
>
> Endeavour to achieve conciseness and directness.

See Appendix A, Contract #2: Sentence Fragments.

Good writers of description will use monosyllabic words to convey a sense of what is crisp, clean, or clear, and sequences of multisyllabic words to create a sensation of the meandering, indirect, or languorous. You may also choose to write a sentence fragment or extremely short sentence or paragraph for dramatic effect to draw something important to your reader's attention. On the other hand, you may write extremely long and complex sentences to create a sense of complexity, variety, or wonder in your reader.

Spatial transition words will link descriptions as you move from left to right or top to bottom. These include the following: *above, on top of, below, underneath, beside,* and *next to.*

Temporal transition words clearly indicate chronological order: words such as *then, next, after, subsequently, lastly/finally, as a result,* and so on make clear the relationship between events in a story. These will very effectively create a flow to your narrative.

Exercise 8

Below are very brief examples of descriptive/narrative writing.

1. Unify them by adding appropriate transitional phrases and combining sentences to improve unity.

2. Move sentences or phrases around as needed for spatial or chronological unity.

3. Underline any phrases or items that seem vague or imprecise (look for words like *big, nice, good, a lot*) or places where the author seems to be telling more than showing. Rewrite them using precise, vivid, and concise language that appeals to the senses. Create new specific examples where they are needed.

   A. When the teacher came over to him at recess, Miguel looked scared. Miguel thought he had done something wrong. The teacher could tell Miguel wanted to run away. The teacher asked Miguel if he could show a group of students how to throw a frisbee the right way. Miguel was happy.

B. The building was big. It had a nice garden in front and a big patio behind it. On the roof there was another garden with some trees and barbecues. The building had lots of reflective windows above the second floor.

C. People steal things for survival. Wade stole food and clothing for his daughter. Other people steal things they just want. Rahim stole electronic equipment from the store where he was working. Others like Marc steal because of peer pressure.

D. In August, Jane started being unreliable at work. Her friends said that they couldn't count on her. She borrowed a lot of money from her parents. She couldn't pay the rent for her nice place. She was taking drugs.

Sample Essay of Description

WHAT A CERTAIN VISIONARY ONCE SAID

"A PORTRAIT OF CANADA" IN *BANK OF MONTREAL ANNUAL REPORT*
BY TOMSON HIGHWAY

As you travel north from Winnipeg, the flatness of the prairie begins to give way. And the northern forests begin to take over, forests of spruce and pine and poplar and birch. The northern rivers and northern rapids, the waterfalls, the eskers, the northern lakes—thousands of them—with their innumerable islands encircled by golden-sand beaches and flat limestone surfaces that slide gracefully into water. As you travel further north, the trees themselves begin to diminish in height and size. And get smaller until, finally, you reach the barren lands. It is from these reaches that herds of caribou in the thousands come thundering down each winter. It is here that you find trout and pickerel and pike and whitefish in profusion. If you're here in August, your eyes will be glutted with a sudden explosion of colour seldom seen in any southern Canadian landscape: fields of wild raspberries, cloudberries, blueberries, cranberries, stands of wild flowers you never believed such remote northern terrain was capable of nurturing. And the water is still so clean you can dip your hand over the side of your canoe and you can drink it. In winter, you can eat the snow, without fear. In both winter and summer, you can breathe, this is your land, your home. (1)

Here, you can begin to remember that you are a human being. And if you take the time to listen—really listen—you can begin to hear the earth breathe. And whisper things simple men, who never suspected they were mad, can hear. Madmen who speak Cree, for one, can in fact understand the language this land speaks, in certain circles. Which would make madmen who speak Cree a privileged lot. (2)

Then you seat yourself down on a carpet of reindeer moss and you watch the movements of the sky, streaked by endlessly shifting cloud formations by day. You watch the movements of the lake which, within one hour, can change from a surface of glass to one of waves so massive in their fury they can—and have—killed many a man. And you begin to understand that men and women can, within maybe not one hour but one day, change from a mood of reflective serenity and self-control to one of depression and despair so deep they can—and have—killed many a man. (3)

You begin to understand that this earth we live on—once thought insensate, inanimate, dead by scientists, theologians and such—has an emotional, psychological and spiritual life every bit as complex as that of the most complex, sensitive and intelligent of individuals. (4)

And it's ours. Or is it? (5)

A certain ancient aboriginal visionary of this country once said: "We have not inherited this land, we have merely borrowed it from our children." (6)

If that's the case, what a loan! (7)

Eh? (8)

Questions

1. In your own words, state the point Tomson Highway is making. What is the purpose of the description: entertainment, instruction, warning?

2. Can you identify the thesis of the essay? Where is it?

3. This is a descriptive essay, but are there any narrative elements in it? If so, where?

4. Is this objective or subjective description? Why?

5. Is it organized chronologically or spatially? Why?

6. What transitional devices are used to unify this descriptive essay?

7. Examine the first paragraph carefully.

   a. Locate at least five examples of specific, vivid detail appealing to the senses—one for each sense.

   b. Locate at least three examples of alliteration. What is their effect on the description?

   c. Locate at least three examples of listed items. What is the purpose and effect of using these?

   See Appendix A, Contract #2: Sentence Fragments, Contract #3: Run-on Sentences.

   d. Locate a sentence fragment and a comma splice. Why does Highway use these ungrammatical constructions?

   e. Locate the second-last sentence. What do you notice about the length of the words here compared with the other sentences? Given what Highway is discussing, is this change effective? Why?

8. Who are the "madmen" discussed in paragraph 2, and what is their relationship to the description in the first paragraph?

9. Assess the conclusion of the essay. What is its relationship to the description with which the essay opens?

10. What is the significance of the final, one-word paragraph?

Sample Essay of Narration

THE KASE-HIGHWAY TO RAIN

BY ROBERT LAWRENCE

To Tom Highway. In memory of our friend, E.H. (Doc) Kase.

There is a photograph. I am solo in a cedar strip canoe, my left hand pushed back and my right shoulder forward; the bow of the canoe lifts above the lap of lake. I pass a stand of pines and aim towards the camera. Dimly, the background shows the bush creeping over the straight line of an embankment—a line that defines a logging artery abandoned over thirty years ago, when Brûlé Lake was the centre of logging operations, before Lands and Forests burned almost everything to the ground to create Algonquin Provincial Park, twenty years after Doc Kase built his cabin. This is the line of the Kase-Highway to Rain. (1)

We started our loop at Rain Lake; planned six days north-east through Misty, south through Macintosh and Timberwolf Lakes, south-west through Brûlé and Potter's Creek, west to McCraney and north again to Rain. We knew portages—last year we tripped lakes and mountains to Misty—and we knew bugs. Weekend trips since spring prepared us: arms were strong from the paddle; my shoulders were hard from the rub of a portaged canoe. Even the water was high. We could paddle the marshes. (2)

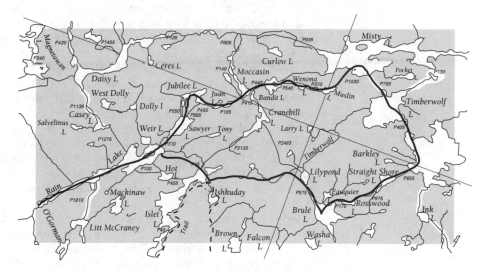

Coureur de bois: *A Canadian fur trader, accustomed to travel on rivers and through forests.*

Four days into the trip, we were a day behind. We stopped when we wanted, swam naked when we were hot, dozed in the afternoon bush to the hum of insects and listened to evening loon-calls. We were modern "coureurs de bois," but with a few easy days and the flow of water, rather than laden lives and a continent ahead. So we continued, that afternoon, rounding the J of Straight Shore Lake, over a kilometre portage, into Rosswood, heading towards Brûlé Lake. (3)

"Wouldn't it be great," my partner said, halfway down Rosswood, "to round this corner and find a pub serving cold beer?" We laughed and dipped our cups. But we wondered why the lake was so shallow and dark; you could see mud-banks at shore; there was silt in our cups. Approaching the Brûlé portage, the water shallowed more. Using paddles as poles we pushed towards shore and wondered where the water went. We ran aground and then could only wade our loads, knee-deep and running-shoes, through muck to solid ground and shoulder our gear for the next leg beside the creek between the lakes. (4)

It is a short portage to Brûlé, only 175 metres. Halfway down was a broken beaver dam—water spilled strong through the middle—built at the sides with sand bags but flowing fast through the centre. A sign in red and black was nailed to a tree:

Brûlé Lake Construction Company Unlimited
Waterways Division
E.H. (Doc) Kase, Proprietor (5)

At the Brûlé end of the portage, we found a lake, black, silted dirty, and a case of lake-cooled beer on the shore, looking alone, strangely manufactured, out of place on this edge of the bush. Across the lake, a canoe approached, paddled closer, ground ashore and two young men with New York accents, talking more like traffic than Canadians, climbed out and began to offload sandbags. (6)

They told us that last spring, the melt-water rose over the top of the long abandoned beaver dam, and the flow, trickle by stream, had taken everything with it—mud, twigs, logs tail-slapped to place, and finally, even silt—emptying Rosswood into Brûlé, flooding south through Potter's Creek to Canoe and Smoke Lakes. Here was damage and immediate aftermath; here repair was underway. (7)

They told us that there was a cottage on Brûlé, owned, even now, by old Doc Kase, a retired theology professor from Princeton University. Doc had been coming to the Park area since before the park was created; he knew the old rangers and the stories of the Algonquin. He collected canoeists, or hikers, or anybody who came this far. That was why they were rebuilding the dam. They first came here last year on a canoe trip that Doc had organized. They loved the bush and wanted to save the lakes for Doc and his wife. (8)

We helped drag sandbags to the broken dam; shared beers and the afternoon. In the evening, they took us to Doc. He had one of the last cabins in the park; when the Department of Lands and Forests had expropriated the land, they had agreed that Doc could keep his cabin for as long as he lived, but they burnt the rest of Brûlé station and let it grow. When Doc died, they would burn his cabin too. We met people: Americans mostly, mostly young except for Doc and his wife who had brought the city people here. We also met Tom Highway. He smoked hand-rolled cigarettes near the wood-stove and spoke only sometimes. (9)

Talk isolated into darkness and a moment of fellowship. We talked about canoes and loons, and Doc, in his 90s, spoke stories of the park. He told us that there was an old bush road from Highway 60 to Brûlé, largely overgrown, passable only by four-wheel drive and luck. That's how he came in now. My partner described the route that brought us to Brûlé, and the route we planned to take out. (10)

"There's a problem." Tom stated, as simple as that. "The route you want to take is impossible. When the Rosswood dam broke, it flooded everything south from here. Potter's Creek is always bad but now it is impassable. I've seen canoeists sink to their armpits in ooze this year. And bugs! You just can't do it." He was right, Doc told us. "Young, strong city-boys, no matter how well prepared, are just not ready for avoidable catastrophes." (11)

"But there is a way out without going south," Tom said. He drew a map out of his backpack, spread it out on the floor, and traced a line from Brûlé to Rain, along a consistent topographical line. "It's the old railroad bed from logging days," he said. "It's mostly passable, overgrown in parts. This trestle over Islet Lake is down. But it's how I hike in and, if you want a way out, I'm hiking back tomorrow." (12)

Options? Muck, maybe days! or a day and twenty kilometres with a canoe or full pack on the shoulders? I asked how much bushwhacking was involved—balancing a canoe on your shoulders and trying to push it through dense growth while it pushes you every direction. "Some," Tom said, "A few miles maybe in all." (13)

Sunrise. The lake is still. Three of us climb into the canoe and say goodbye to Doc. Three of us paddle to the end of Brûlé, offload, and walk—twenty minutes of sweat, mosquitoes and deer flies, five minutes rest and more. (14)

At 2:00 PM, we reach Islet Lake; hop-scotch our packs and our canoe on my sore shoulders down the fallen trestle, across the gaps between

the railroad footings, finally to the climb on the other side. At four, we stop at Hot Lake for a rest, and my partner and I decide that we will stop here for the night. After all, we are only a kilometre from our starting point at Rain Lake. We know the rest of the way. We have time. We can stop. (15)

There is a photograph. It shows Tom Highway and me sitting on a log, drinking coffee at the bottom of the railway embankment on Hot Lake. We are hot. Tom's T-shirt is stuck to his body; his glasses grainy with sweat. He is smoking a hand-rolled cigarette. I have one foot in the canoe, holding it against the log upon which we are sitting; the breeze is blowing through the cotton, long-sleeves I wear to protect me from black-flies. Gear is strewn down the embankment. (16)

Doc Kase is dead now; Tomson Highway is famous. We have passed through Brûlé and portaged to Rain again. We call the portage the Kase-Highway to Rain. And I have written a poem for my friends:

darkness creeps into camp and there is no moon
only our occasional words jar the silence
shape shadows in brush as broad as the black
and our eyes reach stars beyond fingertips
map lights with nods

expansion focuses on this grey rock
beginning to feel cold through our clothes
tonight will not sleep but our perception drowses
everything as safe as care and luck

night turns the constellations raising mists

in the moment a tree falling in the bush
tears branches
thudding hard
and an echo of leaves settles back

sense has already tested
distance
will not drowse again in this
silence

heartbeats

swallow

stillness

only eyes rest (17)

Questions

1. In your own words, state the "point" of Robert Lawrence's story. What is the purpose of the narrative: entertainment, instruction, warning?

2. Can you identify the thesis of the essay? Where is it?

3. This is a narrative essay, but can you identify descriptive elements in it? If so, where? What senses does Lawrence appeal to? For example, how tangible is the muck in the story? How sore are his shoulders during the long portage? How does he make you feel these things?

4. Is this objective or subjective narration? Why?

5. By what principle is the essay organized?

6. What transitional devices are used to unify this narrative essay?

7. Examining specific words and ideas, evaluate the essay's tone.

8. Lawrence shifts the verb tense of this essay twice. Where does he do this? Why do you think he changes his tense? What is the effect? How does this contribute to the point?

9. Assess the conclusion of the essay. Compare it with the introduction. What is their relationship? What is the purpose of the poem? Explain why you do or do not like it.

10. What is the "final thought" Lawrence leaves the reader with? Is it effective? How does the poem achieve its purpose?

OTHER APPLICATIONS OF DESCRIPTION AND NARRATION

As with all rhetorical modes, you may very effectively use moments of description or narration within essays written in other rhetorical modes for different purposes. The following example shows description being used for persuasion: this is the text of a radio advertisement for the Upper Canada Brewing Company, a microbrewery that produces high-quality beer from all-natural ingredients. A man's voice is heard slowly reading the following description, which is intended to attract you to this beer. The faint sounds of a still evening in rural Ontario are heard in the background.

Description/narration can be used effectively to create a persuasive argument. See Module 10.

> Somewhere, north of here, there is a green Adirondack chair. It sits beneath a maple tree, that sits on a hill, overlooking a perfect and pristine lake. It is precisely nine seventeen p.m. Darkness gathers. A cooling breeze rises gently. A distant train calls softly. A loon weeps. In the hand of the man in the chair, is a glass. He raises the glass, holding it up to the light of a Coleman lantern. He pauses to contemplate the moment. Its elusiveness. Its ephemeral nature. Its perfection. The moment is pure. And so is the beer held in the glass, held in the hand of the man, in the chair beneath the maple tree. The beer is called Rebellion. Summer has returned to Upper Canada. And so has the man.
>
> The Upper Canada Brewing Company. A pigheaded resistance to mediocrity.

Questions

1. How would this description persuade a beer drinker to buy Rebellion beer? Is this an effective strategy? Would you buy the beer?

2. What senses are appealed to in the description?

3. Are the details of the description organized into a coherent point of view? If so, how?

4. What transitional devices can you see at work?

Exercise 9

Using the six-step method, write an essay on one of the topics from your Top Ten List. Justify your choice of mode: is this a descriptive or a narrative essay? Will it be inductive or deductive? Will you organize it chronologically or spatially? Why? Remember, choose a topic that you are interested in and/or know a lot about. Be specific in your essay. Try to come to some logical conclusion related to your purpose.

SUMMARY

In an essay of description you communicate your sense of an object or experience— something seen, heard, smelt, tasted, touched, and/or felt—through words. In an essay of narration, you are telling the orderly (probably chronological) story of a series of events that are probably real-life occurrences. In both cases, your goal is for the reader to understand and/or be able to empathize with the situation described. In both cases, you are using the description or narration to make a point about your subject. Description and narration often work together: a story without vivid description offers little sense of reality, and description often includes stories as explanation.

When you are given a specific writing task at school or at work, common cues can indicate that descriptive or narrative writing is appropriate. Similarly, appropriate stylistic devices, such as alliteration, repetition, varied word and sentence lengths, and temporal or spatial transition words will help unify your essay and highlight the linkages among details or events. Brief descriptions or narrations can provide effective examples or explanations in an essay written predominantly in another rhetorical mode.

CHECKLIST

- Does your introduction explain adequately the topic—that is, the nature, the importance, and the result of what you are describing or narrating?
- Is your essay description, narration, or a combination of the two?
- Have you adopted a clear and consistent point of view that is objective, subjective, or a combination of the two?
- Is your essay clearly organized, chronologically or spatially?
- Is the point or purpose of your essay clearly conveyed? Is the essay deductively organized with the thesis at the start, or inductively organized with the thesis first appearing in the conclusion?
- Do you provide sufficient vivid, sensory detail to make the reader understand completely?

- Are you showing, rather than telling—that is, have you used sufficiently clear, exact, specific detail and language, rather than vague generalities?
- Are your verb tenses consistent?
- Is your essay sufficiently unified through techniques such as temporal/spatial transition words, alliteration, repetition, and word and sentence length/variety?

Process Analysis

LEARNING OUTCOMES

By completing a series of written and oral exercises and writing a process essay using the six-step method, students will

1. *distinguish when use of the rhetorical mode of process analysis is appropriate;*
2. *distinguish between process direction and process description essays;*
3. *use chronological or logical organization as needed;*
4. *use the transitional devices that most effectively unify a process essay.*

OVERVIEW

Your friend Nuala, frustrated by her difficulties with the company computer's spreadsheet software, throws up her hands and asks desperately, "Can you please show me how to use this?"

At night school that evening, you are thrilled to receive an "A" on your economics assignment. Knowing the difficulties you were having at the start of the course, your friend Gus elbows you, smiles, and then asks, "How did you manage to get that mark?"

In both of these situations, you are being asked to perform a **process analysis**. In the first scenario, you are being asked to describe or explain the **process**, or general sequence of steps, that must be followed to employ successfully the spreadsheet software. In the second scenario, you are being asked to explain the specific series of actions that led to your improved grade. Process analysis is the explanation of the steps that must be followed or that were followed to complete a specific task. As such, process analysis itself is a process that you often perform.

Process analysis is all around you: it is the recipe you follow when cooking your dinner, the self-help book that explains how to do your own renovations or how to improve your relationships, the rulebook that explains how to play a sport, and the manual that tells you how to use your new computer, power tool, appliance, or child's toy. The newspaper is filled with process analysis: articles give tips on how to protect your home from burglars, demonstrate how to have younger-looking skin in four easy steps, explain how to eat wisely, and discuss how to compost table scraps. Indeed, the primary means by which you acquire new skills of any kind is through reading or hearing successful process analysis. This textbook is an extended process analysis explaining how to write various kinds of essays.

PURPOSE AND FUNCTION

The *Gage Canadian Dictionary* defines the word *process* as follows:

> *n.* 1 a set of actions or changes in a special order: *By what process or processes is cloth made from wool?*

In a process essay, you explain in detail *how* something works or something can be done. In order to do this, you need to break down the process into its component "actions or changes," and to present these in their proper "order."

In process analysis, you are the teacher and your readers are the students. Thus, the learning outcome you want to achieve is for your readers to be able to perform the process themselves, or explain exactly how the process was or is completed. Thus, after reading your memo on what to do in the case of a fire at your company, your reader should know exactly what to do should such an emergency arise. Similarly, after reading an article explaining how a surgeon reconstructs a torn anterior cruciate ligament in the knee, you may not be able to perform the operation yourself, but you should understand the principles and steps involved.

THE TWO TYPES OF PROCESS ESSAY: DIRECTION AND DESCRIPTION

When writing an essay using process, you have two distinct choices. In a **process direction** essay, you provide general instructions to your reader on *how* to do something. The purpose here is practical: to teach audience members a new skill that they will be able to utilize. Thus, nurses read about nursing process therapy, library information students learn how to provide various types of information to library users, and resources technology students read texts teaching them how to do surveying and structural design.

In a **process description** essay, you describe how a specific action or event occurs. The purpose here is to teach someone to understand in detail how something happens. Examples might include the early childhood teacher who learns different theories of a child's socialization process, the hotel manager who must explain the steps in the guest cycle, or the business student who must describe how credit bureaus function.

Process description analysis can also apply to a historical event. A history text-book on the War of 1812 is a process description that seeks to uncover and explain all of the steps involved in the progression of that conflict. In a court case involving a traffic accident or a murder or other criminal event, investigators and other parties attempt to reconstruct the various stages of what happened—that is, to describe the precise process of the event in order to determine who is responsible.

You will determine which of these structures to use based upon your topic and purpose. For instance, a student studying esthetics and taking an aromatherapy course might choose to write a process description essay explaining how the aromatic substances and essential oils used for facial and body treatments are obtained for use in esthetic salons and spas. The same student might also choose to write a process direction essay explaining how to recognize these substances and oils by smell, and how to incorporate them into treatments given at a salon or spa.

Exercise 1

In groups of four, examine the following topics. Decide which ones would require a process direction and which ones would require a process description. Then divide up the topics so that each person has one process direction and one process description topic. Taking no more than ten minutes, each group member should write out in point form the series of steps needed to explain each topic.

1. How your family came to settle in Canada, and how it has grown since.
2. How to get to your home from school.
3. How the average day unfolds for you.
4. How to prepare your favourite food.
5. How to know when you have found your ideal mate.
6. How you spent your summer vacation.
7. How to select a program for postsecondary study.
8. How you decide what movie to see at the theatre.

Once you each have your two topics completed in point form, have each person read the series of steps aloud. Start with all the process directions, and then proceed to all the process descriptions. Answer the following questions:

1. How did you know where to start your direction or description?
2. How did you know where to finish?
3. How did you organize the material between the start and the finish?
4. Is the process clearly understood by the rest of the group?
5. How would you clarify or elaborate upon the process in response to the group's concerns?

Writing a good process essay of either of these types hinges on a number of key factors: clear organization, appropriate tone, sufficient detail, and clear, exact language.

CHRONOLOGICAL/LOGICAL ORDER

A reader will not be able to use your process essay as a guide unless you organize all the steps in the process or explanation chronologically, or in order of time, from start to finish. This means that the first step is always the first thing you tell the reader, and then you present the remainder of the process in the order in which the actions are to be completed (direction), or in the order in which the actions occur (description). The following two examples show how this might work.

Imagine you are required to write a process direction essay on how to become an "A" student. The first thing you will need to do, of course, is to figure out how many steps you are going to include in this process. Suppose you decide upon seven steps; you now have to order those steps from 1 to 7 to ensure that they give the reader the information chronologically. It would make little sense to start this process essay with the advice, "Make sure you study for the final exam," since this is a step that comes after most other necessary ones.

The same basic rules apply in a process description essay explaining how something functions or operates. If you are describing how an internal combustion engine works, you need to break down that process into stages and then explain these stages in order of occurrence. Thus, you are unlikely to begin by stating that exhaust fumes are produced, as this is one of the last stages.

Sometimes, however, you may not be able to employ strict chronological order. If you are explaining how to reduce stress, for example, you cannot use chronological organization to order steps like the following: prioritizing things to do, getting a good night's sleep, and being certain to set aside specific intervals of leisure time no matter how much work you have to do. These are separate guidelines that need to be followed at the same time. Here, it is important to determine a logical order to present these steps: the most significant of the tips should come first, and so on. This will require critical thinking.

 GIVING WARNINGS

Listing steps to avoid, or warning of common errors, will also be extremely helpful to readers. Sometimes explaining what not to do—particularly if it is an easy error to fall into—is the most useful advice of all.

TONE

Process direction essays are generally written in the second person, addressed to "you." As such, much process writing consists of commands to your reader. Think about the directions that come with a new toy: "Recharge battery pack by removing it and plugging it into adapter, as seen in diagram A." This kind of command is useful and effective because it simulates the voice of a speaker giving one-on-one instructions.

Be careful, however—when someone orders you around verbally, you may become irritated. Similarly, readers can be annoyed by process writing that simply shouts "Do this! Do that!" Be careful to offer polite directions rather than bark orders:

phrases like "You may want to ...," "It may be useful to ...," and "You may find it help-ful to ..." can ensure that your tone is cordial and supportive. Rather than issue direct commands to readers ("Don't enter the restricted area at any time"), you can also rephrase these impersonally ("It is important not to enter a restricted area)."

Finally, use of a verb like "should" instead of a verb like "must" conveys the same message in a less authoritarian manner: "You should try to be as considerate of your readers as possible by not ordering them around."

Exercise 2

Return to your rough notes for process direction and process description from Exercise 1. Now write these notes out as single paragraphs. Be sure to organize each paragraph chronologically or logically. Concentrate on your audience—make every effort to ensure that your readers will completely understand the process.

When this is done, you will teach or explain the process to a single classmate. Slowly read the paragraph aloud one or two times to your classmate, who cannot ask questions, but should simply take notes. Then, using the notes and his or her mem-ory, your classmate will explain the process back to you. When this process has been completed, discuss together the following questions:

1. In what places is your classmate's account of your process paragraph accurate?

2. Where is it inaccurate?

3. Did any parts of your original paragraph create problems for your classmate? What was the nature of the difficulty?

4. Is there anything you would concentrate on doing differently to increase the effectiveness of future process writing?

OCCASIONS FOR PROCESS ANALYSIS

When faced with a topic, you need to be able to identify occasions when the process rhetorical mode is appropriate to your purpose. Obviously, if you are asked to detail the process of filing an income tax return by e-mail, or to explain the process of becoming a Canadian citizen, you will utilize process as your rhetorical mode.

You will not always, however, be so clearly told to write a process essay. The fol-lowing word cues call for a process direction essay:

1. If you are asked to describe **how to** do something, or to provide **directions** or **instructions,** you are being asked to direct your reader in completing a process.

2. If you are asked to explain **procedures, rules, guidelines, or regulations,** you are generally being asked to direct your readers in their behaviour. For example, the sanitation regulations at a restaurant are guidelines explaining steps that must be carried out to ensure the sanitary handling of food and dis-posal of waste.

3. **Explanation** of a code of behaviour or code of ethics calls for direction of the reader in what is acceptable and what is not.

4. If asked to explain **what to do** if something happens—for instance, what employees should do in case of an emergency—you are being asked to direct your readers as to how to behave in a particular set of circumstances.

Word cues for a process description essay are a little less obvious. Generally, the word *how* is a good clue. If you are asked to **describe how** something happens or happened, or are asked to **explain a procedure**—for instance, explain how erosion works—you need to respond with a process description.

Exercise 3

Fill in the Top Ten List below with situations in your field in which the process mode might usefully be employed in a writing task. Indicate whether the topic would call for process direction or process description. Use the cue words listed earlier to describe these topics. For instance, the business administration student might choose the topic

1. The industrial relations process (process description).

The student of geriatric nursing might choose the topic:

1. Providing palliative care in the home (process direction).

Fill in as many as you can, and then continue reading the module. As other possible applications occur to you, return to this list and finish it.

TOP TEN APPLICATIONS FOR PROCESS WRITING IN MY FIELD

1.
2.
3.
4.
5.
6.
7.
8.
9.
10.

APPLYING THE SIX-STEP METHOD TO PROCESS WRITING

Step 1: Imaging the Essay with the Rhetorical Triangle

Follow the usual steps. Begin by imaging your essay with the rhetorical triangle. When considering topic and mode, you should decide what kind of essay you are writing: given the cues in the wording of the assignment, is it process direction or process description?

In process writing, your audience analysis is particularly crucial. Before you can begin generating content, you need to consider very carefully what your readers already know and how much you will have to tell them. If you are explaining how to make a Sri Lankan dish like nasi goreng to a group of professional chefs, you will need to provide less detail in your instructions than you would for a group of people at a mid-level cooking class. Similarly, if you are explaining the same recipe to a group of introductory hospitality students, some of whom have never before made rice, you will provide far more detail.

The worst thing you can do in terms of detail is to make faulty assumptions about your audience's level of knowledge. Yes, professional chefs know a lot about cooking, but if you do not specifically explain how much of each ingredient they should add, how hot the oven should be, or how long the dish should cook, you cannot expect them to produce a tasty finished product from your recipe.

Exercise 4

How would you describe the audience for this paragraph? What assumptions about their knowledge is the writer making? Is this an example of process direction or process description?

> When you replace or change an old ceiling light fixture, turn off the power at the wall. It is also a good idea to pull the appropriate fuse or trip the circuit breaker so you don't get a nasty shock. Then, remove the old light bulbs. This can be awkward, so you will want to have two sets of hands or other supports available to you. Have a helper hold onto the fixture while you work, or bend old coathangers into hooks so you can suspend the fixture from the ceiling box while leaving your hands free to work with the wires.

Step 2: Content Generation

The next thing to consider is the amount of detail you will need to provide in order for the reader to carry out the task or comprehend the process. Generate content using more than one method; focus on breaking the process up into its logical component steps and explaining these thoroughly. Be careful to define, explain, and simplify any terms your audience may not understand.

Step 3: The Outline

Outline your essay in the following fashion.

See Module 3: How to Say It, Introduction, p. 49.

INTRODUCTION

Begin with your grabber as usual. Be certain to explain adequately the topic—that is, the nature, the importance, and the result of the process you will be directing the reader how to accomplish (process direction), or the background to the event or phenomenon that you are explaining (process description). Your thesis statement should clearly indicate the process to be analyzed, and may provide an overview of the number of steps or components. For example, "Proper batting in baseball requires preparation in four areas: footwork, the hips, a level swing, and a complete follow-through."

See Body, p. 57.

BODY

The body should consist of detailed explanations of the chronologically or logically organized separate steps that make up the process. Be certain you have defined, explained, and simplified all terms and concepts that may be unfamiliar to your audience.

See Conclusion, p. 60.

CONCLUSION

Summarize the steps, and then consider the results of the process. You might describe the savoury flavour of nasi goreng and the compliments bestowed on the chef; you might describe how, in batting, technique is so much more important than strength that a perfectly hit ball flies off the bat with a sense of almost no effort. Give a sense of the worth, outcome, or effects of successful completion of the process.

Step 4: Writing the Rough Draft

When writing your rough draft, one crucial element is clear and exact language. While this overlaps the idea of detail in some ways, the focus here is a little different. Put yourself in the position of explaining a process such as how to start up a new small business. In explaining this kind of process, precision of language is crucial, because the smallest slip or confusion could spell the difference between success and failure.

This means that instead of the vague instruction, "It is a good idea to make a business plan with different ranges," you will get your message across more effectively by saying, "It is crucial to your new enterprise that you create a comprehensive business plan, which indicates specific short-, medium-, and long-range objectives and goals." This adds a new level of detail to your explanation (the three types of objectives that, presumably, will then be elaborated and defined); furthermore, the use of *crucial, enterprise,* and *comprehensive* clarifies these elements importance.

Through exactness in the wording of your instructions or explanations, you minimize the risk of readers going astray; moreover, you make it easier for readers to comprehend and digest your material.

Step 5: Revising

When revising, check for completeness of explanation, adequate definition of terms or concepts that may be unfamiliar, and a sufficiently specific vocabulary. Consult the list of transition techniques for methods for tightening your essay's coherence.

SAMPLE READER

Particularly with process writing, it can be very useful to have a reader who is unfamiliar with the process and is a representative of your target audience read your essay. With an eye to whether he or she understands the process, such a reader will indicate very clearly any areas in which your explanation needs adjustment.

Step 6: Editing

Looking for your most common errors, edit your process essay carefully.

TRANSITION TECHNIQUES FOR PROCESS WRITING

Sharpen the focus of your process essay by using transitional phrases like the following to highlight your linkage of one step to the next:

- **Numbering:** Numbering your points 1., 2., 3. helps to give a sense of tightly organized steps arranged in a deliberate and useful sequence. Frequently, a process essay will number the steps in addition to splitting them into separate paragraphs. This can be done either to emphasize chronological ordering or to highlight the logical order of importance. Similarly, using key words like *first, second, third* helps readers keep track of where they are in a chronological process, particularly if your thesis has already established the specific number of steps.

- **Temporal transition words:** Transition words clearly indicating a relationship in time—*then, next, after, subsequently, lastly/finally, as a result,* and so on—also make clear the relationship between steps or stages.

STEPS OUT OF ORDER

Poor instruction manuals sometimes make the mistake of discussing a complete step and only then telling you, "Before you do this, you should make sure you do something else first." Because such a step comes out of order, it confuses and frustrates the reader, who has been painstakingly following the process step by step.

See Module 4: Summary Skills.

- **Internal summaries:** Internal summaries help to unify process writing, particularly if the process is intricate or extensive. In an internal summary, you remind your reader of the steps you have just discussed as a way of consolidating this information before moving on to the next steps. As an example, "Now that you have completed *x* and *y*, it is time for *z*."

Exercise 5

Below are three brief examples of process writing.

1. Unify them by adding appropriate transitional phrases and combining sentences to improve unity.

2. Move sentences or phrases around as needed for logical or chronological unity.

3. Check the tone; where necessary, rewrite orders into polite directions.

4. Underline any phrases or items that seem vague or imprecise (look for words like *big, nice, good,* etc.) and rewrite them using precise, concise language where necessary.

   A. When you arrive at the campsite, remember these things. There is a swift river running through the northeast quadrant of the campground. Bring your own wood or purchase it at the camp store. Stay away from the banks. Your campsite is clearly defined, so stay in your boundaries. When you obnoxiously extend the boundaries, you ruin the area and intrude on other groups' sites. Campfires are fun. Do not light a fire anywhere outside the permitted area in your camping area. Do not cut trees and do not use dead wood found in the area. The person registering for the camping permit will be banned from future camping if the site is left in an unacceptable state.

   B. A strike is a union's most effective way of exerting pressure on management. The union erects picket lines around the company's premises. Picketers carry signs advertising that a strike is occurring. They prevent nonunion workers from entering the company. Suppliers from other unionized companies often refuse to cross the picket lines. The strike ends when both sides' principles, economic needs, and willingness to give concessions coincide. The employer's sales revenues are reduced unless the employer can sell accumulated inventory while the strike goes on. Customers have to go to other suppliers for their goods. Union members lose their paycheques during the strike, in exchange for much-reduced strike pay from the union. Each side measures its costs against its benefits in various time frames.

   C. Follow these five easy steps from the supermarket to the kitchen table, and you will be sure to reduce fat in your diet. Avoid putting butter and margarine on your vegetables at dinner. Buy low-fat versions of everyday products like peanut butter, salad dressing, and mayonnaise. Reduce the amount of margarine, butter, or mayonnaise you put on bread, bagels, or buns. Buy skim, part-skim, or reduced-fat milk products to use in recipes where you are unlikely to notice any difference in taste. When cooking, do not fry your meat, poultry, or fish; bake, broil, or microwave it.

Sample Process Essay 1

Hey, You, Mind Your On-line Manners: The Ps and Qs of Netiquette

Technology in Government 2.4 (April 1995), 18–19.

by Lawrence Hopperton

Because of the speed, convenience, and informality of electronic communication, we tend to equate it with verbal communication. However, since it is a form of writing, its advantages and restrictions are more like those of memos. Electronic communication does not incorporate any elements of body language. You cannot tell by the tone of voice that the sender is joking. You cannot see by the furrowed brow that the receiver is confused. Only the words convey the message. Another difference between electronic and oral communication is that you lose the instant interaction that often clarifies oral communication, but you gain the ability to make complete statements without interruption and then give the listener time to decide on a thoughtful response. (1)

A key to successful communication is to have consideration for your readers. With the amount of information pushed upon individuals continually increasing, you can save them time by being clear and concise. A well-organized, to-the-point message is more inviting than five screens full of long, single-spaced text. Below are ten guidelines to help you to use the strengths and avoid the problems of electronic communication. (2)

1. Length of Message
Brevity is a definite virtue. Try to restrict a message, if possible, to a screen; two screen pages are still tolerable. Brevity is recommended if only because reading long text on the screen can be tiresome for both the eye and mind. (3)

2. Writing Style
Use short sentences and simple English. Avoid rambling, running prose with complex syntax and a multitude of co-ordinate and subordinate clauses. While the nature of on-line discussion means that some inconsistent grammar will slip through, try to keep your writing clear. Notes should still be written using normal sentence and paragraphing structures. (4)

3. Spacing
Neat, meaningful spacing can ease mental processing. (5)

4. Numbered Items
Ideas, arguments, etc. are clearer if they are numbered. This will make cross-referencing easier. (6)

5. Annotation
When you want to refer to a previous note, make direct reference to it in the first line of your note (for example, "re:#5 in Literature"). It's also a good idea to paraphrase or summarize the original so that readers can understand the background of your entry and follow the argument. (7)

6. Upper Case

The upper case is often used among networkers to denote emphasis, but using too much of it can produce what is known as the "BANG" effect. Words in upper case shout at you and generate a "noisy" reading environment. THIS SENTENCE SEEMS TO STICK OUT AS IF SOMEONE WERE SHOUTING AT YOU, AND THIS CAN MAKE THE SENTENCE MORE DIFFICULT TO READ. (8)

7. Subject Line

A subject line is incorporated by many popular e-mail programs, such as Eudora. But it is a good idea to include subject headings in your note itself to help others follow your thoughts. (9)

8. Wit and Humour

A small and occasional dose of wit and humour does wonders for a message or on-line conference that is beginning to take itself too seriously. It can also break the ice for a conference with a hesitant start. Too much clowning around and too many flippant jokes or remarks, however, can be irritating and offensive to most people. (10)

If you are attempting sarcasm or any other humour, clearly indicate so. A common convention is to place a "smiley face" icon at the end of non-serious passages. Using "face" icons can help generally to clarify your tone and intention. For example, turn the page 90° clockwise to view the following examples:

:–)	I'm happy, or making a joke.
:–(	I'm sad.
;–)	Say no more! A nod is as good as a wink.
>;–I	I'm wrestling with this problem. (11)

9. Spontaneous or Considered Response

While much can be said in praise of spontaneity, if you are dealing with a sensitive or controversial topic, it would be better if you could give yourself a little more time to reflect on the arguments and counter-arguments, rather than compose a considered response that you will regret or feel embarrassed about afterwards. (12)

10. Etiquette and Protocols

a. Acknowledge and thank people for their comments on your views. Avoid digressing in a conference. (13)

While the content of your Internet message is, of course, up to you, following these ten rules of basic "netiquette" should help make your communication on the Internet clearer, more reader-friendly, and therefore more effective. ;-) (14)

Questions

1. Identify the thesis of the essay.

2. What type of essay is this: process direction or process description? Why?

3. Is it organized chronologically or logically? Why?

4. How does Hopperton keep his tone cordial and helpful?

5. What transitional devices are used to unify this process essay?

6. What technique is used as a grabber?

7. How does the introduction establish the importance or relevance of the process that will be discussed?

8. How does Hopperton "practise what he preaches" in writing this essay? Is this effective?

9. Assess the tone of the essay.

10. Assess the clarity of the instructions. Are they phrased and organized in such a way that you could follow them?

Sample Process Essay 2

HOW TO FAIL ENGLISH

BY SHARON BOLTON-SMITH

Although the ultimate aim of most students is to graduate, get a good or better job, and make heaps of money, there may be some times when a "fail" grade in a particular course presents some benefits. Perhaps you are just not ready to face that meat market called the job search, or perhaps that good-looking guy next to you is failing, and you want to do another stint beside him drinking in the smell of black leather and motorcycle grease. Whatever the reason, you will need some helpful hints, because failing a course is not as easy as you might think. I am going to be specific here and concentrate on English because it is a subject we all have to face, as opposed to Fluid Mechanics, Financial Planning, or French. (1)

Moving right along, here is the first tried and true method: do not show up for class! If you never cross the threshold of your English class, you will never get any assignments or complete any assignments—get my drift? However, you have to be careful with this, as not showing up right from the start may get you a "Did Not Attend" grade, which does not carry the same cachet as a "fail." This is another reason you may want to seek out a "fail" grade. Suppose you intend to be a famous (or infamous) writer; how interesting if your book jacket or psychological profile notes that you failed English. This gives you a real human touch —no stuffy academic propriety for you. I see, however, that I am wandering off here, envisioning the glories of failure when I have not yet told you how to accomplish this task. To continue, should you reject the disappearing act, you still have plenty of options, which I will outline. (2)

Sprinkling plenty of incomplete sentences and punctuation errors consistently throughout your assignments. Works for most students. If you have trouble writing an incomplete sentence with punctuation errors. Just remember: when in doubt, end your sentence. It may pain you to write sentences like this, but let me assure you that it is a necessary evil if you are to accomplish your goal. (3)

Despite your whole-hearted efforts, you may find you are faced with an instructor who sees you as a challenge he or she must conquer, or perhaps your stumbling attempts at prose evoke a passionate sympathy. You can be in real trouble here, as no matter how badly you mess up, this teacher probably wants to help you fix it. The thing to do here is to make yourself as thoroughly unlikable as possible, thereby negating any of these do-gooder impulses. Addressing your teacher with a title unusual in academic circles, such as "Hey, guy" or "Hey, lady," can help—or try continually stringing your gum out of your mouth and wrapping it around your pen. The point is to make yourself as unworthy of human compassion and understanding as possible. This can be a delicate balancing act, particularly if you are trying to attract that black leather type beside you. You want to come across as antisocial but not repulsive, sort of like the offspring the Madonna/Sean Penn union would have produced. (4)

Now imagine it: finally, after submitting countless essays as jumbled as a two-year-old's toybox, and fine-tuning a personality that only Sid Vicious could relate to, you hold in your hand the letter with your grade report. You anxiously rip open the envelope, carefully sliding out the computer print-out that foretells your future. There, in all its rare glory, you find the "F" you have striven for. Another semester of English stretches before you. Will you pass next time? Perhaps, or you may be found on the back of a motorcycle, hanging on to that leather-clad guy, recreating Jack Kerouac's journey *On the Road* for the 1990s. (5)

Questions

1. Identify the thesis of the essay.

2. What type of essay is this: process direction or process description? Why?

3. Is it organized chronologically or logically? Why?

4. Is this a personal or a formal essay? How can you tell?

5. What transitional devices are used to unify this process essay?

6. What technique is used as a grabber?

7. How does the introduction establish the importance or relevance of the process that will be discussed?

8. How does Sharon "practise what she preaches" in writing this essay? Is this effective? (In particular, examine paragraph 3.)

9. Assess the tone of the essay.

10. Assess the clarity of the instructions. Are they phrased and organized in such a way that you could follow them?

OTHER APPLICATIONS OF PROCESS

As with all rhetorical modes, you may very effectively use moments of process analysis within essays written in other rhetorical modes for different purposes. For example, a newspaper article from *The Globe and Mail* is a cause and effect essay discussing the problem of grass clippings from suburban lawns and the need to divert these clippings from overfilled landfill sites. One such attempt involves government subsidies of homeowners' purchases of mulching lawnmowers. The essay's sixth paragraph reads as follows:

> The recycling mower has blades that chop grass finely. The cuttings are then blown to the ground with sufficient force that they can't be seen. "People say that even if their kids and dogs play on the lawns, they don't track clippings into the house," Mr. Bellmont says. The mulch helps hold moisture in the lawn, which eventually helps break it down into fertilizer. [From Wallace Immen. "Mulching Mowers Offer Green Solution to Problem of Clippings Disposal." *Globe and Mail* 27 May 1995: D8.]

Process as a way to organize a body paragraph. Using process to explain a point can provide helpful clarification in an argument.

This paragraph is a process description of how the mulching mower functions, how it makes the clippings disappear, and how the clippings, in turn, help the lawn. This brief explanation, unified with temporal connection words (*then, eventually*), clarifies the argument by illustrating exactly how this solution to the problem functions.

Exercise 6

Using the six-step method, write an essay on one of the topics from your Top Ten List. Justify your choice of format: is this a process direction or process description essay? Will you organize it chronologically or logically? Why?

CHOOSING A TOPIC

Remember, choose a topic that you are interested in and/or know a lot about. Be specific in your essay. Try to come to some logical conclusion related to your purpose.

SUMMARY

In a process essay, you are seeking to explain in detail how something works or how something can be done. To do this, you break down the process into its component actions or changes, explain these thoroughly and clearly, and present these in chronological or logical order.

There are two types of process essay. In a process direction essay, you provide general instructions to your reader on how to do something; that is, you teach your reader a skill. In a process description essay, you describe how a specific action or event occurs: you teach your reader to understand the intricacies of how something works or exactly how something happened.

When you are given a specific writing task at school or at work, common cues can indicate that a process essay is appropriate. Similarly, appropriate transitional phrases in your writing will help unify your essay and highlight the linkages between steps in the process. A moment of process analysis can provide an effective example in an essay written predominantly in another rhetorical mode.

CHECKLIST

- Does your introduction provide a) an adequate overview of the nature, the importance, and the result of the process you will be directing the reader how to accomplish (process direction), or b) the background to the event or phenomenon that you are explaining (process description)?

- Does the body include every discrete step in the process?

- Have you clearly and sensibly organized the steps in the process chronologically or logically?

- Have you provided sufficient detail and explanation of terms and concepts, given the level of your audience's knowledge of the subject?

- Have you used sufficiently clear, exact, specific language, rather than vague generalities?

- Does your conclusion both summarize the steps and give a sense of the worth, outcome, or effects of successful completion of the process?

- Is the tone of your essay appropriate? Have you been careful to sound knowledgeable but cordial, rather than demanding and commanding?

- Have you used appropriate transitional techniques (numbering, temporal linkages, internal summaries) to signal chronological or logical linkages between steps?

Comparison and Contrast

LEARNING OUTCOMES

By completing a series of written and oral exercises, and writing a comparison/ contrast essay using the six-step method, students will

1. *distinguish when use of the comparison/contrast rhetorical mode is appropriate;*

2. *distinguish among comparison, contrast, and comparison/contrast essays;*

3. *distinguish between informative and evaluative comparison/contrast essays;*

4. *assess and evaluate related ideas, events, or objects;*

5. *use the block or the slice method to structure a comparison/contrast essay;*

6. *use the transitional devices that most effectively unify a comparison or contrast essay.*

OVERVIEW

How do you decide what optional courses to take each year at school? Before making that decision, how do you decide whether to be a full-time or a part-time student, and what program you should enter? For that matter, how do you decide on what school to attend in the first place?

The answer to each of these questions is the same: you compare and contrast a set of options. After analyzing and evaluating the differences, you select the school, the program, and the courses that best meet your needs.

Comparison/contrast is a process you engage in daily. Determining what to wear for a job interview or dinner party, what kind of car or computer to buy, or where to go and what to do on the long weekend are just some of the decisions you make by comparing the benefits and disadvantages of a variety of alternatives.

As such, comparison/contrast is one of the most significant and powerful tools for structuring an argument in order to communicate effectively with an audience. For example, an aspect of everyday life utilizing a more deliberate and structured style of comparison is marketing. A company will often emphasize the benefits of its product in comparison to that of a competitor: the advertising of a restaurant, a car company, or a bank is often based upon demonstrating its lower prices, better value, or superior consumer satisfaction.

PURPOSE AND FUNCTION

The *Gage Canadian Dictionary* defines *comparison* as follows:

> *n.* 1 the act or process of comparing; finding the likenesses and differences: *The teacher's comparison of a heart to a pump helped the student to understand its action.*

Comparison, then, is measuring objects, ideas, individuals, or other entities against one another in order to determine how they are similar or dissimilar.

In essence, what a comparison and contrast essay is doing is setting up a structure where two things are viewed in relation to each other in order to determine their likenesses and differences. The early childhood teacher might compare and contrast the social skills of groups of children to produce developmentally appropriate programming for each child. The fashion designer, retailer, or marketing expert might compare the advantages and disadvantages of various media such as radio, television, print, and direct mail in order to determine which will be most effective.

THE THREE TYPES OF COMPARISON/CONTRAST ESSAY

When writing an essay using comparison/contrast, you always have three distinct choices. In *comparison,* you focus solely on similarities. In *contrast,* you stick completely to differences. Finally, in *comparison/contrast,* you examine both similarities and differences in the same essay.

Clearly, you will decide which to use based on which of the three possibilities best serves your topic and purpose. If asked to write a paper on the sports of baseball and cricket, you might stick to similarities. On the other hand, you are more likely to contrast life in the city vs. life in a small town. If asked to write about high school vs. college or university, you might be more apt to both compare and contrast. These are, however, only examples, and you might also do the opposite if you are looking to have a particular effect on a reader.

In order to achieve its purpose, the successful comparison, contrast, or comparison/contrast essay subdivides a larger topic into smaller topics that are carefully evaluated in relation to both subjects.

EVALUATIVE VS. INFORMATIVE

As well as choices of whether to compare, contrast, or do both, you also have to make a second fundamental choice: are you going to write an **evaluative (judg-**

mental) essay, in which you recommend one place, thing, or practice over another? Or are you going to produce a purely **informative** essay that provides your readers with the pertinent information and allows them to decide which of the choices is more appropriate for them?

Think of it this way. As a travel and tourism student, you might write an essay about two vacation spots—Cancun and Orlando—in which you tell readers about each and then recommend one as a better place to spend two weeks. In a second essay, you might provide readers with the same general information. This time, however, rather than advising them on which is better, you could let the readers draw their own conclusions on the basis of what you have written. The first essay is evaluative; the second essay is informative.

Exercise 1

In groups of four to six, decide whether you would compare, contrast, or compare and contrast the following pairs of ideas:

men	women
cars	trucks
English classes	professional classes
immigration	emigration
introductions	conclusions

Exercise 2

Two brief comparison/contrast paragraphs follow. Read each of them carefully, and answer briefly the following questions:

1. For each, determine whether it is a comparison, a contrast, or a comparison and contrast paragraph.

2. Identify what two items are being compared.

3. Does one of the items being compared seem to be better than the other? Does the author seem to feel more strongly about one of the items? What is it specifically that gives you this impression?

4. If one item seems to be better than the other, what do you think is the purpose of the writer's comparison/contrast?

5. If neither item seems superior, what was the purpose of the writer's comparison/contrast?

6. Based on these answers, is the paragraph evaluative or informative?

   A. The following paragraph was written by Lassissi Ayano, a visa student who was asked to describe his experiences using a computer conferencing system to take an economics course. Computer conferencing is like an electronic discussion group on a computer network linking teachers and learners.

   I was surprised to find that computer conferencing is very similar to the classroom learning experience. In the traditional classroom, the instructor disseminates information to the class as a whole, and individual students respond and ask questions. Group work and work with other individual students take place both in class and out of class. When you want to see your classroom professor individually, you do this after class or during office hours. You consult your professor or other students about any assignments or notes that you have missed or not understood. Analagously, in a computer conferencing system, your professor places notes for all members of the class in a computer "inbox" for them to read at a convenient time. Like a class discussion, when you respond to a note, your response is then placed in the other students' "inboxes" for them to consider. Similar to group work or homework with friends, you can send your notes to only a few people or even to just one person. Further, if you need consultation, you can just drop a note in your professor's inbox, and you will receive a private response. Finally, you cannot really "miss" anything: in the conferencing system you always have access to the full course for assignments, essays, or tests because all notes are filed electronically for you to consult at any time.

B. The following paragraph is by Rhona Goldstein, an interface designer for a software company. She is explaining the idea of the hypertext.

The traditional text works in stodgy linear fashion: it assumes that the reader starts reading at the beginning of the book and reads the pages in numerical order through to the end. Hypertext, on the other hand, is nonlinear: it could be read in a linear fashion, but it is filled with marginal references and notations that create instantaneous links to other parts of the book or document. These show the reader who is interested in some specific topic where to go for more information on that topic. The linear text assumes that every reader wants to read the whole book in the same order that the creaky old author conceived it. By contrast, hypertext knows that readers have their own agendas—that in the information age, each reader needs different data and has to be able to get it quickly. To accommodate the awesome variety of actual readers, hypertext creates an awesome variety of ways to read, a whole web of links within the text. Instead of one frozen linear text, which must always be read in the same boring way, we have an endless variety of texts that can be programmed in an instant, like a computer, to do what the reader-programmer needs. The linear text is dead; long live the hypertext!

COMPARATIVES AND SUPERLATIVES

As you work with comparisons and contrasts, remember that, as you describe things, the language provides you with three different categories for adjectives (modifiers of the actor of the sentence) and adverbs (modifiers of the action of the sentence). These are the **positive, comparative,** and **superlative** forms. Think about this example:

a. She is good at physics.

b. She is better at physics than most of her classmates.

c. She is the best physics student this semester.

The first statement is positive. The second statement implies a comparison to some others, and the third statement implies a comparison to all others. In an evaluative comparison/contrast essay, you will often need comparatives and superlatives to indicate your judgments.

Fill in the following chart:

POSITIVE	COMPARATIVE	SUPERLATIVE
bad		worst
fast	faster	
	more horrible	most horrible
clever		most clever
	nicer	nicest

How would you describe the difference among the positive, comparative, and superlative forms based upon this chart?

BLOCK AND SLICE METHODS

When you are putting together the outline for your comparison and contrast essay, you have a choice of two methods of organizing the body: the **block method** or the **slice method**.

Block Method

When you use the block method, you organize your comparison into two complete blocks. The first block provides all relevant information about all subtopics related to the first item or idea. The second block then furnishes all relevant information about these subtopics related to the second item or idea. For instance, in one of the sample essays in this module, Andy Manson compares the Canadian and American immigration philosophies. In this block-method outline, he discusses all of the features of the Canadian philosophy of "multiculturalism," and then addresses all of the features of the American "melting pot" philosophy.

para. 1: Introduction

• challenge of immigration, cultural difference

• how to serve immigrants/own citizens?

Thesis: Canadian multiculturalism vs. American melting pot; different aims and effects, problems and virtues

para. 2: Top. sent. multiculturalism
- definition, positives
- Canada as the example
- immigrants retain own culture; Heritage Language Program
- Canada enriched; tolerance

BLOCK 1: The Canadian System of Multiculturalism

para. 3: Top. sent. multiculturalism—possible negatives
- people feel Canadian second
- Quebec: history; desire for separation
- separate cultures with no connection

para. 4: Top. sent. melting pot
- definition, positives
- U.S. as the example
- uniformity of culture: teach English language and American history
- Americans first: blending together

BLOCK 2: The American Melting Pot System

para. 5: Top. sent. melting pot—possible negative
- encourages racism, intolerance
- ignores changing reality; EXAMPLE: Hispanic situation in some U.S. states

para. 6: Conclusion
- summary
- both have flaws but in global marketplace, world of constant change, spirit behind Canadian model preferable because adaptable, more forward-looking to world of twenty-first century

Even though multiculturalism and the melting pot are being examined separately, notice how within each block the same subtopics are being discussed. Thus, the first paragraph of block 1 (paragraph 2) defines the Canadian model of multiculturalism and explains how it works, while the first paragraph of block 2 (paragraph 4) defines the American melting pot model and explains how it works. Similarly, the second paragraph of block 1 (paragraph 3) discusses problems stemming from multiculturalism, and therefore corresponds to the second paragraph of block 2 (paragraph 5), which discusses the problems of the melting pot.

☀ DANGERS OF THE BLOCK

You may be tempted to use the block method simply because it seems to take less planning and less effort to organize. In this case, you would simply write down everything that comes to mind on the subject of multiculturalism, followed by everything about the melting pot. Don't be fooled into making this mistake. Deliberate selection and organization of your information are essential. Just as you must compare two ideas or items that are alike in the first place, so too you must compare the same details about each item. This is why you must construct your outline very carefully. As you can see in the sample outline, the details within the two blocks closely correspond to one another, right down to the specific examples provided.

Slice Method

When writing your essay according to the slice method, you do not discuss each of the items separately. Instead, you make your comparisons and contrasts more directly, on a topic-by-topic basis. The body of your essay is divided up into paragraphs, each of which examines a subtopic relevant to both items being compared.

The general model for the organization of your body paragraphs in a slice method comparison/contrast essay is as follows:

para. 2: Issue 1 Multiculturalism vs. Melting Pot
para. 3: Issue 2 Multiculturalism vs. Melting Pot
para. 4: Issue 3 Multiculturalism vs. Melting Pot

The following is an outline of the same multiculturalism vs. melting pot essay organized according to the slice method. Notice that the content is the same as the content of the previous outline, but the information has been rearranged under subtopic headings. As a result, the differences between multiculturalism and the melting pot are much more explicit.

para. 1: Introduction—challenge of immigration, cultural difference

- how can a country best serve immigrants and its own citizens?
  Thesis: Canadian multiculturalism vs. American melting pot: they have different aims, effects, problems, and virtues, as can be seen in the two countries' education systems, their different senses of national identity, and their different degrees of tolerance of racial and cultural difference.

para. 2: Top. sent.—compare definitions: multiculturalism (Canada) vs. melting pot (U.S.) • definitions contrasted: Canada's distinct cultural groups vs. U.S.'s expected assimilation • different expectations of immigrants in each system	*SLICE 1: Aims and Effects of Multiculturalism vs. Melting Pot*
para. 3: Top. sent.—education system as example of different expectations • Canada bilingual (recognizing two founding cultures); French mandatory in school vs. U.S. English only mandatory • Canada's Heritage Language classes vs. U.S. one common American history and culture • Canada inclusive vs. U.S. exclusive	*SLICE 2: Education System in Canada vs. United States*

(handwritten margin note: examples in boxes not necessary)

para. 4: Top. sent.—compare senses of national identity

- Canada: retain own culture but be Canadian

- U.S.: become American, original culture "melted down"

- this enriches Canadian identity BUT some say people feel Canadian second, while the melting pot makes people feel American first

- firm, unified sense of the American identity vs. the less-defined, more fragmented sense of what a Canadian is

SLICE 3: Sense of National Identity in Canada vs. United States

para. 5: Top. sent.—compare racial, cultural harmony and tolerance under Canadian and American systems

- multiculturalism: accept one another's inevitable differences; understand and appreciate (Quebec: proof of good and bad)

- melting pot: intolerance of difference?

- racism encouraged and evident

- ignores changing reality; EXAMPLE: Hispanic situation in some U.S. states

SLICE 4: Racial Harmony in Canada vs. United States

para. 6: Conclusion

- summary: differences and problems

- on basis of varied education, less rigid, more inclusive sense of national identity, and greater tolerance of difference, Canadian model seems superior

- in global marketplace, world of constant change, spirit behind Canadian model preferable because adaptable, more forward-looking to world of twenty-first century

ADVANTAGES OF THE SLICE

In general, the longer and more detailed your comparison/contrast paper is, the more sense it makes to use the slice method. The slice method is easier for a reader to follow. The block method forces the reader's memory to match up the individual differences and similarities—something that becomes more difficult as the blocks become longer. The truism "The harder readers have to work, the less likely they are to finish reading" is one to remember when you decide to use the block method.

Exercise 3

Following are two brief comparison/contrast paragraphs. Read each of them carefully, and answer the questions that follow.

A. This is a paragraph from Susanna Moodie's introduction to the third edition of *Roughing it in the Bush*. First published in 1852, this account describes the hardships and small victories that she and her family encountered as Canadian pioneers. Here, she discusses how European "public newspapers and private letters" in the 1830s sang the praises of Canada.

> The general interest [in Canada], once excited, was industriously kept alive by pamphlets, published by interested parties, which prominently set forth all the *good* to be derived from a settlement in the Backwoods of Canada; while they carefully concealed the toil and hardship to be endured in order to secure these advantages. They told of lands yielding forty bushels to the acre, but they said nothing of the years when these lands, with the most careful cultivation, would barely return fifteen; when rust and smut, engendered by the vicinity of damp overhanging woods, would blast the fruits of the poor emigrant's labour, and almost deprive him of bread. They talked of log houses to be raised in a single day, by the generous exertions of friends and neighbours, but they never ventured upon a picture of the disgusting scenes of riot and low debauchery exhibited during the raising, or upon a description of the dwellings when raised—dens of dirt and misery, which would, in many instances, be shamed by an English pig-sty.

B. This paragraph was written by Shuk Liu, a former hospitality student, to describe some of her observations during food preparation.

> Before it is dropped on the barbecue, the hamburger is like a frozen puck awaiting the faceoff. Once dropped, the flames battle to possess it, and reduce it to a bloody mess. Fat and animal juices ooze out, bursting into greasy flame on the barbecue coals below. The puck starts out a dull brown-red hue, but, as it softens, it takes on a chalky grey pallor, before blackening into some charred offering to the twin gods of animal slaughter and cancer of the colon. The veggie burger, by contrast, is cleanly, quietly, and consistently captivating. It starts out as a rainbow coalition of discernible, wholesome vegetables suspended in patty form: golden kernels of corn, emerald and crimson splashes of bell pepper, delicate white rice, and verdant peas. Rather than disintegrating or distorting it, exposure to the flame only crisps and confirms this cornucopia of colour and nourishment.

1. Is the paragraph a comparison, a contrast, or a comparison/contrast?

2. Is it evaluative or informative?

3. Draw up a point-form outline of each paragraph. Is it organized in the block or the slice method?

4. Rewrite each paragraph in the other organizational style.

5. Is there anything you like or dislike about the styles of writing?

Exercise 4

1. Return to the paragraphs in Exercise 2 and draw up a point-form outline of each. Is each organized in the block or the slice method?

2. Rewrite each paragraph in the other organizational style.

Exercise 5

1. Write one or two paragraphs in the block style comparing the pros and cons of the block and slice methods of organization.

2. Rewrite this in the slice style.

3. Which method is more effective for completing this task?

OCCASIONS FOR A COMPARISON AND CONTRAST ESSAY

Comparison and contrast is the rhetorical mode of an essay; it is not the subject in and of itself. When faced with a topic, then, you need to be able to recognize occasions when using the comparison/contrast mode will enable you to achieve your purpose.

1. Obviously, if you are asked to **compare and contrast** or to examine **similarities and differences** in two characters, two policies, or two methods, you will use the comparison/contrast mode.

2. Similarly, you may be asked to analyze one option **versus** (as opposed to) another. For example, a library and information student might be asked to examine the Dewey Decimal System of cataloguing vs. the Library of Congress System. This "vs." suggests confrontation: you are being asked for an evaluative judgment of the virtues and flaws of each system. You will likely conclude with a judgment in favour of one vs. the other.

When given a specific writing task at school or at work, you will not always be so explicitly told to write a comparison/contrast essay. Here are some other common cues that indicate a comparison/contrast essay is appropriate:

3. If asked to evaluate the **pros and cons, advantages and disadvantages,** or **positives and negatives** of a policy, you are being asked to compare its positive and negative aspects in order to evaluate its effectiveness and value.

4. In a **cost/benefit analysis,** you compare and contrast the expenses (money, time, and labour) vs. the advantages or benefits of a new procedure or purchase. Your ultimate purpose is to determine whether your company or organization will benefit from adopting the procedure or making the purchase.

For comparatives and superlatives, see pp. 132–33.

5. When **comparatives** (words like *better, worse, greater, lesser, more*) or **superlatives** (words like *best, worst, greatest, least, most*) are used, you should use the comparison/contrast mode. For instance, a travel student might be asked to determine the *most* affordable vacation destination for Canadian families. The student is effectively being asked to compare and contrast the accommodation,

food, travel, and entertainment costs of a variety of destinations in order to determine which represents the best value.

Exercise 6

Fill in the Top Ten List below with situations in your own field where the comparison/contrast mode might usefully be employed in a writing task. Use the cue words discussed earlier when you are describing these topics. Specify whether the essay would be evaluative or informative, and whether the topic would lend itself more to the block or the slice method of organization. For instance, a business student in human resources management might choose

> 1. Cost/benefit analysis of wage vs. non-wage benefits in the workplace (evaluative—slice)

Fill in as many as you can, and then continue reading the module. As other possible applications occur to you, return to this list and finish it.

TOP TEN APPLICATIONS FOR COMPARISON/CONTRAST WRITING IN MY FIELD

1.
2.
3.
4.
5.
6.
7.
8.
9.
10.

APPLYING THE SIX-STEP METHOD TO COMPARISON/ CONTRAST WRITING

Step 1: Imaging the Essay with the Rhetorical Triangle

See Module 8: Definition and Classification.

Follow the usual steps, beginning with imaging your essay with the rhetorical triangle. When focusing your topic, make certain that you are comparing items or ideas of a similar class. For instance, you might compare two types of software, two brands of automobile, two different vacation destinations, or how two writers develop characters in short stories. It might, not, however, be logical to compare Orlando, Florida, with Mexico as vacation destinations. While these are both destinations, Orlando is a single city, while Mexico is a nation. It would be more appropriate to compare Orlando with a single Mexican city, such as Cancún or Acapulco.

You should decide now exactly what kind of essay you are writing: is it comparison, contrast, or comparison/contrast? Is it evaluative or informative? Of course, you may revise these ideas when you actually begin generating content, but it helps to have an initial plan.

Step 2: Content Generation

As usual, generate content using more than one method. Be certain, however, not to give more emphasis to one item than another. Such an imbalance creates a flawed logic in the essay because it suggests that you are prejudiced in preferring one item over another. Imagine that you are a travel agent writing an article for your company's newsletter comparing Orlando and Cancún as winter getaway destinations; for every one line you write on Orlando, you write four lines on Acapulco. Your readers may well suspect that you did not seriously research Orlando. They may assume that you are only pretending to do a fair comparison, when you are really trying to convince them to go to Acapulco because this will benefit your company somehow. As a result, readers may not trust you. Much advertising utilizes this kind of discrepancy to make a certain product seem ideal. For your writing to be effective, in most cases a balanced treatment of both items is essential.

PARALLEL POINTS

When generating content for a comparison/contrast essay, you want to make parallel points about both items. This means that when you are coming up with details, it is useful to try to think of the two items in tandem so that you cover the same ground for each. If you are working on paper, create parallel columns; for every entry in one column, make an entry about the same issue in the other column. If you are working with a computer, open two files, one for each item, and when you enter an element into the first file, enter a related element into the second file.

See Module 8, Choosing Parallel Categories of Classification, p. 156.

Exercise 7

In groups of four to six, brainstorm in point form some parallel subtopics or points about the topics listed below. Try to identify key issues that would uncover the major differences or similarities between the topics. For instance, if asked to compare credit with cash, you might draw up a chart like the following:

Time factor   *Credit:*   You have up to 60 days to make payment; this is very convenient.

Cash: Payment at moment of purchase; you may not always have the cash in your pocket.

Credit rating   *Credit:*   Intelligent use of credit builds your credit rating, which is very important for major purchases, loans, and even renting an apartment.

Cash: To a credit bureau, the person who pays only cash does not really exist.

Debt problem   *Credit:*   It is deceptively simple to go into major debt with crippling interest payments.

Cash: You can only buy what you can afford; this forces you to live within your means.

1. Voice mail vs. receptionists
2. Criminals vs. "normal" humans
3. Quebec vs. the rest of Canada
4. Renting vs. owning
5. Racism vs. sexism

Step 3: The Outline

Outline your comparison/contrast essay in the following fashion:

See Module 3: How to Say It, Introduction, p. 49.

See Module 3, Thesis, p. 53.

INTRODUCTION

After your "grabber," introduce and define the two issues or items for comparison or contrast. Provide any background explanations your audience is likely to need. Your thesis will make your major point about these issues.

THESIS AND MODE

It is easy to mistake the rhetorical mode for the point of the essay. The danger is that your thesis statement becomes the mechanical "this essay will compare Florida and Mexico as destinations." This is a rephrasing of your topic and rhetorical mode from the rhetorical triangle, not a thesis statement. The reader of such a thesis has no indication of what the point of the essay is. Remember, your thesis needs to

1. indicate your focused topic;
2. indicate your rhetorical mode;
3. map out the essay's subtopics;
4. make your main point.

One thesis satisfying all of these requirements is as follows: "For the cost-conscious Canadian traveller, Mexico is clearly a better vacation destination than Florida given the difference in Mexican and American currencies, the predominance of bartering in the Mexican marketplace, and the availability of superior package deals."

See Module 3, Body, p. 57.

BODY

Use the block or the slice method to compare the issues or items according to smaller, relevant subtopics.

*See Module 3,
Conclusion, p. 60.*

CONCLUSION

Draw logical conclusions from the process of comparison—about which option is preferable, about what can be learned from the similarities or differences, or about each option's different flaws and virtues. It is never enough simply to show that differences or similarities exist; if you do this, you will leave your reader wondering "What is the point of this essay?" You must analyze and explain the significance of these differences, as they are exactly the concerns that form the purpose of writing in this rhetorical mode.

Step 4: Writing the Rough Draft

When you write your rough draft, your primary concern should be with ensuring that you have sufficiently developed your subtopics. If you are not careful, your comparison/contrast writing may resemble an essay less than a list or "greatest hits" package of unexplored similarities and differences: "There's this similarity, but then there's that difference. Now this is a little different, but this is the same. That is the same, too. And then there's this other likeness." Poor comparison/contrast writing has the quality of a breathless flood of superficial spoken words. Try to ensure that each subtopic is amply developed with detailed, specific examples and analysis, and that you omit trivial or incidental similarities or differences.

Step 5: Revising

When revising your comparison/contrast essay, you should use transitional phrases that heighten specific differences and similarities. These help to focus the essay as a comparison/contrast by highlighting specific moments of similarity or difference. This may be particularly useful in a block essay where, if you are not careful, you may accidentally produce two separate and unconnected blocks of information. Consult the list of transition techniques for examples.

 UNNECESSARY AMPLIFIERS

One common error that writers encounter is that of using unnecessary amplifiers, or trying to describe something "really really important." The problem is that such statements become meaningless. If something is "more better" than something else, then it is either just plain better, or it is the best. Your normal comparatives and superlatives will work for you. Expressions like "It was so big ... " or "It was really big ... " or "It was awfully big ... " really mean so awfully little.

Step 6: Editing

Looking for your most common errors, edit your comparison/contrast essay carefully.

TRANSITION TECHNIQUES FOR COMPARISON/CONTRAST WRITING

Judicious use of some of the following words or phrases will help suggest the conclusions that are the purpose of the piece:

- Some useful linking or transitional phrases suggesting likeness or similarity are *similarly, analogously, likewise, too.*

- Some useful linking or transitional phrases indicating contrast or difference are *but/yet, although, however, still, nevertheless, on the contrary, on the other hand.*

Exercise 8

Given the transitional phrase being used, complete the following sentences appropriately and logically. This requires a clear understanding of both the transitional phrase and the kind of similarity or difference being expressed.

1. Most Canadians want to retire with the same standard of living as they possess now, but ...

2. Instead of being so competitive and insistent upon winning every argument, ...

3. "I'm only one person. There's nothing I can do about the problem of the homeless," people always insist. Nevertheless, ...

4. ... By contrast, the automatic response of many students when faced with writing an essay for English class is "How long does it have to be?"

5. The primary caregiver in a family should not be determined by gender. Still, ...

6. Everyone knows about the dangers of alcohol, yet alcohol abuse is rampant. Likewise, ...

7. Although buying the latest Paris fashions is not in the budget of every student, ...

8. When a worker takes a twenty-minute break instead of the fifteen-minute break that is allowed, he or she is stealing from the employer. Similarly, ...

9. Costa Rica can be an unbearable swampland in the rainy season. On the other hand, ...

10. Writing a response to a customer complaint may not be the easiest task; however, ...

Following is a proofread final copy of the multiculturalism vs. melting pot essay written for an introductory liberal studies course. Read this final draft carefully, and note the way the essay has been assembled.

Sample Comparison and Contrast Essay 1

MULTI- OR MELTING: IMMIGRATION POLICY IN CANADA AND THE U.S.

BY ANDY MANSON

We inhabit a world filled with people of different colours, different races, different religions and different backgrounds. Naturally, immigration from one country to another is a constant phenomenon, and represents a complex challenge. There is much disagreement about how a country can best serve both its citizens and its immigrants. Indeed, in many ways it seems impossible to satisfy everybody, but in North America, two different approaches have been implemented. The Canadian and American policies—known as multiculturalism and the melting pot respectively—represent different philosophies with unique virtues and problems. (1)

Under multiculturalism, Canadians expect new immigrants to become Canadians but simultaneously to retain a sense of their old culture. In fact, the government encourages them to do this. For instance, where there are enough students, the Ontario government funds "Heritage Language Programs" in public schools. Here, students spend part of their classroom day learning the specific language and culture of their ancestors. Canada was built by immigrants from all nations and backgrounds, and this spirit of acceptance and understanding defines an important aspect of Canadian culture. When immigrants retain a sense of their Asian or African or Australian cultures, the theory says, Canadian culture is enriched. Therefore, Canadian culture is always changing and growing, because Canada has more and more different traditions, knowledges and backgrounds to draw on. (2)

Critics, however, argue that multiculturalism has fostered division and discontent in Canada today. They say that initiatives like the Heritage Language Program teach people how to be different from one another, rather than how to share certain common Canadian values. Therefore, immigrants will think of themselves firstly as Greek, or Japanese, or Indian, and only secondly as Canadian. As another example, these critics note that Canada has had two official languages and two official cultures (French and English) since the country was formed in 1867. Some see this as a source of problems which continue to this day. For example, the desire of many French Quebecers to separate from Canada and form a nation of their own is an inevitable and continuous phenomenon. According to some critics, we would have fewer such "problems" today if the conquering English population had assimilated the French, instead of allowing them to retain their language and culture. (3)

By contrast, the American response to immigration is the "melting pot" or assimilation. In this system, immigrants to the United States are expected to learn the official language of the United States (English) and are taught American history and culture almost exclusively. If immigrants want their children to learn their mother tongue and culture, this must be done on their own time and with their own money. The theory of this system is that immigrants become first and foremost Americans: people of various backgrounds are blended or "melted" together into one

American people. As a result, many Americans have an extraordinarily strong, self-assured sense of their national identity and an extraordinary pride in it. (4)

Critics of the American system, however, argue that America is a less tolerant society than Canada. They say that most people, like the government, make little effort to understand people from faraway places and different ethnic backgrounds. Instead, immigrants are expected to simply change and blend in. Critics also argue that the "melting pot" model fails to deal with reality: for example, some experts have predicted that if immigration rates remain constant, by 2000 there will be several states with more Americans who speak Spanish as a first language than who speak English as a first language. To force everyone to conform to the present system and learn only English is not only unrealistic, they argue, but racist, and therefore a source of almost inevitable racial conflict. (5)

The virtues and potential flaws of both systems are readily apparent. Canadian multiculturalism emphasizes diversity in education, tolerance and understanding as the basis for living together—perhaps at the expense of a unified, coherent sense of national identity. Canadians have tremendous difficulty explaining what Canada is and what its place in the world is. On the other hand, the American "melting pot" insists upon a strong, single version of American history, culture and national identity—but this expectation that all peoples and cultures should be "melted" into one broth can lead to intolerance of difference. In this light, the adaptable spirit of Canadian multiculturalism may, in fact, be more suited to the world of the twenty-first century. Increasingly, countries have to learn to trade with merchants and companies from all corners of the globe, while dealing with rapid-fire technological and cultural change. By knowing and respecting different languages, cultures and beliefs within Canada, and all the while not depending on some inflexible, unchanging definition of the "Canadian" way, Canadians are already coping with the challenging, changing cultural and economic realities of our global marketplace. (6)

Questions

1. Is this a comparison, contrast, or comparison/contrast essay? Why do you think so?

2. Does this essay use the block or the slice method? Why?

3. Is this an evaluative or an informative essay? Why?

4. When you consider the argument, how is the choice of this particular method effective or ineffective? Is it a strong or weak argument? Why? How does the argument lead to the conclusion?

5. Underline transitional phrases indicating similarity or contrast.

6. Rewrite the conclusion of the essay in favour of the American model.

Sample Comparison and Contrast Essay 2

THAT LEAN AND HUNGRY LOOK

NEWSWEEK, OCTOBER 9, 1978

BY SUZANNE BRITT JORDAN

Caesar was right. Thin people need watching. I've been watching them for most of my adult life, and I don't like what I see. When these narrow fellows spring at me, I quiver to my toes. Thin people come in all personalities, most of them menacing. You've got your "together" thin person, your mechanical thin person, your condescending thin person, your tsk-tsk thin person, your efficiency-expert thin person. All of them are dangerous. (1)

In the first place, thin people aren't fun. They don't know how to goof off, at least in the best, fat sense of the word. They've always got to be active. Give them a coffee break, and they'll jog around the block. Supply them with a quiet evening at home, and they'll fix the screen door and lick S&H green stamps. They say things like "there aren't enough hours in the day." Fat people never say that. Fat people think the day is too damn long already. (2)

Thin people make me tired. They've got speedy little metabolisms that cause them to bustle briskly. They're forever rubbing their bony hands together and eyeing new problems to "tackle." I love to surround myself with sluggish, inert, easygoing fat people, the kind who believe that if you clean it up today, it'll just get dirty again tomorrow. (3)

Some people say the business about the jolly fat person is a myth, that all of us chubbies are neurotic, sick, sad people. I disagree. Fat people may not be chortling all day long, but they're a lot nicer than the wizened and shriveled. Thin people turn surly, mean, and hard at a young age because they never learn the value of a hot-fudge sundae for easing tension. Thin people don't like gooey soft things because they themselves are neither gooey nor soft. They are crunchy and dull, like carrots. They go straight to the heart of the matter while fat people let things stay all blurry and hazy and vague, the way things actually are. Thin people want to face the truth. Fat people know there is no truth. One of my thin friends is always staring at complex, unsolvable problems and saying, "The key thing is...." Fat people never say that. They know there isn't any such thing as the key thing about anything. (4)

Thin people believe in logic. Fat people see all sides. The sides fat people see are rounded blobs, usually gray, always nebulous and truly not worth worrying about. But the thin person persists. "If you consume more calories than you burn," says one of my thin friends, "you will gain weight. It's that simple." Fat people always grin when they hear statements like that. They know better. (5)

Fat people realize that life is illogical and unfair. They know very well that God is not in his heaven and all is not right with the world. If God was up there, fat people could have two doughnuts and a big orange drink anytime they wanted it. (6)

Thin people have a long list of logical things they are always spouting off to me. They hold up one finger at a time as they reel off these things, so I won't lose track. They speak slowly as if to a young child. The list is long and full of holes. It contains tidbits like "get a grip on yourself," "cigarettes kill," "cholesterol clogs," "fit as a fiddle," "ducks in a row," "organize," and "sound fiscal management." Phrases like that. (7)

They think these 2000-point plans lead to happiness. Fat people know happiness is elusive at best and even if they could get the kind thin people talk about, they wouldn't want it. Wisely, fat people see that such programs are too dull, too hard, too off the mark. They are never better than a whole cheesecake. (8)

Fat people know all about the mystery of life. They are the ones acquainted with the night, with luck, with fate, with playing it by ear. One thin person I know once suggested that we arrange all the parts of a jigsaw puzzle into groups according to size, shape, and colour. He figured this would cut the time needed to complete the puzzle by at least 50 percent. I said I wouldn't do it. One, I like to muddle through. Two, what good would it do to finish early? Three, the jigsaw puzzle isn't the important thing. The important thing is the fun of the four people (one thin person included) sitting around a card table, working on a jigsaw puzzle. My thin friend had no use for my list. Instead of joining us, he went outside and mulched the boxwoods. The three remaining fat people finished the puzzle and made chocolate, double-fudged brownies to celebrate. (9)

The main problem with thin people is they oppress. Their good intentions, bony torsos, tight ships, neat corners, cerebral machinations, and pat solutions loom like dark clouds over the loose, comfortable, spread-out, soft world of the fat. Long after fat people have removed their coats and shoes and put their feet up on the coffee table, thin people are still sitting on the edge of the sofa, looking neat as a pin, discussing rutabagas. Fat people are heavily into fits of laughter, slapping their thighs and whooping it up, while thin people are still politely waiting for the punch line. (10)

Thin people are downers. They like math and morality and reasoned evaluation of the limitations of human beings. They have their skinny little acts together. They expound, prognose, probe, and prick. (11)

Fat people are convivial. They will like you even if you're irregular and have acne. They will come up with a good reason why you never wrote the great American novel. They will cry in your beer with you. They will put your name in the pot. They will let you off the hook. Fat people will gab, giggle, guffaw, gallumph, gyrate, and gossip. They are generous, giving, and gallant. They are gluttonous and goodly and great. What you want when you're down is soft and jiggly, not muscled and stable. Fat people know this. Fat people have plenty of room. Fat people will take you in. (12)

Questions

1. Identify the essay's thesis, and state in your own words the purpose of the essay.

2. Is this a comparison, contrast, or comparison/contrast essay?

3. Does this essay use the block or the slice method? Why?

4. Is this an evaluative or an informative essay? Why?

5. When you consider the argument, how is the choice of this particular method effective or ineffective?

6. Underline any transitional phrases that indicate similarity or contrast.

7. How do you respond to the argument? Is it valid?

8. Is Jordan talking exclusively about fat and thin people in this essay, or is she making a more general argument?

9. Can you imagine an audience being offended by this argument? What would you say to this audience?

10. Examine Jordan's conclusion: how does she leave the reader to ponder the larger implications of her issue?

OTHER APPLICATIONS OF COMPARISON/CONTRAST

As with all rhetorical modes, you may very effectively use moments of comparison/contrast within essays written in other rhetorical modes for different purposes. A 1995 advertisement inserted in Toronto newspapers had the following sentence written in large red type on its front page:

> We can fight youth crime with guns, handcuffs, and longer jail terms.

For the rest of this essay, see Module 10, "Sample Essay of Persuasion 2," p. 213.

Comparison/contrast as a grabber

Upon opening the insert, the reader saw three pages of attractive type and photographs, beginning with the following text:

> Or we can use baseballs, hockey pucks and minnows.
>
> We can fight youth crime by pursuing and punishing the guilty. That's a vital part of what Metro's police force does. But what we can also do is get to innocent kids before their lives take a tragic turn to crime. Before they get caught up in a cycle that ruins individuals and destroys families.

The balance of the essay is persuasive: it explains the many past efforts of an organization called ProAction to bring "kids and cops and sports" together in order to help everyone function better as a community and to deter youth crime. The essay ends by appealing to the reader for a donation.

Question

How does this contrast make an effective grabber for this essay?

Exercise 9

Using the six-step method, write an essay on one of the topics from your Top Ten List. Justify your choice of format: is it a comparison, contrast, or comparison/contrast essay? Is it informative or evaluative? Is it organized by the block or the slice method? Why?

CHOOSING TOPICS

Remember: choose a topic that you are interested in and/or know a lot about. Be specific in your essay, and be certain to compare the same types of specific details. Try to come to some logical conclusion related to your purpose.

SUMMARY

A comparison/contrast essay analyzes items or ideas of a similar class. A comparison essay focuses solely on similarities, a contrast essay deals with the differences, and a comparison/contrast essay examines both similarities and differences. Each of these formats can be either evaluative (judgmental)—in which case you conclude by favouring one item or idea over the other—or purely informative, in which case you provide your readers with all relevant details and allow them to choose the better option.

When you write any of these essays, it is essential to subdivide your topics into relevant subtopics. There are two ways to organize these subtopics: the block method and the slice method. In the block method, the body of your essay consists of two distinct blocks, one about each item being compared. When using the slice method, you make comparisons and contrasts between your two subjects more directly on a topic-by-topic basis.

When you are given a specific writing task at school or at work, common cues can indicate that the comparison/contrast essay is appropriate. Similarly, appropriate transitional phrases in your writing will help unify your essay and highlight the actions of comparing and contrasting. A moment of comparison/contrast can provide an effective grabber or other part of an essay written predominantly in another rhetorical mode.

CHECKLIST

- Does your thesis clearly establish whether this is a comparison, contrast, or comparison/contrast essay?
- Are you comparing/contrasting items of the same class?
- Have you given more emphasis to one item than another, creating a flawed logic in the essay?
- Have you clearly structured your essay using either the block or the slice method?
- No matter which method of organization you have used, have you compared/contrasted the same details about each item?
- Have you used sufficient appropriate transitional phrasing to clarify the logic of your argument?
- Does your conclusion suggest the larger implications of the process of comparison?

8

Definition and Classification

OVERVIEW

Imagine 2-year-old Julia, her face shining with delight, pointing at a dazzling orange Monarch butterfly as it swoops and flutters through a field. "Bird!" she shouts. "No," you reply with a smile. She looks at you curiously. "What is it?" she asks. "It's a butterfly," you respond.

Julia's question and your answer deal with two important, related rhetorical modes. Because the butterfly is flying, and the only creatures that Julia has seen fly are birds, she classifies it as a bird. **Classification** is the grouping of items into categories by similarities and differences. When Julia is told that her classification is, in fact, incorrect, she looks to you for clarification of what this strange, colourful flying object is. In response, you provide a **definition** or explanation—it is a butterfly.

Definition and classification are two common, related processes of explaining and understanding ideas and things. Much education depends specifically upon the definition or classification of concepts. For instance, a social service worker student specializing in gerontology will likely take a course on aging; this course will define aging by classifying it into biological processes, psychological processes, and social dynamics. An office administration student might take a course on the sociology of work; this course deals with the nature of work (definition) and establishes criteria for evaluating the different kinds of job satisfaction (classification) that are likely to exist in these jobs. The textbook you are currently reading classifies essays into different rhetorical modes, and then defines each.

DEFINITION: PURPOSE AND FUNCTION

If you do not understand the meaning of a word, you look it up in the dictionary. The dictionary is a tool that ensures that when two people discuss "entrepreneurship," "hydrology," or "torts," they are both talking about the same thing. In this sense, it is a kind of rulebook of language meanings.

The *Gage Canadian Dictionary* defines *definition* in the following way:

> *n.* **1** the act or process of explaining or making clear the meaning of a word or group of words. **2** a statement that makes clear the meaning of a word or group of words; explanation.

Definition, therefore, is a process of clarification or explanation; more simply, it is a process of using different, generally simpler words in order to explain the meaning of a word or idea. In all likelihood, Julia will not be satisfied with your answer "butterfly," but, like any child (and any student skilled at using the five "Ws" and one "H"), she will ask you further questions: "What is a butterfly?" or "Why is that a butterfly?" In order to answer this question, you will need to define what a butterfly is. Perhaps, in order to do this, you will consult the dictionary for its definition.

> *n.* **1** any of a large group of about six families of diurnal insects (order Lepidoptera) having a slender body, long, slender antennae with thick, knoblike tips, and four large, often brightly colored wings. Compare **moth.**

Here you have a very specific definition of a butterfly in terms of the characteristics or details that distinguish a butterfly from other insects. The second part of the definition literally takes the butterfly apart in order to look at the components that make it unique: the "slender body," the "long, slender antennae with thick, knoblike tips," and the "four large, often brightly colored wings."

Definition is a fundamental process in learning about a subject. When you write a definition essay, you are explaining an uncertain or ambiguous idea by breaking it down into its smaller or component parts. A biological technology student might write a definition essay for a virology class; the essay might begin from a general definition of the word *virus*, and then explain and analyze a virus's structure, growth, and effects. A law enforcement student might write an essay defining the notion of criminal responsibility, the complex concept upon which our whole legal system is founded. To define *criminal responsibility* would, in turn, require the definition and explanation of the specific defences of insanity, age, provocation, and duress, all of which affect whether or not a person can be held responsible for a criminal act.

Exercise 1

Form groups of four to six. In separate paragraphs and without using the dictionary, define as specifically as possible each of the following terms. Pretend you are describing the term to someone who has never heard of it before.

1. Your program or career goals (for example, define *nursing* or *agriculture* or *business*)

2. Maturity

3. Computer literacy

4. Fun

5. Employment equity

   In your group, compare your definitions. Are they similar or different? Are some more effective than others? Why? As a group, decide upon at least three characteristics of a good definition.

Denotation and Connotation

As you have likely discovered, the process of defining an idea or a word is not necessarily as straightforward as it may first seem. This is caused by a variety of reasons, one of which is the difference between denotation and connotation.

Exercise 2

Look at the words below. Each pair of words means the same thing if you look them up in the dictionary. Nonetheless, do you detect any differences between the type of words on the left and the type of words on the right? Hint: does one suggest a stronger (more positive or negative) feeling?

average	mediocre
unusual	exceptional
job	task
school	academy
restaurant	bistro

DENOTATION

Language works on two levels. In **denotation**, also known as the "literal meaning," a word signifies a specific object. For instance, *house* refers to a specific type of building with four walls and a roof where a person lives. When most people think about a house, they visualize a generic, nondescript building.

CONNOTATION

In **connotation,** however, a word suggests or involves something more than it specifically refers to. It creates expectations and associations in the reader's mind. For instance, the word *home*—just like *house*—means the place where a person lives. But when most people think of home, they think not simply of a building, but of a variety of emotions and ideas they associate with home. For many, home connotes, or makes them think about, love, security, comfort, belonging, ownership, and family. For others, home may connote pain, violence, or poverty. It conjures up unique personal and cultural associations. As such, connotations are extremely powerful tools in creating meaning.

Some connotations are cultural; for instance, to various Canadians, maple syrup, ice hockey, wheat fields, multiculturalism, railways, or unspoiled forests may connote a powerful, patriotic sense of what Canada is.

Even the same word can have negative or positive connotations depending upon the context in which it is used. For example, if you consult a thesaurus for synonyms for *proud,* some of the words you will find are *conceited, smug, vain, arrogant,* and *haughty.* These, of course, have negative connotations. Other synonyms you will find are *magnificent, splendid, principled,* and *dignified,* which have more positive connotations. To be an effective writer and reader, you must understand a word's denotative and potential connotative meanings.

SYNONYMS

In reality, there is no such thing as two words that mean exactly the same thing—otherwise, there would be little reason for having two different words. This is why you have to be extremely careful when using a thesaurus. When you select a synonym from a thesaurus, always look up the new word to ensure that you understand some of the consequences of using it. Select your words carefully with an eye to connotations; otherwise, your definition may confuse or mislead rather than clarify.

Generally, the dictionary definition of a word deals with denotation—that is, with the literal meaning. If we only had literal meanings, there would be no need to write definition essays. When someone used a term like *Generation X,* or *bribe,* or *addiction,* everyone would understand exactly the same thing. This is not the case, however. Language functions equally by connotation. The connotations that you associate with the term *Generation X* may be very different from someone else's. In a definition essay, you organize information and thoughts (often about your connotations) into separate groups or categories in order to illustrate a point.

Exercise 3

In your group, and using a dictionary, look up the original five words or phrases from Exercise 1.

You now have the denotative meanings; write these down. Now re-examine the definitions you initially created. What individual connotations distinguish your definitions from the denotative dictionary definitions?

CLASSIFICATION: PURPOSE AND FUNCTION

The *Gage Canadian Dictionary* defines *classification* in the following manner:

> *n.* **1** an arranging in classes or groups on the basis of similar qualities or features; grouping according to some system.

We use classification to "group" similar items together in order to organize the world around us. Think about a weekly television listings magazine: it uses two different systems of classification to make the listings accessible to you. First, it will classify all programs by time. Second, the listing may have separate pages classifying sports, movies, and pay-per-view listings. Another example would be a college or university course calendar. This does not simply throw all of its course information at you randomly, but classifies it by program and course so that you can easily discover what is relevant to you.

In a classification essay, you are taking a subject and dividing it into smaller classes or groups in order to make a point or to simplify the subject for your reader. Libraries are based upon classifying information by category so that all of the material on small engine repair, or fire protection, or microcomputers is in roughly the same location. Thus, a library information techniques student might write a classification essay on subject cataloguing in the Library of Congress cataloguing system. A design arts or visual arts student might write a classification essay on the physical, psychological, and optical properties of colour. A civil engineering student might write a classification essay on types of automatic sprinkler systems or types and applications of automatic fire detectors.

STEREOTYPES

In the effort to classify types of people, it is possible to cut corners so much that we forget that people are individuals with unique virtues and failings. This is sterotyping. Stereotyping is irresponsible and inaccurate classification. Be very careful not to stereotype; Module 9's discussion of qualifiers (words or phrases that turn absolute statements into general statements) may help you to find more diplomatic and accurate ways of phrasing such classifications.

Exercise 4

Break down the five categories below into at least three different types, and make brief notes of the characteristics of each type. This is not the same as providing three examples; refer to the following example:

Category: Student Jobs

Type 1: Highly Relevant Course Placements—excellent hands-on, practical work experience; prove that you can do the kind of work you are being trained for in school; can sometimes lead to a full-time job after graduation;

Type 2: Relevant Part-Time Jobs—sometimes useful and practical; may help you develop broadly useful work skills; on rare occasions may help you get a full-time job by showing you are responsible and have had a variety of positions;

Type 3: Irrelevant, Menial McJobs—never useful and generally unpleasant; not very helpful in developing job skills, except to show you are willing to work; will likely not lead to a full-time job.

1. Benefits of education

2. Students

3. Vacations

4. Necessary job skills

5. Role models

Choosing Parallel Categories of Classification

See Module 7: Comparison and Contrast, Parallel Points, p. 140.

When planning a classification essay, you must be careful to divide your topic into equal or parallel categories. For instance, suppose you are given the dreaded topic "types of cars," and you choose to subdivide the categories in the following fashion:

automobiles

luxury cars   economy cars   sports cars   Ford cars

In this case, the first three groups are "types of cars according to drivers' expectations." The luxury-car driver wants comfort, size, and elegance in an automobile. The sports-car driver wants stylish design, speed, and power. The economy-car driver wants a low price and efficient fuel economy.

However, to quote the television show *Sesame Street,* "one of these things doesn't belong." The fourth category is not parallel. Ford is an automobile manufacturer; as such, Ford makes a complete line of automobiles, including luxury cars, sports cars, and economy cars. This fourth category, then, is not parallel, but in fact overlaps the first three. It should be excluded from the essay.

The principle of classification becomes in large measure the principle by which the essay is organized: each body paragraph in this case could deal with a different subgroup.

Exercise 5

1. Return to your types from Exercise 4. Are they all parallel?

2. Play the *Sesame Street* game: in the five lists below, one of the things does not belong in the category. Pick it out and explain why it does not fit.

3. Name the classification in which the remaining four items should be grouped.

4. Give two more examples that would fit into this classification.

   A. Nursing, Business, Math, Law Enforcement, Agriculture

   B. Roses, orchids, begonias, petunias, weeds

   C. Canadian, Asian, French, Brazilian, Australian

   D. Clustering, rhetorical triangle, brainstorming, dictionary method

   E. Money, rent, gas, food, parking

Providing Parallel Information

Not only do your categories need to be parallel in a classification essay, but your discussion of each category should address the same kind of information about each. A reader can only appreciate the differences among different classes if the same type of information is being provided about each class. For example, if you return to the example given in Exercise 4, you can see that within each of the three types of student jobs discussed, the exact same information is presented:

1. information on the usefulness of the job experience;

2. its impact on a student's job skills; and

3. its helpfulness in getting a full-time job.

Exercise 6

Return to your classifications from Exercise 4, and evaluate the characteristics you listed there to define each category or type. Are they parallel? Have you provided the same kind of information about each? Revise your explanations so that they are parallel in structure.

PARALLEL STRUCTURE

Parallel structure in a sentence refers to equal elements that are constructed in the same way. They help your writing to flow and make it more interesting and understandable to read. Consider the following two sentences:

See Appendix A, Contract #8: Parallelism.

> Adrian went to the bookstore, cafeteria, and the classroom.
> Adrian went to the bookstore, to the cafeteria, and to the classroom.

Notice the equal elements (bookstore, cafeteria, and classroom) in both sentences. Notice that in the second sentence, each of these uses the same basic format. Which of these sentences is more effective?

Rewrite the following sentences so that equal elements are parallel.

1. Ajani is wealthy, attractive, and a bachelor.
2. In this subject we are asked to write legibly, to acknowledge our sources, and that we should be accurate.
3. Petroleum is used for fuel, for engine lubricant, and when you are manufacturing plastic.

RELATIONSHIP OF CLASSIFICATION AND DEFINITION
Definition by Classification

Definition and classification are intimately related rhetorical modes, as you can see by this simple example. Suppose someone says to you, "Tell me something about yourself." When it comes to defining who you are as a person, you will likely start classifying yourself in various ways, such as by gender, nationality, marital status, geography, and occupation. You are a man or a woman. You are a Canadian, not an American. You are single, dating, or married. You come from Battleford, Vancouver, or Truro. You are a legal assistant, a technologist, or a computer programmer.

Indeed, in one form or another, classification is the key to everyone's sense of identity. In different conversations, you may define yourself by the sports you like ("I'm a tennis player"), the program and educational level you are studying at ("I'm a college student in building environmental technology"), your likes and dislikes ("I'm a big fan of grunge music"), or your politics ("I'm a conservative"). Quite naturally, even inevitably, when you seek to define who you are you look for categories to which you belong. You are "grouping according to some system." If you examine the dictionary definition of *butterfly* again, you can see that it, too, like any dictionary definition, works by classification: by classifying the word *butterfly* as a noun, and then by explaining the various groups of insects to which a butterfly belongs.

Exercise 7

Brainstorm answers to the question "Define yourself." Then examine your answers and write down the classification or larger category to which each detail belongs. For instance, you might start by quoting the Molson beer commercials, "I am ... Canadian." Then move on to other aspects of yourself.

Classification by Definition

The reverse is also true: for classification to be effective, each unique class must be defined. For example, after someone has been killed, several different kinds of criminal charges, ranging from first-degree murder to involuntary manslaughter, can be levelled. Explaining these classifications means defining them. For example, *first-degree murder* is premeditated, planned, cold-blooded murder. *Involuntary manslaughter* is a lesser charge; the person charged is responsible for the other person's death, but the death is deemed to be unplanned and unintentional. These belong to the same category ("possible charges in the event of a wrongful death"), but without a definition, the distinction between them would be unclear. Within a classification essay, the explanation of each classification will read like a miniature definition.

Exercise 8

Take your classifications from Exercise 7 and define whatever you mean by them. Be creative as well as literal; use connotation as well as denotation. Use the five "Ws" and one "H" if you are stuck. For instance, "I am Canadian—meaning I live in the land of universal health care, trout-filled lakes, and the Northern Lights."

THE DEFINITION/CLASSIFICATION ESSAY: OBJECTIVE OR SUBJECTIVE

When writing an essay of definition/classification, you may adopt an **objective** perspective, in which you attempt to define, describe, and distinguish actual and apparent categories or classes of objects or things. Here, you deal in the denotative quality of language and in information and ideas that are measurable. Such an essay is an excellent way to present factual subject matter in an informative way. For example, an ECE student could write a classification essay on types of children's literature and their uses in early childhood education. This would involve identifying and distinguishing the types of children's books under headings such as fiction and nonfiction, or by the age level of the intended reader. By making distinctions among items and defining the categories, the student would present information or ideas in an accessible and orderly fashion.

Equally common is the **subjective** perspective, in which your definition or classification, although still supported by examples and evidence, is coloured by your personal opinion. Here, you express a new, individual perspective that challenges the reader's usual understanding of an issue. In Module 1, Bruce's essay on types of television programs (programs we watch but do not admit we watch; programs we do not watch but say we watch) is subjective and personal.

In many ways, we all experience the same things differently. Imagine two people in the same room. One says "I'm hot," while the other says "I'm freezing." Both are telling the truth from their own subjective perspectives. This subjectivity, coupled with the connotative nature of language, means that different people define and classify things in many different ways; thus, the subjective essay of definition or classification is quite common as well. For example, imagine an essay with the topic "Define a child." Now imagine how different the essays might be if written by a teenager with overprotective parents, a child youth worker, and a corrections officer familiar with the Young Offenders Act.

Exercise 9

British Columbia author Douglas Coupland's famous 1991 novel *Generation X* first coined the term "Generation X," which is used widely to describe those people born in the 1960s. In the margins of the book's pages, Coupland frequently creates various new words and definitions appropriate to the experiences of this generation. One example is the following:

> **McJob**: A low-pay, low-prestige, low-dignity, low-benefit, no-future job in the service sector. Frequently considered a satisfying career choice by people who have never held one. [From Douglas Coupland, *Generation X*. New York: St. Martins Press, 1991, 5.]

The *Mc* prefix placed in front of the word *job* is clearly a reference to McDonald's, which mass-produces burgers in disposable packages. Coupland provides a highly personal (and sarcastic) definition of his term *McJob* by classifying the characteristics of a Generation Xer's typical job. His definition could function as a thesis statement for a definition essay on the McJob, with body paragraphs explaining each characteristic.

As a group, add the prefix *Mc* to another term, and define this new idea carefully by classifying its characteristics and providing specific examples as support.

DEFINITION AND CLASSIFICATION MUST HAVE A POINT

The definition/classification essay is a means of explaining in detail your particular understanding or definition of a phenomenon or object. If the essay is factual and objective, the purpose is to present the information clearly and logically, in an accessible and orderly fashion, in order to teach the reader how to understand the subject. If the essay is subjective, once again the purpose is to present your ideas clearly and logically, in an accessible and orderly fashion. This time, however, your goal is to teach the reader your unique understanding of something. What must be remembered is that both kinds of essay have a specific point to make.

STATING THE OBVIOUS

Nothing is less interesting to read than a definition/classification essay that states the obvious for no apparent purpose. Remember Bruce's first essay in Module 1 on types of television programs? Initially, it discussed situation comedies, talk shows, and cable television in order to prove that television programming offered variety. This is self-evident and, quite frankly, boring. An essay on types of cars risks the same fate—yawn!

In order to make your point, use one rhetorical mode to reinforce the other. For instance, a human resources management student, asked to write a subjective definition essay defining *employment equity,* might choose as a thesis, "Employment equity is institutionalized racism" or "Employment equity is the means to achieving fairness in the workplace." No matter which definition is chosen, one way to proceed is by further defining the key terms, and by classifying and analyzing the groups subject to the policy: visible vs. invisible minorities, all minorities vs. the majority, men vs. women, the able-bodied vs. the physically challenged.

OCCASIONS FOR DEFINITION AND CLASSIFICATION

When given a specific writing task at school or at work, you need to be able to identify occasions when classification is appropriate to your purpose. Obviously, if you are asked to classify job prospects for computer studies students, you will utilize classification.

You will not, however, always be so explicitly told to use classification. Here are some other common cues that indicate a classification essay is appropriate:

1. If you are asked to **describe** or **explain** the different *branches/categories/classes/components/groups/kinds/parts/sorts/types/varieties* of something, you are being asked to use classification. For example, "Discuss the components of pharmaceutical analysis."

2. If you are asked to *divide/sort/separate/distinguish/break down* an arrangement or organization, you are probably being asked to **classify** its component parts. For instance, "Distinguish sales strategies appropriate for a small business."

Similarly, if you are asked to **define** mediation, a definition essay is appropriate. Being asked to do an **extended definition** of a complex idea is also a common essay task. There are fewer other cues for definition essays; generally, a variant of the word *meaning* will be involved.

1. If you are asked to explain the **meaning** of something, you should provide a definition. For instance, "Explain the meaning of "arboriculture."

2. If you are asked **what something or someone means**, you are being asked for a definition. For example, explain what Maslow means by *self-actualization needs.*

Exercise 10

Fill in the Top Ten List that follows with situations in your own field in which the definition/classification mode might be usefully employed in a writing task. Use the cue words discussed earlier when you are describing these topics. Indicate with a "D" or a "C" whether the writing would be primarily definition or classification. For instance, a student in retail floristry might choose

1. Types of design style in floral arrangement (C)
2. Explain the meaning of "Art Nouveau" floral arrangement (D)

Fill in as many as you can, and then continue reading the module. As other possible applications occur to you, return to this list and finish it.

 TOP TEN APPLICATIONS FOR DEFINITION/CLASSIFICATION WRITING IN MY FIELD

1.
2.
3.
4.
5.
6.
7.
8.
9.
10.

APPLYING THE SIX-STEP METHOD TO DEFINITION/ CLASSIFICATION WRITING

Step 1: Imaging the Essay with the Rhetorical Triangle

Begin by imaging your essay with the rhetorical triangle. Make certain your topic is not too broad—a frequent problem with classification essays. For instance, an essay classifying job prospects for graduating students is so broad that it would be virtually impossible to say anything meaningful. Classifying job prospects for pharmaceutical technicians would be more manageable. Decide upon your purpose and point of view: are you arranging or explaining objective, factual material in order to help your reader to understand? Are you by contrast presenting a subjective view in order to make your audience see a new perspective on the issue? Finally, assess your audience carefully: you must be certain that they will understand the terms and ideas you are using to create your definition or to define each classification.

Step 2: Content Generation

Whether you are doing definition or classification, you may want to start generating content by using the dictionary method. The dictionary is a particularly logical place to start because it defines words in large part by assigning them to appropriate classes. After using the dictionary and at least one other method, you should have a clear set of classifications to work with, or a clear sense of the many components of your definition.

Step 3: The Outline

When you outline your essay, there is no single pattern to follow for a classification/definition essay, as you can see from the samples provided in this module. Generally, however, your essay can be structured in the following way:

INTRODUCTION

See Module 3: The Essay: How to Say It, Introduction p. 49.

Begin with your grabber as usual. Then present the necessary background—a sense of a general concept's significance. Finally, your thesis will do the following:

1. In a definition essay, it will define the concept's major characteristics, which will be elaborated in the body. For example, "Love is a healthy, respectful, nurturing appreciation for another person."

2. In a classification essay, it will subdivide or classify the concept into parallel subcategories, each of which will be elaborated in the body. For example, "The pharmaceutical technician graduate's job prospects are promising, whether in a community setting, a clinical setting, or a pharmaceutical firm."

BODY

See Module 3, Body, p. 57.

Each body paragraph should clearly and completely explain one aspect of the definition or one classification of the larger subject. Each aspect of the definition or classification should be supported through specific explanations, examples, facts, and images. In a definition essay, remember to define by classifying the concept. In a classification essay, remember to define each parallel classification with parallel details. Be certain to organize these subtopics in order of importance or interest, or in some other logical fashion.

NEGATIVE AND POSITIVE CLASSIFICATION

It is not only possible but advisable and effective to define or classify negatively as well as positively. For example, "Love is not dependence on another person; love is not control of another person."

CONCLUSION

See Module 3, Conclusion, p. 60.

Summarize the main characteristics of the definition or the different classifications of the subject. Then draw a specific, significant conclusion from the definition or classification presented—make your point. Give a sense of the worth, outcome, or effects of the definition or classification, and leave your reader with a final thought to ponder.

Step 4: Writing the Rough Draft

When writing your rough draft, remember that writing a good definition/classification essay hinges on a number of key factors: clear organization, sufficient detail, and clear, exact language.

Step 5: Revising

When you revise your essay, tighten its coherence by adding transitional phrases to clarify the connections among your various classifications or definition aspects, and among the individual sentences making up each of these. Consult the list of transition techniques for examples.

Step 6: Editing

Looking for your most common errors, edit your definition/classification essay carefully.

TRANSITION TECHNIQUES FOR DEFINITION/ CLASSIFICATION

- **Listing:** It may be useful to number the classifications or main characteristics of your definition; for instance, *first, second, third,* and so on.
- **Contrast:** Use linking phrases such as *similarly* or *by contrast* to show how one classification or aspect of the definition links to the next.
- **Examples:** Introduce examples with a phrase such as *for example* or *for instance.*
- **Elaboration:** Add further details to your definition or classification with words like *additionally, furthermore,* or *moreover* or by referring to *another, an additional,* or *a further aspect.*
- **Cause/effect:** Inside an explanation of a particular classification or aspect of a definition, it may be useful to use a transitional phrase suggesting a cause/ effect relationship, such as: *therefore, thus, as a result, consequently,* or *hence.*

Exercise 11

1. Read the following paragraphs. These are the first and second paragraphs of a definition/classification essay called "Adventure!" by Caitlin MacNamara.

2. Choose the appropriate word, or use appropriate transitional devices, to link the sentences and ideas to one another. Do not use any of them more than once.

> I'm bored. I'm tired of life in the big city, and I've had enough of my daily routine of work, eat, and sleep: I want an adventure. What do I mean by this? Well, according to the *Gage Canadian Dictionary,* an adventure is "a bold and difficult undertaking involving unknown risks and danger." I do

want difficulty, risks, and danger, but this basic (Select one: denotation/connotation) does not completely encompass what I mean. Traditionally, the appeal of adventure comes from (Select one: denotation/connotation)—that is, the specific emotions or ideas we associate with adventure._____ when I think of adventure, I think of pioneers or explorers blazing trails across uncharted wilderness. _____, I think of sailors cresting the horizon in quest of new lands, and astronauts hurtling through the frozen void of space. We sometimes need to confront situations that are more vast than we are, and that challenge our smug sense of security and control. As humans, we pretty much get our own way. _____ , we feel we are generally in control of our fate, that we have all the answers. Adventures in nature, _____, place us in danger. _____ , implicit in these romantic images of adventure is an idea not just of danger but of danger on a very large scale. Nature is _____ the most obvious source of danger and, therefore, of adventure because of three qualities: its vastness, alienness, and unpredictability.

_____ , suppose I take my canoe one summer to the immense expanses of the tundra of the Northwest Territories. I may not be actually facing death in the form of unexpected rapids or wildlife; _____, that possibility always exists. _____ the encounter with nature does not actually threaten me physically, it at least challenges and unsettles my sense of psychological and mental comfort. _____, the breathtaking grandeur of canyons, forests, waterfalls, and thunderstorms—the complexity and magnificence of the natural world around me—can force me to realize how trivial and insignificant I am. It can _____ motivate me to grow, to stretch my understanding of the universe and my place in it.

3. Is this a definition or a classification essay?
4. Locate the thesis. In your own words, state the point being made. List the subtopics the essay promises to address.

Sample Essay 1

TEENS NOT THE PROBLEM, AND TIRED OF BEING TOLD THEY ARE

THE TORONTO STAR, DECEMBER 12, 1994, P. A1, 13
BY CARLYN ZWARENSTEIN

Teenagers. These days, we seem to be the favorite topic of English essays: teenagers and parents, teenagers and drugs, teenagers and television. Issues that are said to affect the youth of today—peer pressure, self-image and racism—are explored interminably. Teenagers are analyzed until we begin to seem like another species. To watch television or glance through a magazine, one would think society was made up of citizens aged 13 to 30. North American culture both craves and denigrates youth. Even as young people are idolized, we are blamed for everything and anything. Crime, unemployment, poor educational standards, environmental decay—teenagers are hit over the head with lists of the world's problems. (1)

The fact is, we are tired of being held responsible for all that is wrong with the world. We weren't born when the atom bomb was first dropped. We aren't the ones who carved a hole in the ozone layer. We didn't ask for things like poverty and racism that push people to crime. As for lack of respect for others, poor nutrition, sluggish lifestyle and ignorance, well, we might well ask to see our role models in the adult world. A child is defenceless, a lump of Play-Doh waiting to be moulded by whatever example is provided. The examples teenagers have had have not been good. (2)

The adults of today were the teenagers of yesterday—many of them ignorant, rebellious, promiscuous, intoxicated and rude. Just as they once asked themselves, so we are asking now: what is there for us to learn from our elders? The answer would seem to be selfishness, laziness and a really bad attitude. (3)

They call the 20-something young adults of today Generation X, those who are freshly emerged from adolescence and facing a world that seems without hope. There doesn't seem to be a name yet for the 16- and 17-year-olds who see the same dismal future. A similar symbol of isolation would seem apt. (4)

But, strangely enough, there is no real reason we should despair, any more than our parents once did. After all, our parents were born during the Cold War, when the threat of nuclear annihilation was real. Yet they are called baby boomers, hippies and flower children—all names suggesting vitality and optimism. Perhaps it is the expectations of our elders that have given us our nihilistic, who-the-hell-cares attitude to life. (5)

Despite being constantly criticized and analyzed, we are also our parents' hope for the future. We are expected to go out and find jobs, get healthy and educated, stop pollution and world hunger. Although we see our planet and our civilization going down the tubes, we are being forced into it without support from members of the older generation who are preparing to retire and enjoy a slower pace of life. (6)

The problem is, teenagers are being viewed as a distinct species. Adolescence has become a commodity to be sold along with Diet Coke and Clearasil. "Teenagers" are spoken of as if we were born that way, as if we will stay 16 forever. Where adolescence was once simply a step on the way to maturity, teenagers nowadays are seen as a homogeneous group that will have to make its own way in the world. (7)

If we could pass through adolescence knowing that we were part of a gradual, never-ending stream of kids growing up into adults, we might have a feeling of continuity. If we had the support and compassion of parents capable of loving discipline and of teachers truly able to impart knowledge and understanding, we might be less afraid to grow up. (8)

We don't need to be analyzed from every perspective. We are simply people at a younger age. The only thing that separates us from you is time. (9)

Questions

1. What and where is the thesis statement of this essay? Why?

2. In your own words, state the point of this definition/classification essay.

3. What different classifications are introduced by the author? What is her attitude toward these categories?

4. In the first paragraph, how does the author establish her credentials, or her ability to speak as an authority on this subject?

5. In some ways, this is an essay about the connotations of words. Find at least two places where the author analyzes the connotations of words. What does Zwarenstein argue is the effect of connotations? Do you agree with her assessment?

6. Find at least two examples of negative definition (definition by explaining what something is not).

7. Who is the audience for this essay? How has the writer appealed to this audience?

8. How does the conclusion link to the introduction?

9. What technique does Zwarenstein use as a final thought? Is this effective?

10. Is this a subjective or an objective essay? Why?

Sample Essay 2

GREASING THE WHEELS OF COMMERCE

THE GARDNER REPORT, SPRING 1995

BY ALYSSA DIAMOND

Bribes are so prevalent while conducting business, often we don't recognize them for what they are. Tickets to a Jays game or lunch where a supplier picks up the tab are common examples and hardly cause to raise an eyebrow. But if you are a small business-person who must compete with a large company that whisks clients into a skybox for the game, you are at a disadvantage, with small hope of winning the contract solely on the merits of your proposal. (1)

You have little choice when a client suggests if you have a Christmas gift for him, to deliver it to his home address. If you don't play the game, another supplier will. One more item to bury under "advertising and promotion." (2)

But when does a gift become a bribe, and when does a kickback become a crime? (3)

You know one of your clients wants a new set of golf clubs. You tell her you know someone in the sporting industry and can get the clubs for half price. You pay full price and then resell them to your client at the "discount" price. No crime yet. (4)

Next you get a shipment of Product X that you can sell for $20. Everyone else is selling it for $25. You invoice for that amount and split the difference with the buyer. Good business for you and the buyer, but the buyer has defrauded the company he works for and you are both on the hook. (5)

A simple rule of thumb is do not become involved in a scheme where you invoice for a service or goods that you did not supply, or for goods sold at an inflated price. No matter how good the deal may appear to be, it is fraud. And having a forensic accountant poring over the books will give you a bigger chill than Revenue Canada ever could. (6)

Questions

1. Identify the thesis statement.

2. Is this primarily a definition or a classification essay? Why?

3. Is this a subjective or an objective essay? Why?

4. Evaluate the level of language, style of writing, and tone: what do you notice about them?

5. Keeping in mind your answer to question 3, can you suggest who the audience is for this essay and for *The Gardner Report* from which it is taken? How has the author appealed to the audience?

6. Evaluate the conclusion as a conclusion: does it provide all of the necessary elements, and is it effective?

The following is an essay written by a social work student.

Sample Essay 3

WE ARE A NATION OF ADDICTS

BY LISA FRANKEL

Addict — *n.* **1** a person who is dependent on a drug, especially a narcotic drug, such as morphine or heroin. **2** a person who has given himself up to a habit or obsession: *a movie addict.*

Do you recognize yourself in this dictionary definition? In many ways, it speaks directly to the Canadian experience, for we are a nation of addicts. We don't all put needles in our arms, snort powder up our noses, or squander bank accounts betting on professional sports—but we do live in a society founded upon the exploitation of our various dependencies. (1)

We're afraid to admit this, of course. In fact, we squander millions of dollars every year trying to convince ourselves that we are not addicts, and that we discourage addiction. Our government has given itself up to the habit of spending money—to educate our youth to "just say no" to drugs, and to train police officers and their dogs to sniff out illegal drugs that people are bringing across our borders. Fully eighty percent of the money and energy we spend enforcing drug and alcohol laws is spent to stop illegal drugs such as marijuana, cocaine, and LSD. Yet some researchers estimate these drugs cause less than 1 percent of the drug-related deaths in Canada. (2)

Would it surprise you to learn that most of these deaths are caused by two legal and highly addictive substances—tobacco and alcohol—or more precisely, by the persons who are dependent on these drugs? Over 35 000 deaths annually are directly or indirectly related to tobacco use—mainly cancer caused by smoking or prolonged exposure to someone else's "second-hand" smoke. Every year 18 000 deaths are attributed to alcohol—many of these from diseases related to alcohol abuse, and many from accidents involving alcohol. (3)

Based on these statistics, some researchers argue that we are misusing our funds and energies. For instance, marijuana is a minor recreational drug that is not addictive and that has few side effects. Yet we arrest 40 000 people per year for marijuana offences, and we ruin their lives by giving them criminal records. We have given ourselves up to an obsession with arrests; they make us feel as if we are solving the problem of addiction. But resources used to stop marijuana might be better devoted to a) researching tobacco and alcohol, society's biggest dependencies, and b) devising strategies to stop the waste of health-care expenses and human lives caused by these killers. (4)

More extreme thinkers suggest banning tobacco and alcohol outright. History, however, tells us that even decent, law-abiding Canadians will do anything necessary to satisfy their addictions. For example, during Prohibition in the 1920s, alcohol was banned in many areas. As a result, many Canadians smuggled alcohol into the country from elsewhere or distilled their own. The 1993 increase in the smuggling of illegal cigarettes occurred simply because the taxes on cigarettes had gotten so high. Imagine how bad this problem would become if we banned smoking completely! (5)

Faced with the annual loss of a half-billion dollars in tax revenue due to cigarette smuggling, the federal government and some provincial governments lowered the tax on cigarettes in 1994. A package of cigarettes in Ontario or Quebec, for example, now costs approximately half of what it did in 1993. When criticized, the government is quick to point out that it has also increased spending on anti-smoking education. It is also more strictly enforcing the law, which says that persons under the age of eighteen may not buy or use cigarettes. (6)

This is a clear contradiction that is reminiscent of the way the cigarette smoker or alcoholic or junkie keeps saying, "I'll quit cold turkey tomorrow" or "I'll get help tomorrow." Of course, tomorrow never arrives. When the clock strikes midnight, a new "today" begins, and action is again postponed to "tomorrow." Our government depends on the tax revenues it collects from our addictions. Just like any other addict needing a "fix," it can rationalize any policy and justify any action to ensure that those desperately needed dollars keep pouring in. With dollar signs dancing in front of their hungry eyes, the Ontario government legalized casino gambling in 1993. There is even talk now of making alcohol cheaper to prevent the smuggling of American liquor into Canada! (7)

Canada has a problem. We have given ourselves up to our government's obsession with tax revenue. Like any person dependent on a drug—like any addict—we need to admit the problem exists before we will be able to solve it. Do we have the courage to face up to our national addictions? (8)

Questions

1. What and where is the thesis statement of this essay? Why?

2. Classify and briefly define the different types of addiction that are introduced by the author.

3. In your own words, state the point of this definition/classification essay.

4. Why does the writer use these phrases: "by the persons who are dependent on these drugs?" (paragraph 3); "We have given ourselves up to an obsession with arrests" (paragraph 4)?

5. How does the author establish her credentials, or her ability to speak as an authority on this subject?

6. Examine the length of the paragraphs. How much variety is there? Is this variety used effectively? Give an example.

7. Who is the audience for this essay? How has the writer appealed to this audience?

8. How is the government like an addict? Is this an effective argument? Why or why not?

9. How does the conclusion link to the introduction?

10. Is this a subjective or an objective essay? Why?

OTHER APPLICATIONS OF DEFINITION AND CLASSIFICATION

As with all rhetorical modes, you may very effectively use moments of definition and classification within essays written in other rhetorical modes for different purposes. The following example is taken from a narrative/descriptive newspaper article discussing a controversial Supreme Court of Canada decision. This decision allows assailants to view the private therapy and counselling records of their alleged sexual assault victims. In order to gain access to such records, defendants need to establish the records' probable relevance. The following paragraph defines what constitutes "relevance":

> A relevance threshold, at this stage, is simply a requirement to prevent the defence from engaging in 'speculative, fanciful, disruptive, unmeritorious, obstructive and time-consuming' requests for production [of the counselling records]," Chief Justice Antonio Lamer and Mr. Justice John Sopinka wrote for the majority. [From Kirk Makin, "Court Rules against Rape Victims." *Globe and Mail* 15 December 1995: Al, A15.]

Definition and classification can be used effectively to explain or clarify an important idea in an essay in another rhetorical mode.

Questions

1. How is classification at work in this definition?

2. Is this a clear definition, or do you see any difficulties with it?

Exercise 12

Using the six-step method, write a definition/classification essay on one of the topics from your Top Ten List. Decide whether this will be a subjective or an objective essay, and remember: choose a topic that you are interested in and/or know a lot about.

SUMMARY

In a definition essay, you are explaining and clarifying an uncertain or ambiguous idea. In a classification essay, you are organizing a subject by grouping similar items together, or taking a subject and dividing it into smaller classes or groups. Your purpose in both kinds of essay is either to simplify a subject for your reader or to make a point about your subject. These rhetorical modes are closely related. Most definition essays function by classification; that is, they break the subject down by analyzing the groups or categories into which it fits. Similarly, the discussion of an individual class or group within a classification essay usually reads like a miniature definition of its characteristics. When you are given a specific writing task at work or school, common cues can indicate that a definition/classification essay is appropriate.

When writing an essay of definition/classification, you may adopt an objective perspective in which you define and classify factual categories or classes of objects or things. Here, you deal in the denotative quality of language and in information and ideas that are measurable. You may also adopt a subjective perspective in which your classification or definition, still supported by examples and evidence, is coloured by your personal opinion. Here, you deal more with connotative or suggestive language and ideas and you express a new, individual perspective that challenges the reader's usual understanding of the issue. In both cases, your essay must have a clear point to make.

CHECKLIST

- Does your essay make a clear subjective or objective point?
- Does your introduction adequately explain the background and relevance of your definition or classification?
- Does your thesis clearly establish the main characteristics of your definition or the main categories of your classification?
- Does each body paragraph completely and clearly address a single aspect of the definition or a single classification?
- Is each classification clearly and completely defined?
- Is each definition characteristic clearly categorized?
- Are your classifications completely parallel?

- Do you address parallel information about each classification?
- Are your definition characteristics or classifications clearly organized in order of importance or logic?
- Have you used sufficient appropriate transitional phrases to signal clearly connections between definition aspects or classifications?
- Does your conclusion summarize the aspects of the definition or main classifications, reinforce the point you are making, and leave the reader pondering the issue in a larger context?

The Cause and Effect Essay

LEARNING OUTCOMES

By completing a series of oral and written exercises and writing a cause and effect essay using the six-step method, students will

1. *distinguish when use of the cause and effect rhetorical mode is appropriate;*
2. *distinguish among cause, effect, and cause and effect essays;*
3. *distinguish between the informative and the evaluative cause and effect essays;*
4. *utilize the transitional devices that most effectively unify a cause and effect essay.*

OVERVIEW

What do you do if Jorge, one of your friends, fellow students, or business associates, acts strangely toward you—for instance, by becoming angry over a very minor issue? Perhaps you analyze carefully why this might have happened in order to discover some way to smooth over the situation. Did you do something to upset him? Is he taking his stress from another problem out on you?

Suppose you discover that he is upset that another friend, Zareen, did not invite him to her party on Saturday. You and just about everyone else were invited, but Zareen left out Jorge because, in her words, "He's such a pompous know-it-all." Jorge asks you to tell him why Zareen did not invite him. How will you respond? Should you tell him the truth and risk hurting his feelings and creating resentment? Should you lie and condemn him to continuing unpopularity? Should you pretend you do not know?

In the first scenario, you are analyzing the **cause** of Jorge's behaviour. In the second scenario, you are evaluating the likely **effects** of your possible responses on Jorge. **Cause and effect** analysis is the process of measuring the reasons for and the results of events or facts. As such, it is a process in which you are continually engaging during the most basic personal interaction.

Many government studies and investigative reports by television or print journalists utilize a deliberate structure of cause and effect to organize their subjects. For instance, a news story might discuss the effects of poverty on children's education, or might establish that the cause of an increase in injuries to professional athletes is the increasing use of artificial turf rather than natural grass in stadiums. The cause and effect essay is one of the key tools for uncovering social problems and inducing their resolution.

PURPOSE AND FUNCTION

The *Gage Canadian Dictionary* defines the word *cause* as follows:

> *n.* **1** whatever produces an effect; a person or thing that makes something happen: *The flood was the cause of much damage.*

It defines the word *effect* as follows:

> *n.* **1** whatever is produced by a cause; something made to happen by a person or thing; result.

The interrelationship between cause and effect is obvious, since each word is a part of the other word's definition. You cannot have a cause without an effect, and vice versa: this is the reason for this rhetorical mode.

In a **cause and effect essay** you are seeking to establish the relationship between an issue or event (the cause) and its results (the effect). You are examining the nature of this relationship and analyzing its consequences. You provide reasons to explain why something happened, and explore or anticipate the outcomes or effects of a particular action or policy. Many scientific studies work on the principle of studying cause and effect. The relationship between the two forms is the basis for the "scientific method" of investigation.

The scientific method depends on establishing cause and effect.

See Module 10: Persuasion, Inductive Reasoning, p. 201.

Law enforcement officers must understand the effects of the Charter of Rights and Freedoms on issues of personal responsibility for criminal behaviour. Mechanical engineers must understand the effects of applied forces on the beams, shafts, and columns that make up the structures they are building. Social workers, nurses, early childhood educators, business administrators—anyone teaching, aiding, or supervising others—needs some understanding of psychology, which explains the biological, psychological, and sociological causes of human behaviour.

THE THREE TYPES OF CAUSE AND EFFECT ESSAY

When writing an essay using cause and effect, you always have three distinct choices. In a **cause essay**, you focus solely on the reasons why something happened. In a cause essay, your introduction establishes a given effect or effects, and the rest of the essay investigates and analyzes their possible origins. For example, a cause essay might analyze the reasons for changing fashion trends.

In an **effect essay,** you examine outcomes or results. In an effect essay, your introduction discusses a specific cause or phenomenon, and the body of the essay explores its effects or consequences. For example, you might write an essay exploring the effects of smoking on the health of smokers and nonsmokers or the effects of increasing computerization in the workplace.

Finally, in a **cause and effect essay,** you attempt to explore both the causes and the effects of a phenomenon—generally an undertaking of some length and complexity.

You will determine which of these structures to use based upon your topic and purpose. For instance, imagine three students who are asked to write a paper on drug addiction. The social work student, interested in understanding and ultimately helping drug addicts, might evaluate the social, mental, and physiological causes of addiction. The business administration student might analyze all of the different effects of an employee's drug addiction on the finances, morale, and efficiency of the workplace. Finally, the law enforcement student, wanting both to understand the addict and to examine the addiction's profound consequences, might write a paper evaluating both cause and effect.

Exercise 1

Here are ten topics for cause/effect essays. Identify which kind of essay—cause, effect, or cause and effect—you would write for each of the following:

1. Why is there a crisis in the fisheries?
2. Roots of aboriginal nationalism.
3. Reasons for getting regular automobile tune-ups.
4. Importance of good work habits.
5. Success in business.
6. Compost is good for your garden.
7. The sources of security.
8. The death penalty is a deterrent to crime.
9. Exercise your brain—read a good book!
10. Nuclear energy: will it meet the needs of the future?

EVALUATIVE VS. INFORMATIVE

As well as choices of whether to analyze cause, effect, or both, you also have to make a second fundamental choice: are you going to write an **evaluative (judgmental)** essay, in which you draw your own conclusions about the actual cause or likely effects of a phenomenon or practice? Or are you going to produce a purely **infor-**

mative essay that provides your readers with a factual discussion of a particular practice or problem, and then details the effects that actually resulted—or the causes that have been uncovered by others?

Think of it this way. Suppose that you are a student hoping to learn how to use the Internet. Unfortunately, however, your school offers no Internet training or access. Faced with this absence of resources, you could write an essay in which, through research and logical reasoning, you detail the likely effects of such ignorance in an era when both work and home life will be more and more Internet-related. This would be an evaluative effect essay. On the other hand, suppose that you discover that students in a similar situation at another school lobbied their administration, succeeded in creating an optional course on Internet, and established a World Wide Web site to disseminate information on teaching the Internet. In a second essay, you could describe these particular responses to a particular problem. This second effect essay would be informative.

Exercise 2

Below are three cause and effect paragraphs. Read each of them carefully, and answer the following questions:

1. Is it a cause, an effect, or a cause and effect paragraph?

2. Does the writer limit him- or herself to the known facts of the case?

3. Does the writer draw any conclusions or make any personal judgments?

4. Based on your answers to these questions, is the paragraph informative or evaluative?

   A. The more I study, the more I know. The more I know, the more I forget. The more I forget, the less I know. So why study?

   B. Every month in Canada, there are one or two deaths caused by allergic reaction to food. An estimated 1 percent of Canadians suffer from extreme life-threatening allergies to even trace amounts of certain foods, medications, or insect stings—and the number of people with allergies to peanuts, in particular, seems to be increasing. Exposure can bring on a reaction in two or more body systems (anaphylactic shock), which, in extreme cases, can cause death. [From Virginia Galt, "Severe Food Allergies Sticky Topic for Schools." *Globe and Mail* 23 Sept. 1995: A1.]

   C. Privacy on the job may soon be a thing of the past—and mandatory drug-testing of employees is only the beginning. Today, some American employers track their employees' movements at all times through special badges with microchips. Other companies use chair sensors to measure how long employees are seated and how restless they are. Ultimately, the day is not far off when you may go for brainwave testing rather than a job interview. This testing will determine how well you can concentrate and how suitable you are for a certain job. You will be told what you are capable of accomplishing—and what you are not. An employer may then be willing to hire you only for tasks that suit your predetermined aptitudes. You may have no choice whatsoever in deciding what your career will be.

ROOT VS. IMMEDIATE CAUSES/IMMEDIATE VS. FURTHER EFFECTS

Cause and effect are like a chain of linked events. In life, one event flows out of another in the same way that a tree grows out of a root system below the surface of the ground. When attempting to determine cause, you should not be content with examining merely the obvious or branch causes. Whenever possible, you should attempt to discover a root cause.

Imagine an analysis of the cause of increasing tuition fees for college and university students. The most obvious, immediate cause is reductions in government funding to postsecondary education, which cause individual colleges and universities to increase their tuition fees. If you follow the problem further, however, you come to a variety of other issues: the federal deficit, the lack of a coherent voice for student protest, the fact that the effects of high tuition are long-term whereas the effects of other cutbacks (for instance, to health care) are immediate. Most times, you may not ultimately arrive at the "one and only" root cause, but the further your analysis proceeds, the more depth and relevance it will have.

Similarly, imagine a second analysis, this time of the effects of increasing tuition fees. The immediate effect is that some students may decide not to pursue higher learning because they cannot afford the tuition. But what are the further effects? Does postsecondary education in Canada risk becoming something exclusively for the rich? Are we dooming the less advantaged to menial jobs? What about students who continue but who graduate with bigger student loan debts? It will take them that much longer to become financially stable so they can make the big purchases (car, house, and so on) that drive our economy. The chain of events is, of course, endless, but the wider the range of potential effects your analysis considers, the more valuable your essay will be.

JUMPING TO CONCLUSIONS

See also Module 10, Coincidence, p. 201, and Circular or Repetitive Arguments, p. 203.

Beware of oversimplifying a problem—that is, of prematurely assuming you have arrived at the root cause or the total effects. Be suspicious of quick, easy answers to problems of cause and effect; your readers will be.

Exercise 3

In groups of four to six, examine each of the following topics. Identify an immediate cause and an immediate effect for each. Then try to identify at least five further causes and five further effects. You may wish to represent this visually by using the

See Module 2: The Essay: What to Say, Clustering, p. 29.

clustering technique to show how the various causes and effects connect to one another.

1. The rising cost of health care
2. Good essay-writing skills
3. NHL expansion in the United States
4. Single-parent families
5. The computerization of society

QUALIFIERS

Police are allowed to stop a suspect or search his or her house only if they have "probable cause." Probable cause is no guarantee that the person is guilty, but it is a rule that ensures that police act responsibly. So, too, should you endeavour to act responsibly in cause and effect writing. If you cannot absolutely discover the root cause, or cannot prove unequivocally the likely effects of a particular policy, do not pretend that you can. It is enough for you, too, to demonstrate probable cause (or effect).

You can use certain words or phrases as **qualifiers** in order to indicate the probability of your conclusions, but leave room for the possibility of other conclusions. Phrases like *in general, generally, probably,* and *likely* indicate to a reader the non-absolute nature of your conclusions. Verbs like *should, may,* and *might* instead of verbs such as *must,* indicate the likely but conditional, rather than absolute, nature of your statements.

Exercise 4

In groups of four to six, examine your lists of causes and effects from Exercise 3. Write an "A" beside any that are absolutely true; write a "Q" beside any that you would qualify to indicate their nonabsolute nature. Compare the numbers of "As" and "Qs." What, if anything, can you conclude from these?

OCCASIONS FOR A CAUSE AND EFFECT ESSAY

When faced with a topic, you need to be able to identify occasions when the cause and effect rhetorical mode is appropriate to your purpose. Obviously, if you are asked to analyze the **effects** of recent tax law changes on your company, or to assess **causes** of adult illiteracy, you will utilize the cause and effect structure.

You will not always, however, be so clearly told to write a cause and effect essay. The following word cues indicate that a cause or an effect essay is appropriate.

Cause Cues

If you are asked to analyze or detail the **reasons, sources, roots, grounds,** or **basis** for an argument, action, or policy, you are being asked to assess its cause. Similarly, the word *why* always demands explanation of cause. This is obvious, since one of the main ways of responding to a "why" question is with a sentence using the word *because*—a word with the word *cause* inside it.

Effect Cues

1. If you are asked to analyze or detail the **benefits, consequences, outcomes, results, repercussions,** or **impact** of an argument, action, or policy, you are being asked to assess its effects.

See Module 8: Definition and Classification, Denotation and Connotation, p.153.

Exercise 5

Analyze the effect cue words above. Which have positive connotations? Which have negative connotations? Which are neutral? If you are uncertain, look them up in your dictionary. These connotations offer an important cue as to what the focus of your writing should be.

2. Questions using the words *what if* require that you consider effects. Marvel Comics in the United States publishes a comic book called *What If*, each issue of which takes an important event in the life of its characters (for instance, the death or marriage of a character) and recounts the story of what would have happened if that one key event had not occurred or had proceeded differently. Similarly, when asked "What if ... ," you are being asked to speculate on the effects of some hypothetical event.

3. If you are asked *how* an event, policy, or action has *affected, impacted, influenced, changed, altered,* or *modified* someone or something, you are being asked to evaluate its particular effects on that specific person or thing.

Exercise 6

Fill in the Top Ten List that follows with situations in your field where the cause and effect mode might usefully be employed in a writing task. Use the cue words listed above to describe these topics. Specify whether the essay would be a cause essay, an effect essay, or a cause and effect essay. Indicate also whether the essay would be evaluative or informative. For instance, a nursing student might choose the topic

1. Impact of need interference on community nursing (effect—informative)

Fill in as many as you can, and then continue reading the module. As other possible applications occur to you, return to this list and finish it.

10 TOP TEN APPLICATIONS FOR CAUSE AND EFFECT WRITING IN MY FIELD

1.

2.

3.

4.

5.

6.

7.

8.

9.

10.

APPLYING THE SIX-STEP METHOD TO CAUSE AND EFFECT WRITING

Step 1: Imaging the Essay with the Rhetorical Triangle

Follow the usual steps, first imaging your essay with the rhetorical triangle. You should decide now what kind of essay you are writing: given the cues in the wording of the assignment, is it cause, effect, or cause and effect? Of course, you may revise these ideas when you begin generating content, but it is essential to have an initial plan.

Step 2: Content Generation

Generate content using more than one method. Often, the effects of a cause or the causes of an effect are unexpected and startling. Try to use the variety of methods of content generation to extend your consideration of the causes or the effects as far as possible.

CONFUSING CAUSE AND EFFECT

This may seem obvious, but do not confuse cause for effect. For instance, an essay exploring the causes of racism cannot argue that "the cause of racism is hatred or a sense of superiority one culture feels toward another." These are not causes; these are forms of racism, ways in which racism reveals itself, or, in other words, the effects of a racist attitude. The true causes are the reasons for that hatred.

Step 3: The Outline

Outline your essay in the following fashion.

See Module 3, Introduction, p. 49.

INTRODUCTION

Begin with your grabber as usual. Be certain to explain adequately the background in your introduction—that is, the initial cause that you will analyze the effects of, or the effect whose causes you will be exploring. Be certain your thesis statement clearly introduces the causes or the effects that your body paragraphs will be exploring.

See Module 3, Body, p. 57.

BODY

Support each argument with concrete evidence for the case you are making. The best cause and effect essays provide substantial data to support their claims. They are scientific, not simply argumentative. Quotations from experts, specific examples, charts, statistics, graphs, documents, and facts are useful forms of support.

CONCLUSION

See Module 3, Conclusion, p. 60.

Do not stop at simply summarizing the causes or effects you have documented. Once you have established them in your essay, draw conclusions about the implications of your study so that the question of the causes or effects is redirected to a larger, thought-provoking issue.

Step 4: Writing the Rough Draft

When assembling your rough draft, be certain to support carefully the connection between the event or idea and its causes or effects. Failure to do so often results from a lack of evidence or from a poor (illogical) presentation of the available evidence; such a failure inevitably results in the essay's failure.

Cause and effect essays also explain and document the kind of the connection *between* the cause and effect. For instance, a study of the effectiveness of a new drug for treating angina (a heart condition) would have to be very careful to distinguish the drug's actual effects from the effects of other factors (like diet, age, or fitness). When writing a cause and effect essay, pay close attention not only to the explanations of the causes or effects, but also to the logic of the argument linking the causes and effects to one another.

Step 5: Revising

When revising your essay, sharpen its focus by using transitional phrases that highlight your linkage of causes to effects, and vice versa. Consult the list of transition techniques below.

Step 6: Editing

Looking for your most common errors, edit your cause/effect essay carefully.

TRANSITION TECHNIQUES FOR CAUSE AND EFFECT WRITING

- **Transitional cause indicators.** Some useful conjunctions indicating that a cause is being suggested include *since, because, for.*

BECAUSE

See Appendix A, Contract #2: Sentence Fragments.

This word is used to connect two ideas in a complete sentence, but there can be pitfalls. Often you are told never to start a sentence with *because* since this can lead you to write a sentence fragment. You can start a sentence with *because*, so long as you remember that you are setting up a cause and an effect and you make certain that both the cause and the effect are included in the sentence:

> Because I need to write well in order to pass this subject, I am working on this module.

A second pitfall is not connecting the cause and the effect in a single sentence, but splitting these into two different sentences:

> My daughter is upset with me. It is because I stayed out late.

In this kind of situation, the "easy fix" is to get rid of the "It is" and join the two sentences. These are unnecessary words, and they interfere with the flow of your thinking.

> My daughter is upset with me because I stayed out late.

- **Transitional effect indicators:** Some useful conjunctions indicating that an effect is being suggested are *so* and *so that.* Some useful transitional phrases introducing an effect relationship include *therefore, thus, as a result, consequently, hence.* General phrases such as *clearly, surely,* and *in conclusion* signal a result or effect.

Exercise 7

Below are very brief examples of the kind of cause and effect reasoning that you do in an extended fashion in a cause and effect essay.

1. Complete these incomplete arguments by supplying the missing conclusion (effects) or reasons (causes).

2. Identify with a "C" or an "E" whether you are supplying a cause or an effect, and underline the cue words that indicate this.

3. Not all of the sentences that follow present absolute conclusions or reasons. Underline and write a "Q" above words that indicate that qualifications are being placed on the conclusions or reasons.

   A. Students should receive a failing grade if they are not meeting the basic requirements of a course. I do really well in all my program courses, but I'm failing English; consequently, ...

   B. Children must not play on the grass unattended. Unfortunately, therefore, we cannot allow Naushad onto the grass since ...

   C. Because ... , Brutus cannot possibly be the one responsible. According to the mail carrier, the dog that bit her was a sheepdog.

D. It is unfortunate, but Mahnaz is guilty of hacking into the Cana-Bank central computer to embezzle money. When computer skills are used for fraud, the person responsible must be jailed. Therefore, ...

E. The college with the most modern facilities and equipment will be most successful in attracting the best students. Huron College's brand-new campus was just completed; as a result, ...

F. Once it becomes the off-season, hotel vacancies generally increase and room prices decrease. You should wait until after Labour Day to take your trip, for ...

G. Children who live in poverty may have greater needs than children from more privileged backgrounds. Nancy's mother is a struggling single parent who is on welfare; hence, ...

H. A trained photographer is extremely careful not to expose film to light. After taking his pictures yesterday, Kiran stupidly exposed his film. Clearly, ...

I. A baseball player needs at least two weeks of running, throwing and catching practice prior to playing in actual games. The first game of our season is May 15, so ...

J. Heart disease is hereditary. Since ... , it seems likely that Mukesh, too, will develop heart disease.

Sample Cause and Effect Essay 1

DISTURBING DISCOVERIES ABOUT WHAT CHILDREN RECALL

FROM *CALGARY HERALD*, REPRINTED IN THE *TORONTO STAR*, DECEMBER 4, 1994, D4

BY ALLYSON JEFFS

In Newfoundland, they're not sending their child abuse investigators to school—they're sending them to day care. "We thought, if you're going to be an investigator, maybe you should spend some time with children ... who haven't been abused and aren't in the middle of an investigation," says William Rowe, director of social work at Newfoundland's Memorial University. Rowe says the practice is providing some disturbing insights into the reliability or suggestibility of young children—insights that could have ramifications for sexual abuse investigations. (1)

Once the children were comfortable with their presence, the investigators arranged for a man in a "funny hat" to enter the day care, set up a ladder, and change a normal light bulb to a coloured bulb. Two to three days later, the children—aged 3 to 4—were interviewed about the experience. "The descriptions were as different as night and day," Rowe told professionals attending a conference last week on Organized Sexual Abuse. "They remembered that the light bulb was changed, but one said a clown came into the room, another said someone in a bear suit did it." (2)

Rowe told the conference about an even more disturbing case in which a 31-year-old doctoral student, saying he was sexually abused by his mother and paternal grandfather, went to a therapist. The therapist recommended a men's group for survivors where nearly every other man in the group had suffered abuse at the hands of his parish priest. By the end of 20 weeks, the doctoral student had new memories similar to accounts by other group members. Eventually the man went into treatment and realized much of what he had "recalled" had never happened. (3)

Rowe said such accounts are undeniably fodder for proponents of false memory syndrome—a controversial theory that what people believe to be repressed memories of child sexual abuse are actually false memories planted by therapists. The problem, Rowe insists, is that memory research is new and offers no conclusive evidence. And there are therapists who, due to zeal or poor training, pursue an agenda with their clients. (4)

For therapists seeking to navigate the emotional mine field created by the debate, Rowe has only one piece of advice. "The magic solution is simple: competent practice. Don't worry about false memory syndrome. If you're a competent practitioner, it won't be an issue." (5)

Questions

1. Identify the thesis of the essay.
2. What type of essay is this: cause, effect, or cause and effect? Why?
3. Is it informative or evaluative?
4. Does the thesis suggest that absolute or qualified conclusions will be drawn?
5. Regardless of the actual essay's conclusions, list any conclusions that you can draw about the issues discussed. Are these absolute or qualified conclusions? Why?
6. List the causes and the effects being discussed: how convincingly are they linked?
7. How convincing is this essay's conclusion? Why?

Sample Cause and Effect Essay 2

LEARNING WHERE TO FIND FINANCING: A NEW SERIES OF CASE STUDIES IS DESIGNED FOR POST-SECONDARY STUDENTS—AND TEACHERS.

CANADIAN BANKER SEPT./OCT. 1994: 12–13

BY JUDY MARGOLIS

They may be strong in areas such as management methods and marketing, but small-business courses at Canada's business schools and community colleges seldom pay as much attention to another subject of vital interest to entrepreneurs: financing. Indeed, a typical post-secondary business curriculum devotes only two lectures per term to matters of finance, according to a recent survey conducted for the Canadian Bankers Association (CBA). (1)

That's a telling irony, given the lack of capital and lack of knowledge about where to get it are the biggest obstacles to growth for fledgling enterprises. There's little understanding, for example, that banks, despite press reports and claims by the small-business lobby to the contrary, are just one of several sources of seed money and startup capital. (2)

Two key reasons for the scant attention paid to this crucial topic in business courses are a lack of knowledge of financing on the part of instructors, and a scarcity of resource materials. (3)

Addressing both of these problems is a new resource tool that has been produced on behalf of the CBA by finance professors Barbara Orser of Ryerson Polytechnic University and Allan Riding of Carleton University. Orser specializes in micro-business development and women in management; Riding is an expert on small-business financing and associate dean of Carleton's Faculty of Social Sciences. (4)

Guided by the results of a national telephone and mail poll of business-school instructors and course offerings, Orser and Riding, along with three other case writers, have developed ten real-life case studies that explore various aspects of small-business financing in depth and at length. (5)

"Many of the textbooks currently in use are dated," says Orser. "They often come from the United States where the banking system is quite different, and they look at finance from the point of view of debt only—bank debt, the bad-news story." (6)

The new series of cases is badly needed, she says, particularly since "a lot of the information that instructors are picking up stems from the popular press, which is generally not familiar with equity or other forms of capitalization. What the cases will do is educate faculty—because each comes with fairly extensive teaching notes and other resource materials—as well as students about alternative sources that can complement debt financing by banks." (7)

The survey revealed, says Riding, that "about 80% of the people teaching small-business courses in the colleges and universities come out of marketing, organizational behaviour, or business policy. They have no, or very little, formal education on the financial dimension." (8)

Aware of the concern voiced by several survey respondents that these cases might be seen as an exercise in "bank propaganda," Orser and Riding went out of their way to ensure their independence. "We note that issue in the foreword and the fact that we have been able to develop this kit totally autonomously from the CBA," Orser explains. (9)

Adds Riding: "We made it very clear to the banking community early on that we wanted the latitude to be able to say a bank isn't the place to go for certain kinds of financing, and they endorsed that. In several cases, the solution is for the entrepreneur to look elsewhere." (10)

The end result of their efforts is a binder or kit—a fluid, user-friendly resource tool complete with cases and spreadsheets in hard copy and on disk, and a video. Five hundred copies of the kit are now in instructors' hands, free of charge, slated for use this fall. (11)

The cases were expressly written for use in small-business management, entrepreneurship and new-venture development courses—from community college level up to executive MBA programs—but they're equally applicable to more general business courses. They were tested in classrooms across the country and reviewed by a team of academics and instructors. (12)

Each case covers a wide range of problems and issues, and doesn't shrink from pushing human-resource, gender and other emotional hot-buttons that might influence decision-making by the entrepreneur, lender—or student. (13)

"Because we have to pack a lot into that two- to three-hour period," says Riding, "the majority of cases deal with the Small Business Loans Act, different forms of financing, venture capital, development corporations and so on. Almost no matter which case instructors use, they get a cross-section of financial alternatives." (14)

One of the cases Riding and Orser are most proud of concerns the startup of Knowledgebase Ltd., a software company whose president, Chris MacGregor, is seeking a $400,000 bank loan. (15)

After poring over what's obviously a half-baked business plan and putting themselves in the loan officer's shoes, the class is asked to watch a video featuring Chris in person pitching the case much more convincingly to the account manager. The gender bender is that half the class sees a video featuring Chris as a woman, the other half as a man. Whether that clinches or kills the deal for him/her is a matter for discussion once students learn about the double play and get together afterwards to compare reactions. (16)

This underscores a point that case writer Walter Good, who heads the Marketing Department at the University of Manitoba's Faculty of Management and is also president-elect of the Canadian Council for Small Business and Entrepreneurship, is fond of making to his own classes; there are no right or wrong answers. (17)

"That's why I discourage students from following up on these cases," says Good. "Because then they think there's a right answer, which is whatever the company ultimately did—implying that the people running it had 100% insight and always made the right decisions. What we're trying to capture is as realistic a context as possible." (18)

Questions

1. What kind of grabber is used to get the reader's attention?

2. Identify the thesis: can you spot all of its necessary components—major point, rhetorical mode, and overview of subtopics?

3. What type of essay is this: cause, effect, or cause and effect? Why?

4. Is it informative or evaluative? Why?

5. Does the thesis suggest that absolute or qualified conclusions will be drawn?

6. List the causes and the effects being discussed: is this a useful issue to consider?

7. What do you imagine is the effect of the "gender bender" in paragraph 16?

8. How effective is this essay's final thought? Why?

9. How does the conclusion relate to the cause and effect scenario being explained?

OTHER APPLICATIONS OF CAUSE AND EFFECT

As with all rhetorical modes, you may very effectively use moments of cause and effect analysis within essays written in other rhetorical modes for different purposes. A 1995 article called "Why Not to Worry about Timing the Market" in the Bank of Montreal's *The Strategic Investor* is a process essay describing the most effective strategies for individual clients to manage their investments. The essay's fourth paragraph reads as follows:

Cause/effect as a way to organize a body paragraph. Using cause/effect to illustrate a point can make an effective example in an argument.

> But what if your timing is off? By chasing after the elusive best possible return, you may do serious damage to your portfolio. Frequent changes can disturb the diversified allocations you've so carefully established. Researchers have found that even expert investors typically have little success in timing broad market movements. [From "Why Not to Worry about Timing the Market." *The Strategic Investor* Spring 1995.]

The essay has just described how to "time" the market. It now includes this paragraph to show the negative effects that result from bad timing. The rest of the essay deals with the process of how to manage an investment portfolio effectively, but its effectiveness is in part set up by the effective use of cause and effect in detailing the process of how not to manage an investment portfolio.

Exercise 8

Using the six-step method, write an essay on one of the topics from your Top Ten List. Justify your choice of format: is the essay cause, effect, or cause and effect? Is it informative or evaluative? Why? Should you qualify your cause and effect conclusions? Remember: choose a topic that you are interested in and/or know a lot about. Be specific in your essay. Try to come to some logical conclusion related to your purpose.

SUMMARY

In a cause and effect essay you are seeking to establish and examine the relationship between an issue or event (the cause) and its anticipated or actual results (the effect). You also assess the consequences of this relationship. Investigative journalism and government and scientific studies often work on the principle of studying cause and effect.

There are three types of cause and effect essay. In a cause essay, you focus solely on the reasons why something happened. In an effect essay, you examine the outcomes or results of a specific action or event. In a cause and effect essay, you attempt to explore a certain phenomenon's linked causes and effects—generally an undertaking of some length and complexity.

When you are given a specific writing task at school or at work, common cues can indicate that a cause and effect essay is appropriate. Similarly, appropriate transitional phrases in your writing will help unify your essay and highlight the linkages between causes and effects. A moment of cause and effect can provide an effective example in an essay written predominantly in another rhetorical mode.

CHECKLIST

- Does your introduction adequately explain the initial cause or effect responsible for the causes or effects that are detailed in your thesis and that your essay will be exploring?

- Does the body have adequate specific, substantial data to support the linkage of cause and effect?

- Have you dealt only with branch causes or immediate effects? Should you explore further in quest of root causes or further effects?

- Does your conclusion both summarize the effects or causes discussed in your essay and explore the implications of the argument, so that the question of the causes or effects is redirected to a larger, thought-provoking issue?

- Have you used appropriate transitional words to signal clearly linkages of cause and effect?

- Should you be qualifying any of your statements of cause or effect to allow for other possibilities?

- Is your essay clearly and appropriately informative or evaluative?

Persuasion

By completing a series of oral and written exercises and writing a persuasive essay using the six-step method, students will

1. *distinguish when the use of persuasion is appropriate;*

2. *use deductive or inductive argumentation where appropriate;*

3. *distinguish among emotional argumentation, logical argumentation, establishment of personal credibility, and refutation, and utilize each appropriately;*

4. *employ a combination of strategies to achieve the purpose of a single essay;*

5. *employ effectively strategies of legitimate argumentation and avoid illegitimate arguments;*

6. *use the transitional devices that most effectively unify a persuasive essay.*

OVERVIEW

What do you do if you feel your child should be socializing and exercising rather than watching television or playing so many video games? What do you do if you feel a course's workload is too heavy and the schedule of deadlines in a class is unrealistic? What do you do when your evaluation comes up at work and you feel you deserve a promotion?

In each of these situations, you clearly need to talk to the people involved: your child, your instructor, and your boss. In each of these situations, the goal of your conversation is clear—to convince the other person to agree with your views and to act accordingly. **Persuasion** is the presentation of carefully constructed arguments in order to change the listener's or reader's mind. As such, it is a process in which you engage and by which you are bombarded—continually.

Persuasion is one of the most fundamental elements of modern society. Whether you are watching a television commercial urging you to buy a specific brand of toothpaste or reading a letter from a charity urging you to donate your money, you are experiencing attempts at persuasion. A child begs for your permission to go to the movies. A colleague coaxes you to help on a project: "It will only take a couple of hours, and there's really no one else with your expertise on this subject." A pamphlet urges you to attend a rally against a local polluter. In each of these situations, techniques of persuasion are at work. Naturally, different strategies are employed in each circumstance to try to win you over; whether or not you are persuaded to change your position depends on the effectiveness and arrangement of the arguments.

PURPOSE AND FUNCTION

The *Gage Canadian Dictionary* defines the word *persuade* as follows:

> *v.* **1** cause (a person) to do something by urging, arguing, etc.; prevail upon: *I knew I should study but they persuaded me to go to the movies.* **2** cause (a person) to believe something by urging, arguing, etc.; convince: *They finally persuaded him of the truth of the rumor. We tried to persuade her that we had known all along what she was up to.*

Persuasive writing changes the reader.

As the definition indicates, persuasive writing is writing that literally changes your reader's thoughts or actions. The problem, however, is that most people are reasonably happy with the status quo; people will change only when you give them powerful reasons or incentives to do so. The tangible, verifiable proof of success in persuasive writing is found when your reader has been convinced to agree with you or to undertake the action you propose.

As a result, in a persuasive essay you need to assemble a variety of arguments, examples, and evidence to support your view. When you write persuasively, then, you are a salesperson selling an idea or plan of action. Like the television infomercial that urges "Don't waste a minute; call NOW!" you, too, want to have an immediate effect on your reader. For example, the travel and tourism operator not only dispenses information about rates to clients, but persuades them to purchase specific tour packages. The report or memo written by the office worker is often aimed at influencing co-workers, executives, or other decision-makers to adopt a specific course of action. Your résumé and cover letter are persuasive texts selling the most valuable product of all: you. Thus, no matter who you are, the first impression that a prospective employer forms of you will be based upon your persuasive writing skills.

OCCASIONS FOR AN ESSAY OF PERSUASION

When faced with a topic, you need to be able to identify occasions when persuasion is appropriate to your purpose. Obviously, if you are asked to write a report to **per-**

suade management to hire additional support staff to handle the recent 15 percent increase in volume of sales, you will use the persuasive mode.

You will not always, however, be so clearly told to write a persuasive essay. The following word cues indicate that a persuasive essay is required:

1. A **proposal** of any kind—whether to purchase a new computer, to produce a formal report, or to change a policy (for instance, to allow flexible work hours)—is by nature a persuasive document. Its purpose is to gain approval for some change.

2. If you write a **letter or report of complaint**, or a **formal complaint**, you are seeking to persuade your reader of the validity of your complaint and to elicit some kind of compensation, whether it be money, product, or simple apology.

3. If you do any kind of **advertising**, such as a **sales letter**, you are automatically doing persuasive writing. Your goal is to change the reader's buying habits so that he or she will use your product.

4. If you are asked to write an essay, a letter, or a report explaining, asserting, or defending why something **must, should,** or **needs** to be done, you are being asked for persuasive writing. For instance, an agriculture student might write a paper explaining why farm subsidies must be maintained.

5. If you do any writing designed to **lobby, press, push,** or **solicit** for something, you are by nature seeking to persuade—to affect your reader and change this person's views or actions on a particular issue. For instance, various groups continually lobby the government for favourable policy changes or concessions.

6. The **cover letter** and **résumé** are persuasive texts aimed at convincing prospective employers to hire you.

Exercise 1

Fill in the Top Ten List that follows with situations in your field in which persuasion might usefully be employed in a writing task. Use the cue words listed above to describe these topics. For instance, a small-business management student might choose the topic

> 2. Sales letter about new product to customers

Fill in as many as you can, and then continue reading the module. As other possible applications occur to you, return to this list and finish it.

10 TOP TEN APPLICATIONS FOR PERSUASIVE WRITING IN MY FIELD

1. My cover letter and résumé
2.
3.
4.
5.

6.

7.

8.

9.

10.

PRIMARY PROPOSITION

Every persuasive argument's thesis is formulated as a primary proposition: a statement that affirms or denies an idea and suggests some kind of action in support of this idea. The persuasive essay then assembles arguments, evidence, and examples to prove the truth or falsehood of the proposition. The primary proposition in persusasive writing often takes the form of a *should, must,* or *need* statement. For example, politicians in election campaigns, aiming to persuade you to vote for them, fire off propositions with the regularity of a machine gun: "We *must* reduce the deficit," "We *must* have greater gun control," "We *need* less government, and more individual responsibility," "Welfare recipients *should* work for their benefits." Each of these could become the thesis of a persuasive essay.

Propositions are should, must, or need statements.

💥 PROPOSITIONS VS. FACTS

Primary propositions and statements of fact are different. "College and university tuitions have gone up 30 percent in the last three years" is a statement of fact. This statement in and of itself is neutral; it simply documents reality, but does not propose anything. "We must pressure the government to stop further tuition increases." This is a proposition: it records no facts, but instead suggests a course of mental and physical action. Be certain that in a persuasive essay you use facts to support your proposition, not in place of it.

Exercise 2

Select four topics from your Top Ten List and write the primary propositions for them. Use *should, must,* or *need* statements.

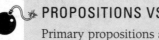

Exercise 3

Divide into groups of four to six people. Each group should take a different primary proposition from the list that follows.

A. Employment equity programs should/should not be legislated by the government.

B. Companies should/should not be allowed to conduct random drug testing on their employees.

C. Upgrading English skills should/should not be compulsory in school and on the job.

D. To save Canada, taxes must be raised/lowered.

1. Divide your group in two; each group will argue a different side of the issue. It is not essential to be arguing in favour of something you believe in; as you will see, an important part of persuasion is being able to understand opposing viewpoints.

2. Each group should brainstorm arguments in favour of their position. These arguments should be written down.

3. Each side should present its arguments before both groups. Being careful not to be biased in favour of the side you happen to agree with, evaluate the arguments carefully. Which ones are particularly effective? Which ones make a particularly strong impact on listeners? Why? Rank your arguments in order of effectiveness.

UNDERSTAND THE CIRCUMSTANCES

Before attempting to persuade someone to do or believe something, you must first be conscious of unique circumstances that will affect the success or failure of your "pitch" or primary proposition. To be effective, an argument must be founded in the demands of a particular situation; therefore, audience analysis takes on particular importance in persuasive writing. For instance, the shape taken by an argument in favour of euthanasia will be very different depending upon whether your audience consists of a) the relatives of suffering, terminally ill patients, or b) members of a religion that preaches the absolute sanctity of all life and abhors the notion of "legalized murder."

The secret to effective persuasion is to recognize and employ the particular arguments, ideas, and statistics that are most likely to impress and convince your specific audience. This is one of the reasons, for example, that advertising companies employ a host of market researchers to figure out what type of advertising campaign will be most persuasive with a given demographic group. Thus, the same automobile or beverage may be advertised in two very different ways to consumers who are 18-25 years old and to those who are over 65. In both cases, however, the crucial factor is to determine what combination of emotional and logical arguments is needed to persuade the audience to share the advertiser's view.

Exercise 4

Take your group's written arguments in favour of and against the primary proposition from Exercise 3, and discuss how you would present these in the following formats:

1. an essay that will be read by all members of your English class

2. a newsletter for unionized automobile assembly-line workers

3. a memo to the head of your school program

4. a memo to workers at your office job

5. a letter to the editor of the local newspaper

See Module 2:
Programming
Decisions, Audience,
p. 4.

You may want to refer to Module 2's more specific discussion of audience analysis. Which arguments would be more effective with each audience? Which would be less successful? Why?

SUPPORTING YOUR PRIMARY PROPOSITION

When we think about how we convince others to agree with our viewpoints or suggestions, we often think exclusively of logic. In fact, you should be using four primary means of argument in persuasion: **emotion, personal authority, refutation,** and **logic.** While logic, the last category, is in many ways the most significant kind of support, it is also the most complex. For this reason, it will be discussed last.

Emotional Arguments

See Legitimate Logical
Arguments, p. 197, in
this module.

While logical argumentation is fundamental to effective persuasion, your readers are not exclusively intellectual creatures. Appealing to your readers' emotions, for example, through a vivid description or a powerful narrative, can help to reinforce logical arguments and complement a more abstract argument with a vivid sense of reality.

For example, during a 1995 conflict with Spain over Spanish overfishing of immature turbot off the Newfoundland coast, Canada seized a Spanish fishing vessel. Canada's Fisheries Minister Brian Tobin made a powerful emotional appeal during a press conference near the United Nations. Holding in his hand an illegally caught baby turbot taken from the Spanish vessel, Tobin discussed Canada's need to defend this "last, lonely, unlovely little turbot clinging by its fingernails to the Grand Banks." Tobin and Canada had (in the eyes of Canada and many other nations) powerfully logical, statistical, and even moral arguments about the need for conservation. Tobin and others repeatedly made these arguments, but this description (which logically is ludicrous: fish do not have fingernails), coupled with the tiny fish in his hand, provided a powerful emotional support to the abstract arguments.

 **EMOTION VS. LOGIC**

Emotion is not a sustitute for logic; it is a supplement to it. Emotion should be used carefully—it is, unfortunately, easy to appeal to some readers' worst emotions by inflaming them with anger or hatred without substance.

 ### Exercise 5

In groups of four to six, construct a purely emotional argument for and against each of the following. Who is your audience? To what emotion of the audience are you attempting to appeal?

1. capital punishment
2. legalizing drugs
3. raising speed limits
4. bilingualism
5. the price of textbooks

Personal Credibility

See Rules to Remember When Using Authorities, p. 198, in this module.

The source of an argument affects your reader's perception of its validity. Imagine the reactions of the Spanish fishing fleet to Brian Tobin's fish fingernails argument. They dismissed his theatrics as biased grandstanding with little substance. Similarly, you will see how the source of arguments or statistics affects the perception of their validity. For example, a combined emotional and logical appeal for tougher safety standards on the job will be extremely effective coming from the parents of a teenage worker killed in an industrial accident.

Your credibility as the writer of the persuasive essay is also a crucial issue. When you complete your rhetorical triangle, you always consider the nature of your point of view. A big part of supporting your primary proposition is establishing why and how you are empowered to speak on this issue and to make this particular appeal. As you will see, some of this authority can be "borrowed" from other sources in your research, but often your particular perspective can be stressed as a means of bolstering your argument. For instance, a student is more credible on student issues than an administrator. A computer engineering graduate is more credible than a recreation leadership graduate when discussing database management. This is not to say that the latter in each case might not be capable of discussing the issues cogently and coherently; their positions, however, do not confer any extra credibility on them, unlike the former.

As an example, in a newspaper article, journalist Bill Radunsky argues in favour of limitations on the public display of evidence in a sensational murder trial. Radunsky argues that the media have a responsibility to practise self-censorship in certain situations. In the essay's third paragraph, Radunsky clearly explains the nature of his authority to speak on this subject: "As both a journalist of almost 20 years, and the brother-in-law of one of the victims, ... I have watched with professional concern on one hand and familial concern on the other, the events and their coverage by the news media over these three years" [Bill Radunsky. "When Journalism Should Avert Its Gaze." *Toronto Star* 20 Apr. 1995: A28]. After highlighting his unique personal credibility, he then proceeds to present separate arguments on personal and professional grounds for media self-censorship.

Exercise 6

In groups of four to six, specify the personal credibility that you would elaborate in each of the following instances. In other words, what specific arguments or examples could you make *because of* who you are in each of these cases?

1. I am a student. Tuition is too high to pay.

2. I am an administrator. Tuition is too low to meet expenses.

3. I am a teacher. My students are unprepared for my class.

4. I am a student. Teachers mark too hard.

5. I am a beggar. Give me a looney.

Refutation: Anticipate Objections

The third major type of argument your persuasive writing should rely upon is refutation, or the anticipation of objections by opponents of your primary proposition. You may have little difficulty coming up with interesting and convincing logical and emotional arguments, examples, and evidence to support your position. Once you have sorted out all the content you intend to use for your essay, however, you need to make a list of counterarguments that your audience might use to oppose your perspective. Think of a tennis game. In tennis, you obviously want to make the best shots possible, but after making your shot, you need to anticipate where and how the other player might return your shot. This allows you to be in the best position to handle that return. Similarly, in persuasion you anticipate your readers' negative mental responses so that you can try to allay their doubts in your writing.

As an example, a six-page form letter on a "multi-level marketing scheme" provides the names and addresses of four people. According to the scheme, a recipient of the letter, for example, Serkalem, sends $5 to each of the four people, who in return send her "reports" on multi-level marketing. In the meantime, Serkalem photocopies the letter, replacing one of the names with her own, and then sends it to as many other people as possible. Then, Serkalem theoretically sits back and waits for these people and others to send $5 each for "reports." In this way the humble Serkalem gets rich! On page 5 of the letter, the author states

> At times you have probably received chain letters, asking you to send money but getting nothing in return. NO product whatsoever. Not only are chain letters illegal, but the risk of someone breaking the chain makes them quite unattractive.
>
> This plan has the feel and appeal of a chain letter but this is legal, since you are offering a legitimate product to your people. After they purchase the product from you, they produce more and resell the product. It's simple FREE ENTERPRISE.

Well, yes and no. It may be legal, but it preys on the reader's gullibility and greed in the same way that a chain letter or pyramid scheme does. The writer here is attempting (not entirely successfully) to anticipate and neutralize the discomfort the reader very likely experiences, because this does seem very much like a chain letter. After all, there is at least some truth to the cliché "If it walks like a duck, and talks like a duck, it probably is a duck."

As a second example, in his article "Fit Yes, Fat No," journalist Michael Kesterton argues, "Being active is almost pure pleasure—more than you can say for some eating behaviours you'll have to learn—and not enough people believe this. Those already tired from lugging bags of fat around all day need to be persuaded that burning energy actually makes them feel more energetic." Anticipating that some readers may react by thinking "Activity is *not* fun; it is painful," Kesterton suggests that disinterest in activity may come from the vicious circle of being out of shape and therefore tired. [From Michael Kesterton, "Fit Yes, Fat No." *Globe and Mail* 31 Dec. 1994: D1.]

Exercise 7

In groups of four to six, consider who would be the hostile audience for each of the following persuasive arguments. What objections would you expect this audience to raise? How would you counter these objections?

1. Abortion should not be legal.
2. Welfare benefits should be reduced.
3. We need stricter gun control.
4. Rock and rap music lyrics must be censored.
5. Refugees should be allowed easy access to Canada.

Legitimate Logical Arguments

Logical, rational arguments carry significant weight with readers—and rightly so, for these arguments can be examined, analyzed, tested, and debated. Legitimate logical argumentation is divided primarily into two parts: authority and reasoning.

AUTHORITY

See Module 4: Summary Skills, and Module 12: The Research Essay, Quotation Integration, p. 254, and Documentation, p. 255.

No matter how brilliant you are, you are just one writer writing from one point of view. Thus, your goal when assembling logical support for your primary position is to expand the range of your authority by introducing other persons and evidence that support your view. You are the lawyer making a case; like a lawyer, to do so, you will need to call a variety of witnesses to testify on your behalf. These witnesses—or authorities—come in many forms, based mostly on research of one kind or another.

Facts are indisputable, externally verifiable nuggets of truth that carry significant weight. For instance, "Canada became an independent nation on July 1, 1867." **Examples** are particular details and concrete illustrations of your point; these show the reader tangible reasons for accepting a certain argument.

Testimony is the equivalent of calling an expert witness at a trial: it is the summary or quotation of the argument or findings of a knowledgeable, reputable expert. This is also known as collaborating support; you quote the argument of an expert, and for the sake of your essay, its authority becomes your own. Television and newspaper stories rely heavily upon the testimony of eyewitnesses and others involved in a story.

Statistics are powerful tools in written persuasion because in the midst of a text that is "just words," they possess the apparent solidity of mathematics, and thus seem to represent tangible, quantifiable reality. While they often carry this kind of weight, you must nonetheless be very careful when using them. In fact, a number of important questions must be clearly resolved when using any authority.

RULES TO REMEMBER WHEN USING AUTHORITIES

See Personal Credibility, p. 195, in this module.

1. **Source.** You must always name your source. Nothing is less persuasive than a statistic or a quotation without a source. The reader wonders if you made it up, forgot the source, or are too embarrassed to admit your source. Further, you must be sure of the impartiality and reputability of the source. For instance, readers will likely be skeptical of a tobacco company's arguments or statistics showing a lack of connection between second-hand smoke and cancer. The tobacco company has an obvious interest in this kind of result, so readers will doubt the validity of this information. You must consider the source and the source's effect on your readers.

2. **Validity of information.** Is the research accurate, up-to-date, and complete? Is the method that was used in conducting the survey or doing the research fair? You will need to explain as much of this as possible to ensure that your readers will accept your evidence. Any number of possible problems can arise. For instance, if you are quoting a survey result, you must ask whether the survey was based on a "leading question." In the months before the 1995 Quebec referendum, there was heated argument over exactly what the wording of the referendum question would be, because there is obviously a big difference between asking "Are you in favour of Quebec separating from Canada?" and "Are you in favour of the Quebec government negotiating a sovereignty association agreement with Canada which retains a common parliament and integrated economy?" Surveys of Quebecers' likelihood of voting "Yes" or "No" fluctuated according to which question the survey participants were asked.

3. **Validity of conclusions.** Do the statistics or testimony or facts really demonstrate what they seem to? Are the conclusions valid or overstated? Have you or one of your sources generalized too much from a specific conclusion? Audrey McLaughlin, former NDP leader and loser of the 1993 federal election, was asked two years later if her defeat, and those of several other contemporary Canadian female party leaders, proved the existence of a bias against female party leaders. Her response was this:

   > There is a great tendency right now, because of four or five of us who have not had startlingly winning campaigns, to say, "Well, that's it, women can't win." But no one ever does the statistics. How many men have lost elections since Confederation? Hundreds, probably, but no one is going around saying, "Gee, I guess men just can't win." [From Kelly Toughill, "Can Women Win?" *Toronto Star* 17 June 1995: B1.]

EVIDENCE

The best advice is to be suspicious of all evidence you want to offer in your persuasive writing—and to be aware that a good reader will also be suspicious. Ultimately, if you always remain conscious of your rhetorical tringle issues, you will not go wrong. You know what your purpose or primary proposition is. Be certain that the authority supports this (topic), expands the reputable range of your authority (point of view), and will have a positive impact on your particular readers (audience).

Exercise 8

Evaluate the validity of the following statistical arguments. Isolate any problems, and the nature of these problems.

1. Food service students doing a taste panel on brand name vs. generic ginger ale (which costs one-third less) expect that the panel will reveal that people find little difference in taste between the two. This, they theorize, will therefore justify people purchasing the cheaper generic brand. Sixty-four participants fill out a questionnaire that asks for ratings of the taste, aroma, and colour of the two brands ("A" and "B" on the form). Fifty of sixty-four prefer the taste of the brand-name ginger ale. When the students present their findings to the class, they discuss their surprise with the results, and conclude that a clear majority (78 percent in this case) of students will buy the better-tasting brand, regardless of price.

2. A television advertisement states "Three out of four Canadian dentists say that flossing and brushing after meals with Pastyface toothpaste significantly reduces the risk of cavities and gingivitis."

REASONING

The second main component of logical argumentation is reasoning, of which there are two main kinds: deductive and inductive.

Deductive Reasoning

Deductive Reasoning: from the general to the specific.

Deductive reasoning takes general premises or assumptions and demonstrates through logic that they apply to specific situations. The basic form of deductive reasoning is the *syllogism*, which is a three-part statement moving from general to specific. The classic example from Aristotle follows:

> All men are mortal. (GENERAL PREMISE about men)
>
> Socrates is a man. (SPECIFIC PREMISE about Socrates)
>
> Therefore, Socrates is mortal. (GENERAL PREMISE about men APPLIES TO Socrates SPECIFICALLY)

Two other examples are as follows:

> The tax rate for small businesses is too high. (GENERAL PREMISE)
>
> Nejat owns a small business. (SPECIFIC PREMISE)
>
> Therefore, Nejat's tax rate is too high. (GENERAL APPLIES TO SPECIFIC)

Syllogisms can be misleading.

Knowledge of Windows 95 is all that is needed for this job. (GENERAL PREMISE)

Julia knows Windows 95. (SPECIFIC PREMISE)

Therefore, Julia is qualified for this job. (GENERAL APPLIES TO SPECIFIC)

If you look up *syllogism* in the *Gage Canadian Dictionary*, however, you will discover that it also means "a specious or very subtle argument; a deviously crafty piece of reasoning." This second meaning comes out of a certain distrust of logic—or, more precisely, of an awareness that logical structures may be manipulated or misused to reach inaccurate conclusions. What do you make of the following syllogism?

All men are mortal. Socrates is a man. Therefore, kill Socrates.

Most problems in syllogistic reasoning come down to questions of whether or not the general and specific premises are valid and the conclusion follows from them. Unfair generalizations are a prime example of the misuse of premises. For instance, examine the following syllogism:

Auto technicians replace car brakes. (GENERAL)

Wilo replaced her car's brakes. (SPECIFIC)

Therefore, Wilo is an auto technician. (GENERAL APPLIES TO SPECIFIC)

This seems to be a logical sequence; however, there is a problem with the initial general premise. While it is true that auto technicians replace brakes, they are not the only people who do this. Wilo may be a systems analyst or student or stewardess who simply followed the instructions in her car's ownership manual. The initial premise is being misinterpreted as "Auto technicians are the only people who replace car brakes," which is, of course, not true.

This is a form of **unfair generalization**, which can lead to **stereotyping**. Think about a stereotype like the "dumb blonde." If blondes are dumb, and Helen is a blonde, then Helen is dumb. Stereotypes like that of the "dumb blonde" represent as absolute truths general premises that are not invalid, but are only partially valid. Of course, some blondes are dumb, just as some redheads, brunettes, greyheads, or albinos are. However, many are also smart, and many have average intelligence—again, just like any group. Be sure, therefore, to test the validity of your own and others' premises, rather than to be swayed by an apparently sound logical structure.

Exercise 9

In groups of four to six, complete the following syllogisms with the missing statement. Are these syllogisms valid?

1. All homeowners pay taxes. I pay taxes. ...

2. Fraud is a serious crime in business that can lead to immediate dismissal. ... Angie was fired.

3. ... Ahmed keeps the company books. Therefore, Ahmed is an accountant.

4. Our children must be cared for professionally. Rozanne is cared for by trained professionals at the Bruckmann sanitarium. ...

5. I will take my vacation only in the most lively locations. I am taking my vacation in the Bahamas. ...

Exercise 10

Select one of the four items from your Top Ten List for which you have written a primary proposition, and develop a point-form deductive argument to support it.

Inductive Reasoning: from the specific to the general.

See Module 9: The Cause and Effect Essay.

Inductive Reasoning

When confronted with a premise that seems to be overly generalized or otherwise questionable, we can verify whether or not it is true by using inductive reasoning. Inductive reasoning works in the opposite fashion to deductive reasoning by beginning with a number of specific observations and then attempting to formulate logical general conclusions from these. The scientific method is based on this procedure. For example, suppose your friend Rosita dropped out of her school program last year. You might think of a variety of explanations. Did she flunk? Was she lazy or disinterested? Perhaps you learn a number of specific facts that come to change your way of thinking.

> Enrolment at postsecondary institutions increased from 1983 to 1992, but dropped in each year after.
>
> In 1992 tuition rises started, and incidental fees also began increasing; in 1991, the government's student aid program changed, so there were no more grants, but just loans.
>
> Numbers of applicants from economically disadvantaged and middle-class backgrounds began dropping, possibly because they would be facing a mounting potential debt load.
>
> Rosita's parents are welfare recipients who insisted she leave her program because they could not afford tuition.

Based on these specific facts and examples, you might formulate a general conclusion that changes in tuition and student aid jeopardize access to school for poorer students.

Jumping to Conclusions. With inductive reasoning like this, you must have sufficient specific, valid, firm information to justify your general conclusion. When we speak of people "jumping to conclusions," or making a "leap in logic," we mean that they are reaching a conclusion prematurely based upon inadequate information. Keep your feet firmly on the ground, and be certain your conclusions are the product of careful, complete reasoning.

See Module 9: The Cause and Effect Essay.

Coincidence. Inductive reasoning is often closely linked to cause and effect reasoning. As such, one possible mistake is confusing coincidence (literally two events occurring simultaneously) for causation. For example, assess the following statement:

> Because it gets cold in the winter, the leaves fall off deciduous trees.

At first glance, this may seem accurate. Certainly when the weather cools in autumn, the leaves do fall off the trees. Science clearly shows, however, that it is not the cold but the reduced amount of sunlight that causes this. Trees depend upon photosynthesis—that is, they process sunlight into food. Less sunlight means less food, causing the leaves to fall off. Be careful; coincidence is easily mistaken for causation.

Exercise 11

Select one of the four items from your Top Ten List for which you have written a primary proposition, and develop a point-form inductive argument to support it.

ILLEGITIMATE ARGUMENTS

In a trial, a judge will decide that certain evidence and certain lines of questioning are inadmissible. This means that for various reasons it is inappropriate or unfair to pursue these arguments. When you are writing persuasively, you should consider the following arguments to be inadmissible. Do not resort to illegitimate arguments like the following:

1. **The personal attack.** Election campaigns too often degenerate into a series of personal attacks in which each candidate seeks to denigrate an opponent's character or morals rather than to argue against his or her views on the issues. It is crucial not to let your essay become a personal attack on readers or others who do not agree with the positions of your essay. Always avoid a statement that can be considered a personal affront; for example, "Anyone who does not believe in the death penalty is neither rational nor open-minded," or "People who believe drug testing in the workplace is acceptable might as well be card-carrying neo-Nazis." Such statements do not forward your argument in any way, and worse than that, they are almost certain to make some readers become hostile and perhaps stop reading. A personal attack upon one of your opponents or readers is not an acceptable substitute for persuasive argumentation.

2. **Questionable examples and non sequiturs.** *Non sequitur* is a Latin term that literally means "does not follow." A non sequitur is, thus, an argument or point that does not logically arise out of the argument you are presenting. As an example, an argument in favour of euthanasia might argue "Abortion is not illegal; therefore, it is hypocritical that euthanasia is illegal in Canada." This is a non sequitur. Abortion is a thorny and complex issue on its own, and revolves around the issue of the definition of human life (is it "murder" to abort a fetus at two months? at six months? ever? At what point is a fetus "human," or is it not human until the baby is born?) as well as questions about a woman's right to control her body.

   Superficially, euthanasia involves similar issues of control over one's body and questions about the quality of life that constitutes "human life." However, euthanasia involves a host of other issues, such as the mental competence of the ill individual, the irreversibility of the medical condition in question, and the ethics of a doctor's involvement. While there is common ground between the issues, this argument can be easily unravelled. Try to stay away from non sequiturs or examples that you know are imperfect; if flaws are easily detected in your reasoning, you will lose your reader almost immediately.

3. **Circular or repetitive arguments.** These are arguments that start in one place and pretend to produce a logical conclusion. In fact, they finish in the same place where they began. Here are three examples:

> The cause of crime is people breaking the law.
>
> People's ignorance comes from not understanding.
>
> To stop a repetitive argument, do not argue in circles.

These arguments can be restated as follows: *The cause of crime is crime. People are ignorant because they are ignorant. To stop a circular argument, do not argue in circles.* However valid-seeming at first, such statements say absolutely nothing. They offer no insight into the situation under discussion, and thus serve no purpose.

4. **The bandwagon effect.** This is a common tactic. For example, signs at McDonald's restaurants tell you of the "billions and billions" of hamburgers McDonald's has "served." Similarly, a child wanting to go to a concert argues, "Everybody's going." Always remember the parent's typical response, "If everybody jumped off a bridge, would you?" Parents are wise (in at least this instance): they realize that the simple fact that others are doing or thinking something is not a logical reason for anybody else to do it. McDonald's has served billions of burgers, but that is no compelling reason for you to eat one. Such arguments play on our insecurities by encouraging us to "jump on the bandwagon" for fear of missing out on something or being considered abnormal. Lacking a logical basis, however, these arguments are ultimately unsatisfactory.

5. **Either/or reasoning.** This is often deliberately and unfairly provocative. For instance,

> We must either restore the death penalty or face an unprecedented crime wave.

The two choices here are presented as the only choices possible—an inaccurate suggestion. This statement assumes an absolute relationship between the death penalty and deterring crime—something that has never been established. The death penalty might be restored, but a crime wave could still occur because of a depressed economy or other reasons. This inflammatory reasoning is a common tactic of politicians and activists.

 ### Exercise 12

In groups of four to six, examine the following arguments. What makes these illegitimate arguments? What type of illegitimate arguments are these?

1. The Minister of Finance says that we must cut the deficit. But it was her party that ran up this deficit in the first place. Moreover, she is a wealthy entrepreneur who will never feel the crunch of the deficit cuts.

2. What does my teacher really know about the business world that I will be entering? He has spent his life in the classroom, and everybody knows that teaching is an easy job.

3. When you consider that the fish stocks on both coasts are dwindling quickly, we must either shut down the fishing industry for the next ten years or lose it forever.

4. You cannot legalize prostitution because it leads to the spread of disease, encourages loose morals, and encourages prostitutes to make money for sexual services.

5. Cigarettes do not cause lung cancer. Smoking causes lung cancer.

6. Guns don't kill. People kill.

7. I am allergic to cats, and my allergies are especially bad in May and June when owners are letting their cats out of the house.

Now, while still in groups, write three more false arguments. One must involve coincidence, one must involve the bandwagon effect, and one must involve a circular argument.

COMBINE TECHNIQUES FOR EFFECTIVE PERSUASION

When you are generating content for any essay, you use more than one technique in order to take advantage of your different thinking processes. When writing persuasively, you similarly need to appeal to your reader's different thinking processes. Good persuasive writing, therefore, combines all of the techniques discussed: logical argumentation, emotional argumentation, establishment of credibility, and refutation.

For example, if you are trying to convince someone to take a CPR (cardiopulmonary resuscitation) course, you might use an emotional argument that touches the person's heart: "Suppose your child is swimming, starts to drown, and is not breathing when you pull her from the water. By knowing CPR, you could save your child's life." You might supplement this with an argument appealing to logic or reason: "This course could also be valuable on a résumé because employers are impressed by people who take the initiative to acquire such knowledge."

A combination of approaches will always be most effective: an essay full of cold reasoning and general statistics may make a good argument, but may not completely convince a reader. A reader may react by thinking, "Yes, I see your point, but I don't *like* that." Similarly, an essay filled with passionate emotional fireworks and heart-wrenching examples may move your readers, but leave them aware of the lack of substance beneath the sizzle. Readers will weary of an argument that hits only one note over and over; when you present a variety of different types of arguments, you appeal to their different needs and sustain their interest.

EXPLOIT OTHER RHETORICAL MODES

As you have no doubt realized, persuasion is one of the most complex rhetorical modes. Persuasive writing can be likened to channel-surfing when watching television: within a persuasive essay, good writers utilize one rhetorical mode after another in order to convey their logical, emotional, credibility, and refutation arguments. In persuasion, you must be willing to deploy any and all other rhetorical modes, such as description and narration (Module 5), process analysis (Module 6), comparison/contrast (Module 7), definition and classification (Module 8), and cause and effect (Module 9). Paragraphs written in these modes can help illustrate or reinforce arguments you are assembling. Use whatever is useful to your argument.

Similarly, be aware that when you are writing an essay in one of these other modes, you are often writing persuasively. For example, in the cost/benefit analysis (comparison/contrast), the accident description (description/narration), or the feasibility study (cause and effect); you are usually seeking to persuade the reader to support your version of what did happen or may happen.

Exercise 13

Using the four items from your Top Ten List for which you wrote primary propositions in Exercise 2, specify how you might use two different rhetorical modes in order to support each argument. For example, is there an anecdote you might tell (narration) or a term you might define (definition)?

DEDUCTIVE OR INDUCTIVE ORGANIZATION

You can use deductive or inductive argumentation not only as a means of constructing a single supporting argument, but also as the principle for organizing your essay as a whole. In a **deductively organized essay,** you introduce your general rule or position, and then proceed to demonstrate its validity by supporting it with specific examples, evidence, and arguments.

General

Introduction: Introduce the primary proposition—the position you want readers to adopt or the action you want them to take.

Specific

Body:

a. Arrange a combination of specific emotional/logical/credibility examples, evidence, and arguments in an effective sequence.

Specific

b. Anticipate reader hostility and counterarguments, and show readers the reasons why your position is preferable to others.

Conclusion: Summarize how you have shown how the general rule applies to specifics.

In **inductive organization,** you begin with a set of specific facts or situations from which you will formulate a general argument or solution in the conclusion.

Specifics

Introduction: Introduce the complex issue's many sides and suggest the different (contradictory) arguments supporting these positions. Reveal a sense of the variety of facts and information.

Specific

Body: Use a combination of emotional/logical/credibility arguments, and go through several possible solutions to the issue while demonstrating the various problems with each.

General

Conclusion: State your primary proposition. Explain it carefully as the only logical, complete solution to the various problems raised by the other positions.

Exercise 14

1. How would a particular audience help you determine which method to use to organize a persuasive essay?

2. Take your Top Ten topics and think of a specific audience for which you would argue inductively, and another for which you would argue deductively.

TONE

Be careful to structure your persuasive essay as dialogue rather than as monologue. No one likes to feel as if he or she is being lectured or told how to think and what to do—a particular danger of persuasive writing. It is vital that your readers feel that they are being engaged in a discussion about the topic or issue. This relates to showing that you understand (and then refuting) the other side of the issue. Remember the tennis game: you are anticipating and responding to the readers' return volleys.

Also, never make a statement that will simply serve to alienate your reader, such as "This kind of thinking is just plain stupid ..." Be diplomatic, even when you are discrediting someone else's position. Count on the substance of your argument. This is particularly important in persuasion because the listeners may be neutral or hold an opinion that is the exact opposite of yours. Do not risk undoing your hard work by triggering negative reader preconceptions.

APPLYING THE SIX-STEP METHOD TO PERSUASIVE WRITING

Step 1: Imaging the Essay with the Rhetorical Triangle

Follow the usual steps, beginning with imaging your essay with the rhetorical triangle. In the rhetorical triangle, you will create your primary proposition (focused topic), determine your personal credibility (your point of view), and uncover what your audience's position on your topic is and why the reader believes in the rightness of this position (audience analysis). Based on this information, you will either be reinforcing this position or trying to convince the audience to change its position.

KNOW YOUR READERS

It is of paramount importance that you have a complete understanding of your readers for the persuasion essay to succeed. A complete profile of your readers' characters and needs will be necessary to ensure that you are adopting appropriate strategies to appeal to them. While assembling each argument, you should almost be able to visualize the readers and their reactions to your various points. Be meticulous about this: errors of audience analysis can completely undermine your ability to convince your audience and can even cause the opposite of your intention.

Step 2: Content Generation

In persuasive writing, content generation is a unique two-step process. You first generate content as usual, using more than one method. Content generation, vital for all effective essay writing, is even more important for persuasion because of the second step now involved.

SUPPORTING YOUR ARGUMENT

There is always a danger that a persuasion essay can degenerate into a series of personal opinions with no evidence, facts, and examples to back them up. Nothing is less persuasive than an unsupported opinion. Make sure that nothing in the essay appears simply to represent your beliefs or feelings. Instead, support and round out each argument with fairly and accurately introduced background material. Just like a trial lawyer, aim to establish the reliability, credibility, and applicability of all evidence to your situation.

See Refutation, p. 196.

The audience for persuasive writing is on some level hostile to your opinion (this is why you are trying to persuade them), so you now have to consider refutation by taking into account the reasons they will disagree with your arguments. Remember that, again like a trial, the opposing side will have its own expert witnesses. Beside the list of your main arguments, then, you need to make a list of all the possible counterarguments someone opposed to your position might use.

After completing your content generation, examine your rough work and categorize your arguments: do you have arguments that make appeals on logical and emotional grounds, as well as clear arguments for personal credibility? Have you adequately refuted opposing views?

Step 3: The Outline

See Deductive or Inductive Organization, p. 205.

When outlining your essay, you will have a number of decisions to make concerning the order that you will use for presenting your arguments. The first is whether or not you will use deductive or inductive organization. Generally, if you anticipate your

Friendlier reader

readers responding favourably to your primary proposition, use deductive organization, where the primary proposition (thesis) appears at the end of the introduction. Within the deductively organized essay, you will then likely move from less convincing (effective) arguments to more convincing (effective) ones. This requires you to rank your main arguments in terms of their relative effectiveness, not from your own perspective, but from that of your reader.

Hostile reader

If you anticipate reader hostility to your position, it will make more sense to use inductive organization and gradually build up the arguments leading to your primary proposition as presented in the essay's conclusion. Here, inside the body of the text, you will likely present the least controversial elements at the beginning and then gradually introduce the more controversial ones at the end. This pattern allows you to gain credibility before tackling the trickiest elements of your argument. Using this method has less to do with the strength of your arguments than with the best method of breaking down the resistance of your audience.

Step 4: Writing the Rough Draft

When assembling your rough draft, be certain to support carefully the internal logic of your arguments. Utilize other rhetorical modes as appropriate; for example, you might use a brief narrative of a personal experience to establish credibility, a brief comparison/contrast example to discredit a common misconception, a brief definition to clarify the parameters of the discussion, and so on.

Step 5: Revising

Because of its complexity, persuasion depends upon the use of all varieties of transition techniques. When revising your essay, sharpen its focus by increasing transitional phrases both to clarify the internal workings of your arguments and to link one argument to the next. Examine your draft carefully, again categorizing your arguments: do you have an appropriate mixture of appeals on logical and emotional grounds as well as clear arguments for personal credibility? Have you adequately anticipated possible reader objections to your arguments?

 THE OUTSIDE READER

It can be very useful to have someone (ideally someone who fits the profile of your intended reader) read your essay. Ask the person to do these two things:

1. **Evaluate clarity.** Do all of your arguments make sense? Is there sufficient detail?
2. **Counter your arguments.** Your reader should look for any gaps in your arguments. Ask the reader to poke as many holes in the arguments as possible.

Then, revise to correct these problems.

COMBINING SENTENCES

See Appendix A, Contract #3: Run-on Sentences, for a discussion of conjunctions.

Having too many short sentences can lead to very choppy and incoherent writing. Combining sentences is the best way to avoid this type of problem. In reality, though, there are numerous ways to combine sentences, and each has a slightly different effect. By using words called coordinating conjunctions or FANBOYS—for, and, nor, but, or, yet, so—it is possible to combine two sentences. Keep in mind that this is only one possible way of making one sentence out of two, and that a comma always precedes the FANBOYS when they are used this way.

> The Student Council voted not to provide free refreshments on graduation day. A group of students ended up serving them by raising money from private and industry sources.
>
> COMBINED: The Student Council voted not to provide free refreshments on graduation day, *so* a group of students ended up serving them by raising money from private and industry sources.

> The proposal you submitted for the research essay looks excellent to me. I have a couple of questions about specifics.
>
> COMBINED: The proposal you submitted for the research essay looks excellent to me, *but* I have a couple of questions about specifics.

Step 6: Editing

Looking for your most common errors, edit your persuasive essay.

Exercise 15

1. Read the following paragraphs. This excerpt consists of the second and third paragraphs of a persuasive essay by Leanne Nierlich in favour of increasing immigration to Canada.

2. Fill in any necessary transitional phrases in the spaces provided in order to link the ideas appropriately.

> One of Canada's fundamental problems is that it is underpopulated. Only 29 million people live in this, the world's second-largest country, which means that vast inhabitable areas have little or no population at all. This lack of population _____ makes it difficult to settle new areas or expand current villages and towns. _____ some argue that the town of Cornwall, Ontario, where my grandparents settled sixty years ago, is dying a slow death from lack of economic and social renewal. _____ we do not want to have the population density of a place like Hong Kong; _____, we do need more people to live in certain areas to make them viable. Larger population bases make offering essential services more feasible. _____ by living on more of the land, we will develop a stronger sense of national identity, because people will see more of

Canada's greatness. _____, we have to strike a balance that will be to the benefit of both the individuals who start lives in these places, and the larger society that gains in very real ways.

_____, this gain is not only cultural because an increase in the population will bring an expansion of the tax base in Canada. More people in the country means more income from taxation for all levels of government. _____, money raised from personal income taxes increases, as the vast majority of new immigrants, if chosen carefully, are fully contributing members of the society. _____, the same is true for the wide range of sales taxes that Canadians pay, and the payroll taxes that Canadian companies pay on behalf of employees. Having a more substantial number of taxpayers will even give the government more ability to modify existing taxes and introduce new ones. _____ one of the most profitable money-making schemes ever devised by governments—lotteries—is certain to be a direct beneficiary of a larger population. More people to draw on allows the government to funnel that money toward reducing or eliminating the staggering debt that Canada has.

3. Now reread the passage carefully, and note in the margins the types of arguments being used: "E" = emotional, "L" = logical, "C" = personal credibility, and "R" = refutation of likely objections. As you are doing this, evaluate the mixture. Is it appropriate for this particular argument? Would you advise the writer to adjust it at all? Take a close look at the logical arguments. Detect at least two syllogisms and assess their validity. Are the premises valid or overly general? Would you rewrite any? Has the writer anticipated and refuted potential objections clearly enough?

4. Rewrite the passage, adjusting the argument mixture as you feel is appropriate: adding, modifying, or deleting arguments; supporting them with refutation; and being careful to provide adequate transitional phrasing.

Sample Essay of Persuasion 1

WHY BUSINESS NEEDS SCIENTISTS

SCIENTIFIC AMERICAN, NOVEMBER 1992, 138
BY MICHAEL SCHULHOF

Twenty years ago I was a physicist working on neutron-scattering experiments at Brookhaven National Laboratory. Now, as the vice-chairman of Sony USA and president of Sony Software, I represent Sony in both the electronics and entertainment business. I spend my days discussing and overseeing projects that range from new developments in high definition to the cutting edge of popular music. (1)

My experience has convinced me that a background in pure science is an ideal preparation for business. I will take that a step further and say that American business would be a lot better if it had more scientists and fewer MBA's running its corporations. (2)

Why do I think the neutron detector prepared me for life at Sony? As a physicist, I was doing work I considered important and working with people I admired. But as I looked around the lab, I asked myself whether this was what I wanted to be doing 20 years into the future. I thought I might like to try business, but I was not absolutely sure. When I shared my uncertainty with my thesis adviser, the distinguished researcher Robert Nathans, he gave me some advice I will never forget. "Don't worry about it, Mickey," he said. "You're a physicist. Physicists don't do anything they really don't want to do. If you get into business and find you don't like it, you'll get out." (3)

Obviously, I liked it. I stayed. But I stayed as a physicist. No matter what it says in my job description, I am still a scientist. And I have approached business problems the same way I approached scientific problems. The lessons I learned as a scientist were excellent instruction for business. (4)

Some of those lessons are as basic as a strong work ethic. The business school yuppies of the 1980s glamorized the idea of working long hours. But that trend was in fashion in labs long before anyone ever heard of Michael Milken. I can well remember sitting up until 3 A.M. baby-sitting our precious high-flux beam reactor through an experiment. The hours didn't matter. It was the result that counted. When you have a meaningful challenge, personal time means little. That is a lesson I have carried over into corporate life. (5)

Science also encouraged my intellectual curiosity. Of course, that was something that attracted me to physics in the first place. But working in the lab at Brookhaven taught me how stimulating it was to make intellectual curiosity the center of your professional life. My responsibilities have obviously changed. But intellectual curiosity is very much a part of what keeps me going in the business world. In science, you accept intellectual curiosity as a given. I wish it were more common in business. (6)

I would also like to see business people develop some of the tenacity that is common in science. People in business tend to be impatient. The scientists I worked with were anxious to see results. But they realized that you had to build the foundation before you could put on the roof. By example, they taught me the importance of mastering the fundamentals of a field before you could do meaningful new work. Shortly after Sony acquired Columbia Pictures, I began to read the scripts for films we had under production. That didn't endear me to some of the operating people. One of them challenged me about why I wanted the scripts. He as much as told me that they were not going to let me take over the creative decisions. But I told him he was missing the point. I was not interested in telling the creative experts how to make films, but I was intensely interested in understanding the process. (7)

Learning as much as you can about the details is a lesson that is actually discouraged in business schools. They promote the misleading idea of the generic manager—the consummate professional whose education has prepared him or her to step into any kind of business and run it. (8)

The myth of the plug-in executive created a generation of migratory managers in American business. Most of them do not have the time or the inclination to learn anything in-depth about the business they are responsible for. Instead they bring their business school theories to each assignment. And quite often they do not stay around long enough even to evaluate whether or not the theories are valid. That is a big difference between business graduates and science graduates. The business graduates accept theory as gospel. The science graduates accept theory as the starting point for experimentation. (9)

An equally dangerous trend in the graduate schools of business is their potential to restrict creativity. And the greater the reputation of the business school, the greater the risk that its graduates will rely on management theory instead of personal creativity. There is a time for doing things the Wharton way or the Harvard way. But there is also a time for doing things your way. (10)

To be truly successful in business, you have to be a creative risk-taker. I have spent about $7 billion of Sony's money to acquire companies such as Columbia Pictures and CBS Records. These were strategic acquisitions that supported our long-term vision for Sony. You have to have your own vision of the future. And you need the confidence to invest in that vision. It is not much different from the approach to scientific research. The people I admired most in science had the creativity to develop long-term visions of the future as well as the courage to stick with that vision unless research proved them wrong. (11)

In the years ahead, business people will be asked to solve complex problems with very high stakes, not just for their corporations but for society as a whole. Some of those problems will involve decisions about technology, about the environment, about the economy and the marketplace, even about government. Scientists understand the process of critical thinking. They know how to analyze problems by concentrating on the important elements and filtering out the irrelevant. They understand that worthwhile results require a long-lived effort. They are willing to admit there are things they do not understand and then take the time to find out what it is they don't know. (12)

Business needs that kind of vision and that kind of intellectual courage. Business could get that kind of thinking by taking some of its surplus MBA's and sending them back to school for PhD's in science. Fascinating, but unlikely. Instead I think business has the responsibility to hire more scientists. (13)

Questions

1. Identify the primary proposition of the essay.

2. Identify three places in which Schulhof establishes his personal credibility on this subject.

3. What rhetorical mode is used in paragraph 3, and for what purpose?

4. What rhetorical modes can you see at use in paragraph 7? What is their purpose here?

5. What rhetorical mode is used in paragraph 9? What is the purpose?

6. Identify a syllogism in paragraph 10. Is it valid?

7. Identify any generalizations in paragraph 9. Are they convincing? Are they based on sufficient specific evidence?

8. Examine paragraph 11: what kinds of argument are at work here?

9. Does this essay contain more logical or emotional arguments? Is the balance of these types of argument effective here?

10. What are two possible counterarguments to hiring scientists for work in business? Does the essay take counterarguments sufficiently into account? If so, how does it do so?

11. How convincing is this essay's conclusion? Why?

12. What worth or validity does this essay's main argument have for someone who is not in either science or business?

Sample Essay of Persuasion 2
PROACTION ADVERTISEMENT

(Pages 213–214 show you how the advertisement originally appeared as a newspaper insert. Pages 215–216 reprint the text of the advertisement for you to read.)

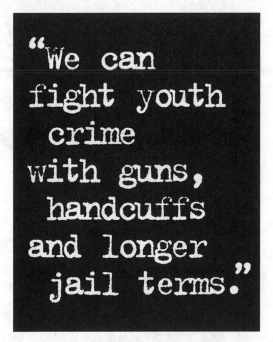

continued

"Or we can use baseballs, hockey pucks and minnows."

We can fight youth crime by pursuing and punishing the guilty. That's a vital part of what Metro's police force does.

But what we can also do is get to innocent kids before their young lives take a tragic turn to crime. Before they get caught up in a cycle that ruins individuals and destroys families.

And that's the purpose behind Proaction.

Proaction is a Toronto citizens foundation whose purpose is to bridge the gap between cops and kids in our community. To get to know each other one on one. To give kids someone to turn to. To see our cops as human beings instead of uniforms.

Proaction funds sports programs, day trips and community events that help cops and kids get to know each other and create a common bond. And it's not just a good idea that could work. It's already is working.

Cops and kids and baseballs.

To date, our projects have involved more than 500 Metro police officers and have reached more than 15,000 kids. Our cops took part in a wide variety of programs all across the city.

We helped run a multi-cultural baseball tournament in East Agincourt. We pitched in when the St. Hope-St. Thomas softball league needed some new equipment. And baseball wasn't the only sport—

we helped our cops get involved in cricket teams, volleyball tourneys, hockey leagues, skiing and even horseback riding.

Kids and cops and sports. We helped them to know each other better as a number of 'community' events held across the city,

Cops and kids and the great outdoors.

We also got involved in events taking Metro police and youth outside of the city.

We helped get them out on town on a day trip to Gananoque. We helped some cops and kids catch some rays at Wasaga Beach. We funded a field trip to Kelso Conservation area as part of the Chinese and Vietnamese Youth Outreach Project of the Scadding Court Community Centre.

and we helped pitch a few tents on a camping weekend for kids and cops from the Jane-Finch and Malvern area.

We even helped some cops take kids ice-climbing up on Lake Simcoe for a day. One way we figure it, if we can take kids outside the normal environment, they can get to know our cops a little better.

Cops and kids and get-togethers.

We put money towards a "Summer Jam" summer festival put on by the Trethewey Residents Group. We lent a hand (and a cheque) to the Community Unity alliance to put two floats in the Caribana Parade. We sprang for school and field trips for the Police/Youth Mentoring Project at George Harvey Secondary school. And we injected some badly needed cash into the annual festival put on by the Bloor Landsdowne Committee against drugs.

These and many more were the sports, day trips and events us got involved with that got our kids together with our cops.

For additional information on Proaction you can call us at 416-252-1508.

Cops and kids and you.

There's no question that we can help create a better understanding between cops and kids in Metro Toronto. But we can't build on our successes without you. Our Metro cops mostly participate as volunteers in Proaction events but we need a little of your money to make it happen.

Your tax-deductible contribution to Proaction goes directly to making these initiatives a success. We'll also give you a window sticker showing you as a supporter of Proaction and a letter of thanks from our Chief of Police.

So give to Proaction and help us in the battle against youth crime. Because the worst crime is doing nothing at all.

We can fight youth crime with guns, handcuffs and longer jail terms. Or we can use baseballs, hockey pucks and minnows.

We can fight youth crime by pursuing and punishing the guilty. That's a vital part of what Metro's police force does.

But what we can also do is get to innocent kids before their young lives take a tragic turn to crime. Before they get caught up in a cycle that ruins individuals and destroys families.

And that's the purpose behind ProAction. ProAction is a Toronto citizens' foundation whose purpose is to bridge the gap between cops and kids in your community. To get to know each other one on one. To give kids someone to turn to. To see our cops as human beings instead of uniforms.

ProAction funds sports programs, day trips and community events that help cops and kids get to know each other and create a common bond.

And it's not just a good idea that could work. It already is working.

Cops and kids and baseballs.

To date, our projects have involved more than 500 Metro police officers and have reached more than 15,000 kids. Our cops took part in a wide variety of programs all across the city.

We helped fund a multi-cultural baseball tournament in East Agincourt. We pitched in when the St. Rose–St. Thomas softball league needed some new equipment. And baseball wasn't the only sport for cops and kids to get together. We gave money for cops to help out the West End Basketball League at Jane & Woolner and the youth league in the Humber Boulevard area. We helped cops shoot hoops with kids in the Flemingdon Park Youth Program basketball tournament. And we helped purchase uniforms for two girls' basketball teams in the Toronto Lithuanian AUSRA Sport Clubs.

In addition, we helped our cops get involved in cricket teams, volley-ball tourneys, hockey leagues, skiing and even horseback riding.

Kids and cops and sports. We helped them get together for a little healthy competition.

Cops and kids and the great outdoors.

We also got involved in events taking Metro police and youth outside of the city.

We helped get them out of town on a day trip to Gananoque. We helped some cops and kids catch some rays at Wasaga Beach. We funded a field trip to Kelso Conservation Area as part of the Chinese and Vietnamese Youth Outreach Project of the Scadding Court Community Centre.

And we helped pitch a few tents on a camping weekend for kids and cops from the Jane-Finch and Malvern area. We even helped some cops take kids ice-fishing up on Lake Simcoe for a day. The way we figure it, if we can take kids outside the normal environment, they can get to know our cops a little better.

Cops and kids and get-togethers.

We helped cops and kids get to know each other better at a number of community events held across the city. We put money towards a "Summer Jam" summer festival put on by the Trethewey Residents Group. We lent a hand (and a cheque) to the Community Unity Alliance to put two floats in the Caribana Parade. We sprung for snacks and field trips for the Police/Youth Mentoring Project at George Harvey Secondary School. And we injected some badly needed cash into the annual festival put on by the Bloor Lansdowne Committee Against Drugs.

These and many more were the sports, day trips and events we got involved with that got our kids together with our cops.

Cops and kids and you.

There's no question that we can help create a better understanding between cops and kids in Metro Toronto. But we can't build on our successes without you.

Our Metro cops mostly participate as volunteers in ProAction events but we need a little of your money to make it happen.

Your tax-deductible contribution to ProAction goes directly to making these initiatives a success. We'll also give you a window sticker showing you as a supporter of ProAction and a letter of thanks from our Chief of Police.

So give to ProAction and help us in the battle against youth crime. Because the worst crime is doing nothing at all.

Questions

1. Identify the primary proposition of the essay.

2. In your own words, exactly what is the purpose of this essay: what are you, the reader, intended to do?

3. What rhetorical mode is used as a grabber for the essay? Do you find this effective?

4. How do the photographs and pictures support the essay's primary proposition? What kind of argument do they represent?

5. What strategies are used to establish personal credibility for this campaign?

6. Is this advertisement organized deductively or inductively? Why? Was this organizational principle a good decision?

7. Does this essay contain more logical or emotional arguments? Is the balance of these types of argument effective here?

8. Analyze the essay's conclusion. Is there a summary? Is there a final thought? How convincing is this essay's conclusion? Why?

See Appendix A, Contract #2: Sentence Fragments.

9. Sentence fragments are used in paragraph 3 and in the last paragraph. Why are these used? Are they effective?

Exercise 16

Using the six-step method, write a persuasive essay on one of the topics from your Top Ten List. Justify your choice of organization: is the essay inductively or deductively structured? Remember: choose a topic that you are interested in and/or know a lot about.

SUMMARY

In a persuasive essay, you are seeking to convince your readers to share your view on a subject or to take action of a very specific kind. In short, you want to change your readers—change their minds and/or influence their actions. The persuasive essay is based upon a primary proposition, usually identified as a *must, should,* or *need* statement. Audience analysis is of paramount importance in a persuasion essay, since different arguments or ideas will have very different effects on different readers. When you are given a specific writing task at school or at work, common cues can indicate that a persuasive essay is appropriate.

To support your primary proposition, you should rely on four distinct kinds of argument.

1. Logical argument is based on a) authority—a combination of facts, examples, testimony of experts, and statistics—and b) reasoning—deductive, which shows how general arguments apply in specific situations, and inductive, which takes specific information or details and fashions general arguments from them. Reasoning is dependent upon the accuracy of its premises or assumptions: if the premises are incorrect, errors such as overgeneralizing, stereotyping, and mistaking coincidence for cause can occur. Illegitimate strategies of argument include personal attacks (where you argue against the person, not what he or she believes), questionable examples or non sequiturs (where your logic is flawed), circular reasoning, the bandwagon effect, and unfair either/or propositions.

2. Emotional argument is designed to appeal to your reader's feelings. This is a useful supplement or reinforcement—but never a replacement—for your logical argumentation.

3. While you will "borrow" authority from other sources through testimony and statistics, your own personal situation and perspective often make you a particularly credible voice on an issue. Some discussion of this can bolster your argument.

4. Refutation is based upon your anticipation of your readers' possible counterarguments and your efforts in your essay to overturn these. Good use of refutation creates a tone of dialogue with your reader, rather than monologue, to which few readers respond well.

A combination of these techniques is necessary to satisfy readers' different needs and to maintain their interest. Furthermore, good persuasive writing exploits other rhetorical modes, wherever useful, in constructing an argument or example. Finally, when you are reasonably certain of a positive reaction from the reader, organize your persuasive essay deductively, introducing your primary proposition in the introduction and supporting it in the body. When you expect readers will be hostile to your argument, gradually establish your reasons, and then conclude with your primary proposition.

CHECKLIST

- Does your essay support a clear, specific, focused primary proposition?
- Have you clearly followed a deductive or inductive structure according to your readers' likely reactions?
- Does your introduction adequately explain the background to and rationale for the primary proposition (deductive) or display the complexity and variety of potential solutions to the problem (inductive)?
- Is your logical reasoning sound and easy to follow?
- Have you avoided personal attacks, questionable examples or non sequiturs, circular reasoning, the bandwagon effect, and unfair either/or propositions?
- Are your premises accurate, or are they unfair generalizations?
- Are your examples, evidence, and testimony—and the conclusions you draw from them—accurate, applicable, and effective for your readers?
- Have you explained all your sources of authority?
- Have you avoided unsupported and inflammatory emotional statements?
- Is your personal credibility adequately established in the essay?
- Do you sufficiently anticipate and refute a reader's potential objections?
- Are the arguments clearly organized in order of importance (least to most effective in deductive organization) or in order of controversy (least to most controversial in inductive organization)?
- Have you used sufficient appropriate transitional words to signal clearly the linkages between points and arguments?
- Is the tone appropriate: does the text read as a dialogue with the reader as opposed to a monologue or sermon?
- Does your conclusion both summarize the supports for the primary proposition discussed in your essay and explore the implications of the argument, so that the question of the proposition is redirected to a larger framework (such as how to implement the policy argued for or what the reader should do now that he or she has been convinced)?

Analysis: Explanation and Evaluation

LEARNING OUTCOMES

By completing a series of written and oral exercises, and writing an analysis essay using the six-step method, students will

1. *distinguish when use of the analysis rhetorical mode is appropriate;*

2. *distinguish between explanation analysis and evaluation analysis;*

3. *determine the appropriate scope and depth—exhaustive or general—of an analysis;*

4. *distinguish between legitimate and nonlegitimate forms of questioning and evidence in an evaluation analysis;*

5. *write in an objective tone and style, employing appropriate diction;*

6. *use the transitional and connecting devices that effectively unify an analysis essay.*

OVERVIEW

You are nervous; it is the first day of your economics class. You look at your classmates and see that except for three or four people, everyone looks about the same age as you, and, in fact, you recognize two people from another school who debated against you last year. This reassures you to some extent, because you are confident that your capabilities are at least as strong as theirs. The course outline, though, is another thing. The list of assignments is almost three-quarters of a page long; the course outline is a reading assignment in itself. Your experience tells you that the teacher attached to this outline is going to have some serious expectations of her students. By analyzing everything you see on your first day of class and connecting the various factors involved, you understand that it will require some serious effort and commitment to pass this course.

It turns out that your teacher is, as expected, hard but also fair; your good work in her class and others lands you an entry-level position at a consulting group specializing in economic, financial, and market analyses for clients in the textile industry.

During the interview process, you never get to meet your direct boss, Mr. Moussadji, because he is in Halifax on a business trip. You arrive at work and are ushered into his office, although he is not yet there. Two minutes later, in he strides carrying a knapsack and wearing shorts and a t-shirt, clearly having either jogged or ridden his bicycle to work. Mr. Moussadji looks about 35 and in excellent physical shape. He tells you to make yourself comfortable and browse through the report on his desk that he wrote for the firm that he visited in Halifax. As he disappears out the door to shower and change (you assume), you quickly think to yourself this certainly was not what you had expected from the interviewers you met over the last eight days. You decide this boss is going to be more easy-going than formal, but after having flipped through the report, you also judge that Mr. Moussadji knows his stuff and is very professional when it comes to the clients and the work. Indeed, when he comes back, he is wearing a professional-looking tie and jacket that would look at home in any formal office setting. You decide that this is someone with whom you are going to enjoy working.

In each of these situations, you are performing an **analysis.** Analysis/evaluation involves breaking down a situation or idea into its constituent parts and then examining the relation of these parts to the whole in order to better comprehend, explain, or evaluate the situation.

In the first scenario, you are trying to comprehend what the class will be like and what you will have to do to succeed; in the second, you are making a judgment about the character of your new boss and the nature of your workplace. In both these cases, you are looking systematically at certain elements of the situation and making a judgment, or prediction, about the situation on that basis.

ANALYSIS IS CRITICAL THINKING

The ability to analyze and evaluate is a fundamental skill required for a majority of jobs in today's economy. Given the complex and evolving nature of many fields for which you are preparing, problem-solving has become a vital qualification on a growing list of job advertisements. More and more, employees are being asked to identify and come up with solutions for problems faced in the daily routine of their jobs. Once a solution has been found, moreover, an explanation of that solution often needs to be transmitted to other employees, sometimes at entirely different work sites. Your ability to do analysis, both as a mental operation and as a written rhetorical mode, has important consequences for success in virtually any career.

PURPOSE AND FUNCTION

The *Gage Canadian Dictionary* defines the word *analysis* as follows:

> n. **2** examination of the parts of a whole to discover their nature, relationship with each other and with the whole, etc. An analysis may be made of a book, a person's character, a medicine, soil, etc.

It defines the word *evaluate* as follows:

> v. **1** judge the worth, quality, or importance of: *to evaluate a statement, to evaluate a new data processing system.*

In an **analysis essay,** then, you are dividing up some item or idea into its component parts, and showing the relationship between these parts in order to be better able to make sense of it. Often you are explaining how something functions, or how something is put together. When you analyze an abstract idea or a proposition, you are **evaluating** whether or not the proposition is true or false, justifiable or unjustifiable. Many analyses have a very practical purpose: they aim to solve a problem, to create a new way of approaching or understanding a situation, or to determine a better method of doing something.

*See Module 10:
Persuasion, Primary
Proposition, p. 192.*

For example, a human resources officer must be able to analyze the required skills for a given position and to evaluate an individual in light of these requirements. A nurse or ambulance attendant must be able to analyze a patient's situation and make a quick decision on the appropriate action. An insurance appraiser must be able to size up a claim and know what the cost of replacing or repairing stolen or damaged articles will be. Every field has specific analytical necessities.

THE TWO TYPES OF ANALYSIS ESSAY: EXPLANATION AND EVALUATION

When writing an essay using analysis, you always have two distinct possibilities. In an **explanation analysis,** you focus on understanding and clarifying how the parts interact to create the whole. In an **evaluation analysis,** you also explain the interaction of the parts, but you base a judgment on your analysis. For example, an explanation analysis might involve analyzing a particular piece of computer hardware to understand and explain precisely how it functions. By contrast, an evaluation analysis might involve analyzing the computer hardware to explain how it functions and to evaluate whether it represents a cost-effective purchase for a company.

You will have to decide which of these two types is most appropriate based on the topic you choose and the purpose of your essay.

Explanation Analysis

If you are writing an explanation analysis, the purpose of your analysis is to help the audience understand something more clearly; for this, you will need to divide the topic up into its natural components. Thus, if you are analyzing a fire truck, depending on the length and scope of your paper, you might have to divide up the truck into all its individual components. If you are doing a broader analysis, this might mean looking at the truck from front to back, looking at the role of the major components such as the engine, the driver's compartment, and any special instrumentation there, and then the actual body of the truck and the equipment there designed for specific tasks. Once you have determined what parts you will analyze, you explain the functioning of each part in relation to the purpose of your

This textbook is an extended explanation analysis of essay writing.

essay, which might be to explain how each part is used when actually on the scene of a fire.

AUDIENCE ANALYSIS

You are already very familiar with audience analysis. For analytical writing, audience analysis will be extremely important. Break down your audience into its component characteristics in order to evaluate exactly how much it already knows and needs to know in relation to what you are analyzing.

Exercise 1

In groups of four to six, complete the following exercises:

1. Do an explanation analysis of a Big Mac, a piece of KFC chicken, or another fast food. Break it down into its component parts, and explain how they fit together.

2. Do an explanation analysis of the following poem, which was written while the author was a student in England. Break it down into its component parts by answering the following questions:

   a. Look at each stanza individually.

   b. What images are developed in each stanza?

   c. What is the relationship of the stanzas, and of the images presented in each one?

   d. Break down the relationship between the two people in the poem.

   e. Based on your answers to a. to d., what is the overall theme of the poem? How do the parts of the poem contribute to this theme?

Stanza: a systematic and regular grouping of lines in poetry.

Image: word picture. A word or expression that appeals to one of the senses.

Theme: the central message or idea of a literary work.

Morning Was Chelsea

by Tatsuji Yanaga

We walked to the airport train
talking of houseboat rows
on a high Thames.

In the station we kissed goodbye
knowing the tide was out
and the boats were stranded.

Evaluation Analysis

Evaluation analysis begins with the same basic steps—namely, dissecting the object or issue into its parts—but the purpose here is somewhat different when relating the parts back to the whole. Here, the goal is to judge the merit or usefulness of the object of analysis. Take, for example, a management class in which you watch a video of a supervisor–subordinate confrontation. On the video, the supervisor confronts the employee about a problem at home that is having a negative impact on the employee's performance. The instructor asks you to analyze the style of the supervisor and decide whether this is the most effective way of handling this particular case. Here, you are being asked not only to split the interaction up into its parts, but also to base a judgment on how these parts fit together to create the whole of the situation.

Exercise 2

In groups of four to six, complete the following exercises.

1. Using Exercise 1's explanation analysis as a starting point, do an evaluation analysis of the components of the Big Mac or other fast-food item.

    a. What is its texture?

    b. What is its nutritional value?

    c. Does it taste good? Why or why not?

    d. What is your overall evaluation of the Big Mac? Why?

2. Using Exercise 1's explanation analysis of the poem "Morning Was Chelsea" as a starting point, do an evaluation analysis of the poem.

    a. What does the title mean?

    b. What do the houseboats and the river tide symbolize?

    c. Why do you think Yanaga has decided to write about these things?

    d. Overall, is this a good poem? Why or why not?

Symbolism: the use of an image to represent something else. A lion is a symbol of courage.

Exercise 3

Examine these five different topics and purposes. Decide whether each calls for an explanation analysis or an evaluation analysis.

1. The first essay is being written for an English literature option called "Romance and Rejection." The essay will be an analysis of symbolism in Michael Ondaatje's novel *In the Skin of a Lion*.

2. The second essay is being written for a course called "Dental Specialties." It is an analysis of the development and normal progression of periodontal disease.

3. This essay is being written for a course called "Leadership in Sports: Recreational Management." The writer is analyzing the job description for a recreational manager from the municipal parks and recreation department and assessing the adequacy of the college training she received to prepare her for this position.

4. This essay is being written for a subject in the School of Technology: "Troubleshooting in Electronics." The task is to write an essay based on a case study, and to determine whether the way the technician in the case study solved the problem was the most efficient.

5. This essay is being written for an early childhood education course called "The Preschooler as Learner." The essay will analyze the observation skills required of the teacher who works with preschoolers.

RANGE AND SCOPE

Analysis can range from exhaustive to general in terms of detail and depth. At one end of the spectrum, you have something like the Chilton's car repair manuals, which list every single part of the car down to the screws and fasteners. Such documents must give the user a complete picture of every element and connection. You can imagine how long essays with this amount of itemization would be; therefore, only rarely would you write them. However, when asked to do tasks such as to produce a manual for a new piece of software, or to devise a better employee evaluation scheme, a great deal of detail will almost certainly be needed because of the nature of the document.

At the other end of the spectrum is a general analysis that looks only at large or broad units in order to generalize on that basis. In this case, rather than dividing the car up into every last component, you might analyze the car by looking at the major functions of the three main units: engine, passenger compartment, and trunk or hatch. Clearly, this type of analysis does not require as many specifics, and makes certain assumptions about the readers' knowledge of the topic.

To make clear the distinctions between these two types of analysis, you use certain qualifying words that indicate to the reader how detailed your paper is going to be. Words such as *partial*, *representative*, *typical*, and *characteristic* all indicate a more general level of analysis, while words like *complete*, *total*, *comprehensive*, and *detailed* indicate that the analysis goes into greater depth.

Exercise 4

The following is the first major section of a controversial analytical essay called "A Practical Path to Transformative Justice" by Ruth Morris. Read it and answer the questions that follow.

1. WHY SHOULD WE CHANGE OUR JUSTICE SYSTEM?

At the 8th UN Congress on the Prevention of Crime and the Treatment of Offenders, in 1990, country after country reported burgeoning prisons, and the absolute failure in reducing crime through this trend. The poorer countries are desperate for better solutions, but creating more "alternatives to prisons" within our existing system usually falls flat because of "net widening." Courts are caught between the cross pressures of public fears, police and Crown anger, victim frustration, and their own fear of bad press. As a result, they constantly find new ways to use planned "alternatives" as add-ons to increase punishment, instead of keep people out of prisons. (1)

So relatively minor offenders face a smorgasbord of alternatives, on top of a prison sentence. A period of prison may be followed by probation, accompanied by 500 hours of mandatory community "service" and a restitution order to the victim, plus a condition of getting drug treatment while on probation. In this example, 4 alternatives have been added to a prison sentence, and have not kept the offender out of prison. (2)

But what is wrong with traditional justice? Basically, 4 things: it is an **expensive, unjust, immoral failure.** (3)

A) Expensive: Prisons are more costly than any of their alternatives. The cost of maintaining a person in prison varies from about $80 to $200 a day, while the cost of alternatives such as probation, bail supervision, and community supervision work orders is $5 to $20 a day. Even halfway houses, the most costly community alternative, with their housing and 24 hour coverage costs, are usually a good deal cheaper than prisons. In general, consistent appropriate use of the best existing alternatives **could save us about 3/4 of our Correction budget!** This fact alone is staggering. (4)

B) Unjust: Native Canadians are 6 times as likely as whites to go to prison in Canada. A research paper I did compared blacks and whites who were being held on detention orders in Toronto while awaiting trial. It demonstrated at very high levels of statistical significance that blacks are more likely to be given a detention order than whites with the same bail characteristics. The book title *The Rich Get Richer and the Poor Get Prison* sums up the major function of prisons in our society. By every measure, poor people and racial minorities have a higher risk of conviction and of going to prison in our society. (5)

C) Immoral: Most countries in the world have moved beyond capital punishment and torture as accepted methods of response to crime. Neither can wreaking revenge on our fellow human beings by caging them be viewed as a progressive response to our social differences. Our retributive justice system is based on a spirit of revenge which does not satisfy the primary health needs of victims, offenders, or society. Moreover, the great majority of offenders are young people whom society has failed to protect from abusive homes, or sterile institutional environments. Having failed to provide them with a safe, nurturing childhood, we go on to exact lifelong revenge toward them for their resulting character defects. Setting limits for their unacceptable behavior is wholly appropriate: exacting a cycle of unending blame and revenge is not. (6)

D) Failure: Recidivism rates from prisons range from about 40% to 85%, and are consistently higher than for any alternatives. Prisons are supposed to deter, protect, rehabilitate and punish, simultaneously. In fact, they do only the last. They fail to deter others, to protect the public from crime and criminals, and they fail abysmally to rehabilitate. (7)

What prisons do best is to INSTITUTIONALIZE, and to embitter angry young men from low income minorities. What courts do best is disempower victims and offenders, so that they are unable to solve the problems that have led to crime, and the problems caused by it. We need to change our justice system, because it does not meet the needs of victims, offenders, or the community. (8)

1. Is this an example of explanation analysis, evaluation analysis, or both?

2. Consider the range and scope of Morris's analysis. Is this a general or an exhaustive analysis? Does she make any assumptions about her readers' knowledge of the topic? Are these assumptions fair?

3. Some audiences have called Morris a "bleeding-heart liberal." Is this a fair assessment? How would you analyze an audience that feels this way? Why would an audience react negatively to Morris's points?

4. Describe how Morris has analyzed the penal system. Is her organization logical? Consider the final paragraph. Does this conclusion flow logically from the analysis?

5. Do you agree with Morris? In a paragraph or two, explain why you do or do not agree with her position.

EVALUATION: APPROPRIATE TYPES OF ARGUMENTS

See Module 10, Supporting Your Primary Proposition, p. 194, for an extended discussion of the legitimate types of argument used in persuasive writing.

Evaluation analysis is by nature persuasive: you are seeking to persuade your reader that your judgment of the situation is the correct one. Thus, using *legitimate logical arguments*, *personal authority*, and *refutation* is appropriate. The only type of argument that should be avoided in analysis is the emotional argument.

Beware of **personalizing** the analysis. Analysis is, by nature, an objective examination not based on personal preferences but rather on an impartial look at the subject. A personal response may be a good way to focus your topic, and should be recorded as part of your content generation; however, it should only appear in the finished essay if it is supported by analysis. For instance, if you are asked to evaluate a classroom instructor, your immediate reaction may be to write down "She's an idiot." If this is the extent of your evaluation, however, it will have little effect on a reader, who may assume you are being spiteful because of a personal conflict. You should instead use this personal reaction as a starting point, but then document specific examples of behaviour that you felt were inappropriate. Evidence and logic are your best friends in an analysis.

See Module 5: Description/Narration, Subjective/Objective, p. 94.

 PERSONAL AND EMOTIONAL ARGUMENTS

One way to detect personal or emotional arguments that may have crept into your analysis paper is the following. Try putting "I think" or "I feel" in front of a statement; if it is appropriate, you should ask yourself if the statement is sufficiently justified. Statements in an analysis paper should be sufficiently verifiable to be able to stand without this kind of introductory phrasing.

 ### Exercise 5

Read carefully the following essay by a resources engineering technician student. Look at the title: do you expect an explanation analysis or an evaluation analysis?

Sample Essay

Why Government Won't Save the Environment

by Steve Inkster

When we realize how bad our environmental problems are, we often look to our governments to provide solutions. Unfortunately, governments simply do not take ecological issues seriously. Regardless of the party in power, the government's priority is the economy. As a result, when the unemployment rate is bad, the government's attitude is "We'll worry about cleaning up the environment once the economy is growing again." (1)

This attitude does not make sense if we consider that our entire economy depends on exploiting our environment: for example, using forests for paper and wood, using oil and gas for transportation, using animals for food, and using water as a dumping ground for chemicals. What the government is really saying is "We'll only worry about cleaning up the environment once we have made it a lot worse." Look at the Conservatives in Ontario: Premier Mike Harris wants big business to destroy all of our forests and lakes. (2)

Governments assume that we are in trouble if new businesses are not starting and existing industries are not expanding. This is the stupidest idea I've ever heard. Economic growth cannot continue forever. The Earth is a very small planet; if each country's economy continues to expand, we will eventually run out of resources. We see one example of this in eastern Canada. The Atlantic fishing industry is almost out of business because the fish stocks have been depleted by overfishing. Government was warned about this years ago, but did not restrict fishing until 1992, when the problem had become a crisis. (3)

On a much bigger scale, many scientists believe that zero population growth must become a worldwide goal in the next thirty years. Otherwise, there will be too many people in the world to support with our limited resources. In fact, people are already starving to death all over the world. Even in wealthy nations like the United States and Canada, the population of homeless and hungry people is growing. Yet how can we get dozens of governments in poor and rich countries to agree to work toward the goal of zero population growth? I think we should restrict families to only one child, like the Chinese government did! The problem is that governments normally encourage population growth, because a growing economy needs more and more people to buy the new products being created. (4)

The biggest problem of all is a very difficult one to solve. The ultimate goal of most governments is a short-term one: to be re-elected. Therefore when a problem arises, the government looks for a quick, short-term solution. To save the environment, however, requires long-term efforts. The problems are enormous and the solutions are complex. For instance, scientists have shown that carbon monoxide emissions from automobiles are causing the Earth very slowly to warm up. The long-term risks are that the polar ice-caps will melt and the oceans will rise, causing massive flooding. In addition, as the planet heats up, more areas of desert will be created by shifts in the climate. (5)

Questions

1. What is being analyzed (broken into its component parts) here? Is it an explanation analysis or an evaluation analysis? Did you expect this?

2. Examine the arguments. Locate and note the following:

    a. Three emotional or personal arguments. What would you do with these arguments?

    b. One syllogism in paragraph 4. Is it valid?

    c. The scope of the analysis: is this exhaustive or general?

*See Module 10,
Deductive Reasoning,
p. 199.*

3. State in your own words the reason "why government won't save the environment."

4. Is the argument of paragraph 3 valid in your view? Write a paragraph analyzing this argument's assumptions and evaluating their validity. Be certain to support your argument.

5. Steve's conclusion has been omitted. Write an appropriate one-paragraph conclusion summarizing the analysis and stating its implications. Should you or can you propose a solution to the problem that Steve has analyzed?

COMPUTER-AIDED ANALYSIS

This exercise is designed to help you argue or comment upon a piece of professional writing. The closest parallel on paper would be the annotation of a piece of writing.

Prerequisite computer skills:
- cut and paste;
- delete;
- CAPS lock.

1. Select a short piece of writing.

2. Turn on CAPS lock and type the whole piece into the computer. Put an extra line or two between the paragraphs of the original.

3. Save the piece to a disk so you can back up later if you want.

4. Turn off CAPS lock.

5. Using small letters, insert personal comments and responses directly into the text wherever they may seem appropriate. You should comment, in particular, upon such things as the thesis statement, topic sentences of the supporting paragraphs, and the conclusion. Explain why you find ideas or rhetorical devices good or bad. How effective are the transitions between paragraphs? How do the paragraphs relate to one another and the thesis? What kind of audience is the writer addressing? Does the argument or explanation make sense? Is it reasonable? Do you agree or disagree? Why? Every comment is worth making, and remember, only you will see this.

6. Save the commented-upon piece to a new file. You may also want to print this annotated reading.

7. Now, delete everything that you originally wrote in CAPS. This will leave you with your comments only, broken into sections that are parallel to the original essay. Do not worry if some comments make no sense right now. You can always refer back to the annotated original, either in electronic form or on your print-out.

8. Now, add to your comments any other facts or observations that you want to include. Expand and explain your comments using other methods of content generation such as brainstorming, clustering, and the five "Ws" and one "H" if you wish. Remember, you can always change anything later. Save this on disk, and perhaps print it out as well.

See Module 2: The Essay: What to Say, The Outline, p. 36.

9. Lastly, using the outlining procedure discussed in Module 2, organize your comments. You now have a formal outline for your own essay that is based upon the professional piece that you were originally given.
   To develop the outline into a full essay:

   a. Call the outline onto the screen.

   b. Write full sentences for each aspect of the outline.

   c. Revise, edit, spell-check, proofread, and print.

OCCASIONS FOR ANALYSIS

When faced with a topic, you need to be able to identify occasions when the analysis rhetorical mode is appropriate to your purpose. Obviously, if you are asked to **analyze** the effectiveness of some process, or to **explain** the meaning or implications of a text, process, or idea, you will use the analysis structure.

You will not always, however, be so straightforwardly told to write an analysis essay. The following words are clues that analysis may be suitable:

1. If you are asked to analyze or detail the **method** or **functioning** of an object or organization.

2. Assignments asking for explanation of **how** or enquiring about a **relationship** often require analysis as the rhetorical mode.

3. As often as not, when asked to **judge, evaluate, appraise,** or **assess** you will be using analysis.

Exercise 6

Fill in the Top Ten List that follows with situations in your field where the analysis mode might usefully be employed in a writing task. Use the cue words listed above to describe these topics. Consider the purpose, and note in brackets whether this would be an explanation analysis (EXP) or an evaluation analysis (EVA). Also, indicate whether the scope would be exhaustive (E) or general (G). For instance, an electronics student might choose the topics

1. Analyze the circuit board of a touch telephone (EXP; E)
2. Judge the effectiveness of test equipment in fault-finding (EVA; G)

Fill in as many as you can, and then continue reading the module. As other possibilities occur to you, return to this list and finish it.

TOP TEN APPLICATIONS FOR ANALYSIS WRITING IN MY FIELD

1.
2.
3.
4.
5.
6.
7.
8.
9.
10.

APPLYING THE SIX-STEP METHOD TO ANALYSIS WRITING

Step 1: Imaging the Essay with the Rhetorical Triangle

Follow the usual steps, beginning by imaging your essay with the rhetorical triangle. You should decide now what kind of essay you are writing. Examine the cues in the wording of the assignment: is it an explanation analysis or an evaluation analysis? You may revise these ideas when you begin generating content, but it is essential to have an initial plan.

When considering your point of view, keep in mind that every object, idea, or process has a "natural" way of being broken down into component parts. This means that one of the key tasks in writing this type of essay is to determine precisely how the topic can be most effectively broken down. As an example, think of a wristwatch. A watch repair person might look at the watch in terms of what mechanical problem might be preventing it from functioning. A fashion consultant might analyze the watch from the perspective of how the watch looks. In your own analytical tasks, carefully establishing your own point of view will often yield such a natural perspective on how to break down your subject.

Step 2: Content Generation

Generate content using more than one method. Often, you will be required to define, explain, or describe some of the components because they are generic and need specific details or because they might be unfamiliar to the audience you have chosen. Try to use the variety of methods of content generation to help make your analysis clear to your target audience.

See Module 8: Definition and Classification.

See Module 7: Comparison and Contrast.

See Module 6: Process Analysis.

See Module 5: Description and Narration.

One effective method for generating content in analysis is to employ the various rhetorical modes as a means of collecting ideas and information. In Modules 5 to 10, you learned the different rhetorical modes of essays: description and narration, process analysis, comparison and contrast, definition and classification, cause and effect, and persuasion. These are simply different means of organizing information or understanding how ideas fit together. You can use these to suggest content. For instance, if, like Ruth Morris, you were analyzing the justice system, you could attempt to create a precise denotative and connotative *definition* of justice. Then, you could *compare and/or contrast* your definition of justice with the actual system. You could describe the *process* by which a victim or perpetrator experiences the system of justice. You could recall anecdotes or *narratives* of these victims or criminals to illustrate your points. While this is only a partial list of the rhetorical modes available to you, it points out the rich possibilities for creating content this way.

Step 3: The Outline

Outline your essay in the following fashion:

INTRODUCTION

See Module 3, Introduction, p. 49.

Begin with your grabber. Be certain to explain adequately in your introduction the necessary background—that is, will your analysis help the reader understand the topic, or does it make a judgment about the topic? In addition, you should indicate to the reader whether to expect a very detailed or more general breakdown of the topic. Be sure your thesis statement clearly introduces the subject being analyzed and the purpose of the analysis, as all your body paragraphs will be relating back to this purpose.

BODY

See Module 3, Body, p. 57.

Be certain that each paragraph sticks to one element of your analysis. If you are doing a general analysis and you have divided the object into four major components, stick to one component per paragraph or writing unit. In conjunction with this, be certain to provide appropriate detail for each part. Do not simply mention the part or unit by name and then rush on to the next one. One of the expectations a reader has for this type of essay is that if it is important enough to be mentioned in the essay, you will explain it in some adequate way, shape, or form.

CONCLUSION

See Module 3, Conclusion, p. 60.

Do not stop at simply summarizing the components you have listed. Once you have shown the relationship among parts, described how they function in terms of the whole, or passed judgment on their usefulness, move beyond the particular subject being analyzed to consider its place, role, or significance within the broader context. You want to leave your reader pondering these larger implications.

Step 4: Writing the Rough Draft

When putting together your rough draft, be certain to emphasize the relationship among components, or between the component and the whole. This means that you will have to use connectives and references that tie back to previous paragraphs or to your thesis statement. Thus, if you are analyzing a new theory on learning patterns in preschool children, you need to link elements of the theory together or back to the guiding purpose of your thesis: explanation or evaluation.

CONJUNCTIVE ADVERB

When we want to show a particular relationship between two complete thoughts in a single sentence, we use a conjunctive adverb, such as the following: *consequently, furthermore, however, in addition, moreover, nevertheless, as a result, by contrast, subsequently, then, therefore, thus*. Sentences of this type require a specific pattern of punctuation: the conjunctive adverb must be preceded by a semi-colon and followed by a comma, as follows:

See Appendix A, Contract #3: Run-on Sentences.

complete thought; conjunctive adverb, complete thought

Identify each complete thought and the conjunctive adverb in each of the following sentences. Explain the punctuation.

1. More than 87 percent of graduates in this program get placed in their field; moreover, within five years of graduation, the average salary for these people is around $46 000.

2. Aquaculture is definitely a burgeoning field; furthermore, as the number of graduates in the field is small, the possibility of becoming an entry-level manager is good.

3. The last five years have seen a definite shift in the demographics of continuing education students in the educational system as a whole; consequently, more and more specialized programs and courses are being offered to meet the demands of this new type of student.

The conjuctive adverbs, with appropriate punctuation, are particularly useful in analytical writing, which, after all, depends upon establishing the connections of various thoughts to one another and to the whole. These must be memorized and carefully distinguished from other transitional devices that require different punctuation.

Step 5: Revising

When revising your essay, assess the quality and legitimacy of your arguments. Tighten the focus by using connecting phrases that highlight the associations among different elements, and between the elements and the whole. Consult the list of relationship and quality indicators that follows.

Step 6: Editing

Looking for your most common errors, edit your analysis essay.

RELATIONSHIP AND QUALITY INDICATORS FOR ANALYSIS

- **Connection.** Some useful connectives that link components together or indicate relationships include the following: *as with, much like, similar to.*

- **Part to whole.** Useful phrases that suggest the part-to-whole relationship are as follows: *one element/condition/component* of, *one part/segment/aspect* of. Also, you may want to discuss a part's particular *function* or specific *role* in the overall scheme.

- **Judgment.** Adjectives and adverbs that indicate a judgment about the topic include words such as *best, worst, more, less, most, least.*

- **Superior/subordinate.** Some words and phrases indicate a superior relationship between elements: *leading, vital, foremost, dominant, major, primary,* and *principal.* Others indicate a subordinate relationship: *inessential, minor, slight, subordinate, inferior,* and *lesser.*

- **General.** General phrases such as *within the larger context, in terms of the bigger issue/situation/process/idea,* and *in the final analysis* indicate a broader contextualization of the part.

Exercise 7

These are very brief examples of the kinds of statements that you might make in an analysis essay. Complete the following sentences by supplying the missing connector or link (the list of relationship and quality indicators above will help).

1. As a _____ of the overall requirements of the course, all in-class presentations must directly involve the class in a discussion.

2. _____ air conditioning, which is a luxury in a car, intermittent wipers really should be considered a necessary safety feature.

3. Only by looking at the issue through its _____ parts can we begin to see why this is such a helpful way of dealing with stress in the workplace.

4. While contrary views are voiced from time to time, _____, second-hand smoke can clearly be seen as the most dangerous by-product of this process.

5. After having analyzed the company's laboratory and its practices and finding only the most up-to-date equipment and procedures, it is clear that this facility is among the _____ of its type in North America.

6. The _____ important aspect of the aesthetician–client relationship is trust, because all other parts of the relationship are built on this.

7. Both these elements, the cost and the quality, play a _____ role in the final decision of the consumer when it comes to purchasing a residential property.

8. _____, a complete overhaul of the ambulance dispatch system in the county is needed, or some people may pay the ultimate price for its current inefficiencies.

9. Although setting and character are important to understanding "Death by Landscape," theme remains the _____ aspect to examine if we want to come up with some of the possible meanings of Atwood's story.

10. _____ context of retraining in general, this analysis makes clear that the current system of retraining individuals between forty and fifty-five for the workforce has been very ineffective.

Sample Analysis Essay

HARD PART OF LANGUAGE IS LEARNING WHAT YOU MAY SAY

THE TORONTO STAR, MARCH 21, 1995

BY ANNA NIKE MINEYKO

It is widely known among teachers of linguistics that every written language has a different logic. But for new Canadians this statement is not necessarily clear. Many immigrants learn English as a second language and after a few years they are able to speak it successfully. They often become so proficient that Canadian-born people who need to improve their spelling or grammar ask them for assistance. However, many newcomers feel uncomfortable with written English, and frequently they don't know why. (1)

Developing an awareness of the different patterns of written languages may take some time. Nearly a year had passed before I finally understood why my written English was not always acceptable. This was also the time when I was diligently trying to examine and become aware of cultural differences. I believe now that my lack of success in this area was due to the extremely different logic between my first and second languages. Certainly, it was not nearly enough to merely acknowledge this; I needed to recognize my own language's pattern of writing and compare it to written English. (2)

Imagine a country where, for many years, censors played the major role in any form of published writing. Journalists couldn't publish their articles without the intervention of the censors. Poets weren't allowed to publish their poems without long discussions and revisions in the censors' offices. Scientists had to obtain permission before they could publish their findings. Writers knew their books were going to spend many months on the censor's desk waiting for the obligatory red stamp granting permission to publish. (3)

However, this same country also held that intelligence, knowledge and university degrees were the most respected features of an individual. A university education was available to anyone who had intelligence and ambition. Students didn't need to pay tuition and many of them could get allowances for their living expenses. These circumstances created an illogical situation where people achieved the best possible education yet at the same time their thoughts were strictly controlled. (4)

What could happen to creative writing in this imaginary country? Year by year writers had to learn how to avoid or reduce the limitations placed on them by the censors. Readers learned how to understand a more intricate and puzzling style of writing that concealed the true meaning securely between the lines. The most talented journalists put enormous effort into their articles, giving them both a superficial and a hidden meaning. Writers used to jump from one subject to another in a short piece of writing, making their stories funny and light on one level and serious on another. (5)

Now try to imagine a journalist who came from this country to North America, where people have the right to criticize the president or the premier and no one is placed in prison for his or her opinions. Where readers expect accurate and concise information about current events. That journalist is totally lost; he no longer needs to hide anything between the lines. Something that was once a preferred and necessary style of writing in one country becomes a weakness in North American writing. He must learn new rules. Readers expect a clear introduction, an informative or entertaining body and a clear and logical conclusion. He should write about one topic at a time, trying not to distract the readers' attention without a clear reason. (6)

(However, somebody who used to build pyramids in Egypt all of a sudden wouldn't know how to build a nice bungalow for the family in our century. Both things are beautiful, but they are created for different reasons, in different points in time and under different circumstances.) (7)

History, culture, and politics definitely influence creative writing. It is not important to name my imaginary country, as there are many similarities and differences between all nations. For many of us immigrants, this imaginary country seems all too familiar. However, I believe that each country has its own circumstances, which usually build different logic in their respective written languages, and every one should find his or her own pattern. (8)

Canada and the United States have immigrants from all over the world. This is the beauty of North America: that we can't ignore our differences and have to understand more and more about one another. Written languages are a part of this challenging knowledge that could bring people together. (9)

Questions

1. What is the issue being analyzed or broken down here?
2. Identify the thesis statement of the essay.
3. Is this an explanation analysis or an evaluation analysis? Why?

4. How does Mineyko establish her credibility on this issue in paragraph 2? Is she guilty of personalizing the analysis (offering personal opinions instead of reasoned analysis) here?

5. What rhetorical mode governs paragraphs 3 and 4 when you look at them together?

6. What rhetorical mode governs paragraph 5? Is this an effective way to organize this information?

7. Why is paragraph 7 in parentheses? What is its connection to paragraph 6?

8. What audience is this piece written for, and how does Mineyko make her subject accessible and interesting for that audience?

9. Why does Mineyko not mention her particular country of origin (paragraph 8)? What does this tell us about the scope of the essay? Is this an exhaustive or a general analysis?

10. State in your own words Mineyko's general conclusion, and write a two- to three-paragraph evaluation analysis of this conclusion's validity and implications. Be certain to support your argument with specific evidence and logic, rather than personal opinion and/or emotion.

Exercise 8

Using the six-step method, write an essay on one of the topics from your Top Ten List. Justify your choice of format: is the essay explanation or evaluation? Will this be exhaustive or general? Why? Remember: choose a topic that you are interested in and/or know a lot about. Be specific in your essay. Try to come to some logical conclusion related to your purpose.

SUMMARY

In an analysis essay you are breaking down an object, idea, issue, or process into its constituent parts in order either

1. to better understand or explain it; or

2. to evaluate it in some manner (i.e., its effectiveness, usefulness, applicability).

As a consequence, this is a particularly useful rhetorical mode in situations that call for problem-solving or adjusting an existing object, process, or approach. Because analysis is both a mode of investigation and a rhetorical mode, its implications and applications are widespread.

Common cue words will indicate not only that an analysis is appropriate, but what scope it should have. Analytical writing tasks are usually (but not always) general rather than exhaustive in nature: they examine larger segments or portions of the subject rather than all of the most minute details. Analysis frequently makes use of the other rhetorical modes as needed to illustrate or explain ideas. Intelligent use of connectives and quality indicators is critical in illustrating the connections of part to part and parts to whole.

CHECKLIST

- Does your introduction make clear whether the essay is explanation analysis or evaluation analysis?
- Does your thesis make clear what elements of the object, idea, or process you are going to examine in the essay?
- Is it clear whether the essay is to be an exhaustive or general analysis?
- Does each body paragraph deal with a single component of the analysis?
- Does the body have adequate specific, substantial details to help the reader understand the analysis?
- Has the analysis made clear the relationship of part to part and whole to part?
- Have you included any unsupported personal or emotional arguments that you should revise or eliminate?
- Does your conclusion both summarize the analysis and mention some implications of the topic for a broader context, so that the topic can be linked to a larger, thought-provoking issue?
- Have you used appropriate connective and indicator words to signal clearly the relationships among elements and, in the case of evaluation analysis, the logic of the judgment the essay reaches?

The Research Essay

LEARNING OUTCOMES

By reconsidering the six-step method and using it to develop and write a fully documented research essay, students will

1. *distinguish when research is appropriate for a writing task;*

2. *understand and utilize library resources in completing research tasks;*

3. *use time-saving devices in every level of the research, development, and revision process;*

4. *correctly integrate quotations and information from research sources in support of a specific thesis;*

5. *document accurately and consistently the appropriate sources of an essay.*

OVERVIEW

Suppose you have an accident while skiing one winter; along with a severely bruised ego, you are diagnosed with a torn anterior cruciate ligament in your knee. After consultation, your surgeon tells you that she will schedule you for "reconstructive semitendinosis," and then dashes off. You are confused about the procedure and more than a little frightened by the idea of major surgery.

As a result, you seek out second and third opinions from other orthopedic surgeons. Both doctors concur with the diagnosis, but the second recommends the bone-tendon-bone method of reconstruction, while the third doctor endorses using a donor tendon. The experts have given you three viable options for the method of reconstruction; now how will you decide what to do? You have only one real option: the library, where you can examine medical texts and studies that explain the procedures, their likely success rates, and the potential risks and complications. Only then, with an understanding of the procedures and their implications, will you be capable of making this important decision.

This is the value of research: it is a common-sense way to solve the basic problem of gaps in your knowledge. When you do research, you broaden the scope of your knowledge by familiarizing yourself with facts, ideas, and opinions in order to be able to answer a question, solve a problem, or develop a clear understanding of a specific issue.

If you are buying a new car, you may consult with friends and relatives and read the current year's *Lemon-Aid* and *Consumer Reports* for expert analysis of the automobiles. You will likely go to more than one dealer to compare prices and packages; otherwise, you will pay an inflated price at the first dealer. If you are lucky enough to save a little money for an RRSP, what will you do with it—invest in mutual funds or GICs? Again, you may consult with friends and family, or you may read up on financial experts' economic forecasts and recommendations. How have you made your decisions about lifetime career and education plans? Deciding to go to college or university or to enter the workforce directly—or some combination of these options—usually involves some degree of investigation. What schools offer what programs? Where are they located? How much do they cost? Are they full-time or part-time programs? What are the job prospects right now, and what are they projected to be in five years? In each case, the situation is the same: you have a specific deficit of knowledge. Your research fills this gap with the knowledge of experts.

As you read this module, you will notice a clock icon in the margins. This indicates tips for time-saving in the development of a research essay.

PURPOSE AND FUNCTION

The *Gage Canadian Dictionary* defines the word *research* as follows:

> *v.—n.* a careful hunting for facts or truth; inquiry; investigation.

"Enquiring minds want to know ... "— The National Enquirer.

As the definition shows, research involves several processes. It is a precise and methodical search for the specific facts—or the "truth" about a subject. You may be looking for information on something you did not know, or you may be looking for details to explain or support something you do know.

It is also an "inquiry" or "investigation"—which means that it is a process of continually asking questions. A question may start the essay process: the law enforcement student may be asked the question: "The Young Offenders Act: Leniency or Stupidity?" The only way to evaluate the value of the Young Offenders Act is to pose further questions and seek answers in research. What were the goals of the act and what are the actual results? What kinds of statistical and anecdotal information about the act's impact exist? Where can you get this information? How reliable or useful is this information? One question almost inevitably leads to another. There may not always be easy answers—or any answers at all—but the research essay asks questions and investigates their implications as far as possible.

See Module 2: What to Say, Research, p. 31, about sources such as a dictionary of quotations, newspapers, magazines, people, and the Internet (World Wide Web pages and their hypermedia links).

The major difference from other kinds of essays is that you are not relying exclusively on your own thoughts and ideas—you are being asked to discover what others have thought and said about your subject, and to present these findings in your research essay.

Use the Rhetorical Modes

See Modules 7, 9, and 11.

The research essay is not a separate rhetorical mode; rather, it is an essay that utilizes research materials or supports an argument developed in another mode or modes. Research essays are very frequently essays of comparison/contrast, cause and effect, or evaluation. More generally, the research essay is an occasion for utilizing a variety of rhetorical modes as they are helpful to your purpose. For instance, within your essay, if you need to define a concept, you will use definition; if you need to describe a specific event in detail, you will use narration/description; and so on. For your research essay to be successful, it should demonstrate not only your mastery of the material you have researched, but also your ability to use a variety of rhetorical modes when appropriate and to link them in a larger paper.

OCCASIONS FOR A RESEARCH ESSAY

You need to be able to identify occasions when research is appropriate for a given writing task. Obviously, if you are asked to complete a research paper on stress management in the workplace, you know that your writing task will involve a trip to the library for research.

You will not always, however, be so explicitly told to write a research essay. Some cues for this kind of task are as follows:

1. If you are asked to write a **formal report,** you must supply a correctly formatted and professional-looking paper based upon legitimate, extensive research.

2. Generally, if you are asked to **investigate, study**, or **survey** an issue, policy, or phenomenon, you are being asked for more than your own thoughts on the subject, and research will be necessary.

3. A business that is about to tackle a big new project, or a professional course dealing with a complex, current issue may ask for a **literature review:** this is a survey of existing studies on a particular issue, their methodologies, and their conclusions. The literature review then becomes the basis for further work and study.

TOPIC CUES

Remember: the research essay is not a separate rhetorical mode; thus, the topic itself is often more of a cue than the wording. For instance, a nursing student asked to write a paper on "transcultural nursing" would immediately understand that this requires research into current nursing theory and application. When a particular topic falls outside the range of your knowledge, you will know that it requires research.

Exercise 1

Fill in the Top Ten List below with situations in your field in which research might be useful in a writing task. You may draw topics from any of your other Top Ten Lists if they would require, or benefit from, significant research. Indicate the dominant rhetorical mode of each topic in parentheses. Where applicable, use the cue words listed earlier to describe these topics. For instance, a legal assistant student might choose the topic

  1. Analyze the effects of taxation on support payments (analysis—evaluation)

Fill in as many as you can, and then continue reading this module. As other possible applications occur to you, return to the list and finish it.

TOP TEN APPLICATIONS FOR A RESEARCH ESSAY IN MY FIELD

  1.
  2.
  3.
  4.
  5.
  6.
  7.
  8.
  9.
  10.

APPLYING THE SIX-STEP METHOD TO RESEARCH ESSAY WRITING

Focus Your Topic Immediately

Focus your topic before you go to the library. When you are assigned a research essay, a temptation that you should resist is to race straight to the library. Do not pass "Go"—remain where you are. As you know from Module 2, research is a method of content generation, which is the second step of the essay-writing process. If you skip the first stage, the rhetorical triangle, you will waste valuable time researching a topic that is far too general to write on. You need to do the following:

  1. Find an approach to the subject that interests you.

  2. Discover what your ideas are on the subject *before* you begin your research; that way, you are less likely to be "taken over" by others' attitudes when you read, and you are more likely to be able to evaluate them fairly.

  3. Decide who your audience is. Obviously, your instructor is, but who else will be able to use your research essay, and for what purpose? This will determine the amount, type, and wording of your information.

4. Determine the mode of the essay. Are you surveying existing information? Are you using research in order to make a recommendation (persuasion) or judgment (analysis)?

FOCUSING RESEARCH

You may not be able to focus your topic completely and specifically before beginning the research. Simply do the best you can; you will naturally sharpen or adjust your focus as you proceed with the research, but it is essential to have as specific a starting point as possible.

Step 1: Imaging the Essay with the Rhetorical Triangle

Below is a description of how one student, Julie Chau, completed this first stage.

During her first semester, Julie Chau, a fashion merchandising student, took EAC150: Essay Skills, a required subject that taught her writing in rhetorical modes. Her major assignment for this subject was a research paper with the following optional topics:

> EAC 150: Research Essay (25 percent)
>
> You will write a research essay of about 2000 words in the area of employment issues. There are many directions that you may take with this topic. A few suggestions include, but are not limited to, the following:
>
> 1. Short and long-term effects of employment equity
> 2. Nontraditional employment opportunities
> 3. Career trends in your field
> 4. The impact of information technology in
>   a. personnel management
>   b. global markets
>   c. retail systems
>   d. your field

Julie decided that topic 3, "Career trends in your field," appealed most to her. She would research a job in fashion, and focus this further by making her topic "How to reach my career goals in the fashion industry." She explained, "I wanted to make it useful to me—and it was a good opportunity to discover what kind of job market I'll be facing when I graduate."

Julie's projected audience was fellow first-semester students: this would be an informative document that could share useful information with them.

Using Julie's topic-focusing as an example, select one of the topics from your Top Ten List and devise a rhetorical triangle. In particular, answer questions 1., 2., and 3. on p. 242. When you are done, write out your rhetorical triangle as a proposal, and then ask yourself: "When I begin my research, do I now know what I'm looking for?"

Step 2: Content Generation

FOCUSING TOPICS FOR RESOURCES

When you are facing a deadline, the sooner you focus the topic, the greater the resources that you will be able to employ. You will have more time for applied research, but you may also quite accidentally run across relevant material in the newspaper or on television. You can also alert friends, relatives, and others to keep their eyes open for useful, relevant material. In Julie's case, her mother works nights, so she videotapes *CBC Prime Time News.* One night, Julie's mother watched a segment called "Internet," which she thought might be relevant to Julie's paper; in fact, Julie did end up using it.

FILTERING INFORMATION IS THE KEY TO EFFICIENT RESEARCH

At every stage of your library research—from the index, to the shelves, to the actual books or periodicals—you want to be focused on your particular topic. You will have no problem obtaining general information on your subject, but your goal is to filter out the irrelevant and get to what is specifically helpful to you as quickly as possible.

Generally, libraries have user-friendly on-line computer indexes, although some may still use a card catalogue or microfiche system. Your library may have databases of periodical articles in various fields, professions, areas, and media, such as business, architecture, science, history, and literature, as well as newspapers and journals. Do not neglect these: they can be invaluable tools in locating very useful articles. All the principles discussed below can be applied equally well to these more specialized information sources.

On-Line Search Catalogue

In all of the above cases, the principle is the same. You can search for information by author, title, or subject/keyword. You will only use the author or title search when you already have a specific idea of an important writer or a useful book in your area. Most useful will be the subject/keyword search: all the library's books (or periodical article titles) are cross-referenced in the subject file by the main subject areas they deal with. Select the key terms that define your topic area (in Julie's case, these were "Fashion" and "Employment"), and punch them into the computer.

Skim the Subject Categories

The more general the topic, the more work it will take to find information specifically useful to you. This is why the topic you punch in will often appear broken down into subheadings. Review all of the subheadings, and then take a close look at offerings only in the most relevant subcategories. Julie searched under the headings of "Fashion" and "Employment," turning up twenty-four records on fashion and fifty-four items on employment; these were scattered through some fourteen different subheadings.

Discover the General Location of Relevant Works
You will notice that many relevant books on a single topic will be clustered in the same general area. Take note of that area; you will do a shelf-search of it.

 ### Skim the Catalogue Information Provided about Each Book
The catalogue will provide you with invaluable clues to a book's likely relevance to your topic:

1. Title: you will be able to reject certain books and sources right away because they deal with nonrelevant aspects of your topic.

2. Date: you can tell right away if the book is out of date and therefore of no use. Seek out the most current, up-to-date material available.

3. Place of publication: based on where they are published, you can eliminate certain books for their likely lack of relevance to your specific concerns. A research essay on Canadian environmental protection law would likely not be advanced by a book on environmental protection published in Bombay, India. Use logic to pinpoint more likely sources of useful information.

Write down the author, title, and call number of any books that appear likely to be helpful.

 ### Exercise 2
The following is a selection of books Julie's on-line search turned up. In groups of four to six, examine the list carefully, and, considering the nature of Julie's assignment, explain which ones you would not bother to locate. Note briefly the reasons for your decisions.

FASHION

Craik, Jennifer. *The Face of Fashion: Cultural Studies in Fashion.* London, New York: Routledge, 1994.

Drew, Linda. *The Business of Fashion.* Cambridge: Cambridge UP, 1992.

Jarnow, Jeannette A., and Beatrice Judelle. *Inside the Fashion Business: Texts and Readings.* New York: Wilby, 1966.

Lambert, Eleanor. *World of Fashion: People, Places, Resources.* New York: R.R. Bowker Co., 1976.

Martin, Richard. *Fashion and Surrealism.* New York: Rizzoli, 1987.

Zoot Suits and Second-Hand Dresses: An Anthology of Fashion and Music. Ed. Angela McRobbie. Boston: Unwin Hyman, 1988.

FASHION—VOCATIONAL GUIDANCE

Chambers, Bernice Gertrude. *Keys to a Fashion Career.* 1st ed. New York: McGraw-Hill, 1946.

Hamburger, Estelle. *Fashion Business: It's All Yours.* San Francisco: Canfield Press, 1976.

ASKING THE LIBRARY STAFF

Do not hesitate to ask library staff for advice or help in using any equipment such as the on-line catalogue, microfiche, or audiovisual materials. The staff themselves are a prime resource for expanding the base of your knowledge; efficient use of your time includes taking advantage of staff whose job it is to help library patrons like yourself.

GO TO THE SHELVES

On the shelves, you will find some of the titles spotted during your electronic search. You will also find others in the same general locations. Once again, as you come across these, ask yourself the simple question, "Will it be useful to me?" Remember: the title, date of publication, and place of publication can give you useful clues. In Julie's case, she explained, "I eliminated the history and social studies topics on women, fashion, and work ... I was more interested in practical stuff on getting a job and what kind of jobs a grad might get. I only ended up using one book on fashion! When I went to the shelves for employment, I was really focusing on two areas: résumé writing and general info on the future of jobs."

Exercise 3

The following is a selection of current books on employment that Julie found on the shelves. In groups of four to six, examine the list carefully, and explain which ones you would not bother to locate, based on the nature of her focused topic. Note briefly the reasons for your decisions.

> Campbell, Colin. *Where the Jobs Are: Career Survival for Canadians in the New Global Economy.* Toronto: Macfarlane Walter & Ross, 1994.
>
> Dietrich, Norma. *The Job Search.* Toronto: ACCISS, 1990.
>
> Feather, Frank. *Canada's Best Career Guide.* 3rd ed. Toronto: Warwick, 1994.
>
> *How to Job-Hunt Effectively: A Guide to Survival and Success.* Ed. Neil A. Macdougall. 7th rev. ed. Toronto: Technical Service Council, 1989.
>
> Karasek, Robert. *Healthy Work: Stress, Productivity, and the Reconstruction of Working Life.* New York: Basic Books, 1990.
>
> Kleiman, Carol. *The 100 Best Jobs for the 1990s & Beyond.* Chicago: Dearborn Financial Publishing, 1992.
>
> Statistics Canada. *Canadian Jobs and Firm Size: Do Smaller Firms Pay Less?* Ottawa: Statistics Canada, 1991.

Scan Table of Contents/Index

After you select a number of likely candidates, it is still not time to read them in full or to sign them out from the library. In order to see whether a book actually addresses useful areas, scan the table of contents at the front and the index at the back for key headings and ideas related to your topic. Quickly skim sections dealing with your topic, and if they seem potentially useful, keep the book.

 ### Read Introductions/Forewords

After you have established that a work deals with relevant areas of your subject, read the introduction or foreword to get a general feel for the book and the approach taken to the subject. You may discover that it will not, in fact, be appropriate for your purpose.

 ### Scan Bibliographies/Works Cited Lists

In order to write their books, the authors of the works that you find on the shelves had to complete significant research of their own. Use these authors' labours to supplement your own. Scanning these books' bibliographies and works cited lists may lead you to other titles that are relevant to your purpose.

As a result of all these processes, Julie eliminated most of the American job titles and narrowed her resources to three books on the future of jobs: one American (Kleiman), and two Canadian. These, along with her "Internet" videotape and single fashion book, were her primary research sources. You likely want more than five main sources, but if they are significant and relevant, as in this case, this is a sufficient amount. Remember how much forethought and effort went into Julie's methodical selection of these five works.

 ### Skim-Read Your Sources

Once you have your stack of likely sources, you will skim-read them. Look for relevant internal headings and first sentences of paragraphs. Slow down, read carefully, and take notes only when you reach information that you are confident will be of use to you. This is how Julie worked her way through 2000 pages in about 18 hours over 2 days.

 ## HIGHLIGHTING

We all love our highlighter pens; they are bright and sassy. With great colour, however, comes great responsibility. If you are highlighting or underlining key points on *photocopied notes* (not in library books!), remember that this is a *critical thinking* exercise, not practice in colouring. Stick to thesis statements, key words, and the most significant arguments; it is easy to fall into the trap of highlighting virtually everything, which does you no real good.

NOTE-TAKING AND RECORD-KEEPING: YOUR RESPONSIBILITIES

During the skim-reading stage, you will be taking notes when you discover material that is relevant. Julie made notes on each of her five works, one at a time, in her research notebook, noting appropriate bibliographic information at the top of each page. In a research notebook or on index cards, you should do the following:

1. Create an accurate record of the source; this way, you will have it when you need it for documentation at the end of the essay. For a book, this means writ-

ing down the following information as it is printed on the book's title page: author's name, complete title, place of publication, publisher, and year of publication. For other items, such as magazine articles, see "Documentation" on p. 255.

See Module 4:
Summary Skills,
Paraphrasing, p. 74.

2. Under this accurate record, start taking down the information you feel is useful. Note the page number you take it from, and whether you have directly quoted, paraphrased, or responded with your own reactions to the text.

There must be no ambiguity about either the publication information or whether your note is a quotation, paraphrase, or reaction. Inaccurate or incomplete records of your sources undermine your credibility and can get you into serious trouble.

PLAGIARISM

A very serious problem occurs when, either by design or by accident, an idea or phrase that is not your own appears in your essay without its true source being acknowledged. This is plagiarism, which is no less than intellectual theft. This is *not* a way to try to save time. When you plagiarize, whether intentionally or not, you are stealing someone else's ideas and pawning them off as your own. While common knowledge (dates, historical events, and so on) need not be annotated, the ideas and arguments put forth by individual writers must be acknowledged as their own, whether you are paraphrasing them or using them word-for-word. The section on documentation (p. 255), coupled with Appendix B: Documentation Styles, show you how to accomplish this.

Plagiarism has dire consequences: often a zero on the assignment is accompanied by a record in your college file, a failing grade in the course, and/or expulsion. As you do not want any of these fates, be rigorous in your note-taking. Also remember that in a research essay you are being judged on the quality of your research and on your effectiveness in assembling it. If you have found extremely interesting or useful sources, then you will receive due credit for this. You need not pretend that every good idea or well-said phrase is yours; acknowledging your sources only shows how well you did the job of researching the subject.

Step 3: The Outline

The outline stage becomes a two- or three-part process for a research essay; the additional step, however, actually saves you time and effort. Because you are juggling so much information, going straight to the refined outline would be extremely difficult. If you have done effective research, at this point you have *too much material;* remember that one of the most important decisions you need to make here concerns what you will leave out.

1. When your notes are complete, read through them in order to group ideas under relevant main topic headings. Write a key word (for example, Technology) beside all material relating to one subject. Then, transfer all the material to separate sheets (one per subject). Use abbreviations to speed up the process. At this point, you have a raw outline with general headings,

quotations, paraphrases, and reactions to all sources now appearing under each subject heading. Supplement these categories with your own additional relevant observations or reactions.

2. Reading through your raw outline, determine your clear thesis and produce your refined outline in the usual fashion. Often (as in the case of Julie), you will use an intermediate stage of main-topic outlining.

One page each of Julie's raw, intermediate, and refined outlines appears below. Note how she carefully notes page references not only for direct quotations but also for ideas and statistics. If you examine all three, you can notice the organization tightening and adjusting as the outlining process develops.

In Julie's words, "For the raw one, I just used the first letter of the writer's last name to explain whose stuff it was." (C = Campbell, F = Feather, K = Kleiman)

RAW OUTLINE

I. Technology

K – stress on high tech

    – heavy demand for electronic/computer literate

F – importance of info tech in economy of the future

C – info tech—changing structure of business, p. xvi

    – 97% of all new jobs 1984–94 = service sector, p. 35

    – greatest in companies using technology

II. General Economy Trends

K – 2 sectors in economy: service-producing & goods-producing: "The service-producing sector ... will create four out five of all new jobs by 2000 ... " p. 43

    – services/retail trade = 75%

    – 90% of 21 million new jobs (intro. p. xiv)

    – includes wholesale/retail

    – in mfg, 18 million new wage/salary jobs in 90s

    – esp mgt w strong financial background

    – heavy demand for electronic/computer literate

    – " ... most of the fields showing the greatest growth are old fashioned ones," p. 43

    – footware expected to be slow

    – most decline in manufacturing due to technical innovation

    – decline need for people

F – switch to service economy—80% of Canadians in postindustrial, service economy, p. 9

    – " ... the information sector is not just spawning an information economy, it is helping to modernize all other sectors of the economy. Computerized information is essential to modern economic activity ... " p. 10

    – new jobs in service sector: "In the late 1990's, Canadians will spend more and more time either at home, with their PC's and home entertainment centres, or outside enjoying all that the leisure and entertainment sector of the economy has to offer," p. 19

- 80% of homes by 2005 will have catalogue/ITV/PC shopping ∴ need for back-up people
- NAFTA, Asia & Pacific Rim
- Cdn mfg down as shift to low-wage world, e.g., Mexico
- C – 25% of all CDNs NOW working from home
  - by 2005, electronic money transfer, most major purchases from home, p. xvii
  - home shopping: direct sell by TV: $100 billion by 2000
    - future = interactive, high-definition TV
  - ability to acquire products, speak to salespeople, order, auto-bill
  - 97% of all new jobs 1984–94 = service sector, p. 35
  - greatest increase in companies using technology
  - ADVICE: seek large, growing corps where advancement includes worldwide
  - emphasis on customer service ∴ marketing strength

III. Personnel Requirements

K – electronic/computer literacy
  - credentials beyond high school = basic requirement
  - service sector to need " ... workers who have specialized skills, are computer literate, intelligent and good communicators," p. xv

Julie included an intermediate step in her outlining:

INTERMEDIATE OUTLINE

"Here, I didn't want any details, just the overall order I wanted my arguments in. If I worried about exactly what quotes to use, I knew I'd lose the overall argument."

I. Introduction
   A. shifting economy
   B. demographics
   C. info tech
   D. Question: how to target for career?

II. The Global Economy
   A. economic sectors
   B. switch to service economy
   C. info tech
   D. working from home

III. The Canadian Economy
   A. service economy
   B. influence of info tech
   C. working from home

   IV. Demographics

      A. age

      B. empty-nesters

         1. profile

    V. Small Business

      A. prior knowledge

      B. women

      C. influence of info tech

      D. growth potential

   VI. Personnel Requirements

      A. the first job

  VII. Fashion Industry

      A. weak areas

      B. potential growth

         1. shift to leisure

         2. empty-nesters

 VIII. Target Job Market

      A. small boutique

         1. sales to management

      B. WWW possibility

   IX. Conclusions

      A. Hamburger quotation

      B. C—stick with demographics

Finally, Julie produced her refined outline by combining the specifics of the raw and the general categories of the intermediate outline.

REFINED OUTLINE

    I. Introduction

      A. shifting economy

      B. demographics

      C. info tech

         K –stress on high tech; heavy demand for electronic/computer literate

         F –importance of info tech in economy of the future

         C –info tech—changing structure of business, p. xvi

           –97% of all new jobs 1984–94 = service sector, p. 35

           –greatest increase in companies using technology

      D. Question: how to target for career?

II. The Global Economy

   – NAFTA, Asia & Pacific Rim

   A. economic sectors

   K – 2 sectors in economy: service-producing & goods-producing

   B. switch to service economy

      K – "the service producing sector ... Will create four out five of all new jobs by 2000 ... " p. 43

      – services/retail trade = 75%

      – 90% of 21 million new jobs (intro, p. xiv)

      – includes wholesale/retail

      K – in mfg, 18 million new wage/salary jobs in 90s

      K – esp mgt w strong financial background

      K – most decline in manufacturing due to technical innovation ∴ decline need for people

   C. info tech

      K – heavy demand for electronic/computer literate

      F – " ... the information sector is not just spawning an information economy, it is helping to modernize all other sectors of the economy. Computerized information is essential to modern economic activity ... " p. 10

III. The Canadian Economy

   A. service economy

      F – switch to service economy—80% of Canadians in postindustrial, service economy, p. 9

      F – Cdn mfg down as shift to low-wage world, e.g., Mexico

      C – emphasis of customer service ∴ marketing strength

      B – influence of info tech

      F – new jobs in service sector: "In the late 1990's, Canadians will spend more and more time either at home, with their PC's and home entertainment centres, or outside enjoying all that the leisure and entertainment sector of the economy has to offer," p. 19

      C – 97% of all new jobs 1984–94 = service sector, p. 35

      – greatest increase in companies using technology

      C – working from home

      C – 25% of all CDNs NOW working from home

Step 4: Writing the Rough Draft

At this stage, if you are using a computer you should print your refined outline and use it to start writing a draft. No matter what, you should keep your outline—printed or handwritten—beside you for reference. This is the roadmap for your thinking and writing.

1. Make certain quotations and ideas are carefully sourced: you do not need full MLA or APA style documentation; having to check formats at this point will waste your time and disturb the flow of your writing. Be certain, however, to include sufficient information so that each source is clear. During the revision stage, you will complete these references.

2. Do not simply dump all of your original raw outline phrasing into the draft; spend your time genuinely pondering how to say it most effectively.

MISUSING QUOTES

Research essays can easily turn into an unfocused stream of other people's thoughts, statements, and ideas. This happens if you simply run one quote or source reference into another. You must demonstrate control of your sources—that you are using them to serve a larger purpose of your own (whether evaluative, persuasive, or informative) that is reflected in your thesis. *Your* voice should dominate, and your sources should be used to reflect your needs.

Sample Research Essay—First Draft

JOBS OF THE FUTURE IN FASHION

BY JULIE CHAU

Julie explains, "I made modifications on the fly—like comparing the U.S. and Canadian economies in paragraph 3 ... I didn't do full documentation yet ... that's a pain."

The economy of this country has shifted dramatically in recent years. In past years, a person could graduate from college, take a job with a company, and expect to retire from that company forty years later. This is no longer the case. As we look at the career market in the 1990s and the next century, people can expect to change their careers numerous times. This is as true for the fashion industry as for any other. Every student asks, "How do I organize my educational career and my professional career of the future?" By considering the global and Canadian economies, demographics, and computer development over the next ten years, I will chart a personal route for success in the fashion industry. (1)

We are moving from local to global economies. Agreements such as NAFTA (the North American Free Trade Agreement) have been expanding, and we have seen rapid expansion of Pacific Rim trade. This is causing a shift in the way we think about jobs. With the shift away from manual labour, there is an increase in an economy that is concerned with leisure time. (2)

There are two sectors in the economy: service-producing and goods-producing. North America, and Canada, is in the process of switching from a goods-producing to a service economy: "... The service producing sector ... will create four out of five of all new jobs by 2000 ... " (K., p. 43), and in Canada, 80 percent of Canadians are expected to work in the service economy of the future (F., p. 9). Manufacturing is expected to expand and employ 18 million new people in the U.S., and Canadian manufacturing is expected to decrease as jobs shift to low-wage areas such as Mexico (K., F.). Canadian strengths will be customer service, and marketing strengths will be important to employees of the future. (3)

High technology and computer-literate individuals (K.) are now important. Information technology will be more important in the economy of the future. It is changing the structure of business and Colin Campbell, in <u>Where the Jobs Are</u>, says the greatest increase in jobs will happen in companies that are using technology (C., p. 35). Frank Feather talks about "... the information sector is not just spawning an information economy, it is helping to modernize all other sectors of the economy. Computerized information is essential to modern economic activity ..." (F., p. 10). (4)

Feather says by the late 1990s, Canadians in the leisure economy will spend more time at home with their personal computers and home entertainment centres, and are "... enjoying all that the leisure and entertainment sectors of the economy has to offer" (F., p. 19). (5)

Exercise 4

Read Julie's draft carefully; in groups of four to six, detect problems for fixing. Remember that everything is open to alteration: organization, language, grammar, and development of ideas.

Step 5: Revising

As usual, when you revise your essay you are "seeing it again"—evaluating and adjusting the coherence and unity of your argument. Two additional areas require attention in a research essay, however:

1. At the essay's end, you must provide a complete, detailed list of all sources, formatted in an appropriate style (generally either APA or MLA: see "Documentation," p. 255).

2. You should thus at this stage flesh out your in-text documentation and verify that you have correctly integrated your quotations.

QUOTATION INTEGRATION

Quotations are the best possible kind of textual support for your argument. However, you must remember the following rules about quotations:

1. Be careful to quote accurately. Your argument, no matter how sound, will be viewed more skeptically if you copy the quotation and its punctuation incorrectly.

2. When you insert a quotation, you must integrate it into your text. For example, this quotation from Julie's paper is not integrated: "Frank Feather talks about 'the information sector is not just spawning an information economy, it is helping to modernize all other sectors of the economy.'"

Quotations should be seamlessly integrated into your own writing so that the sentences and ideas flow together. The current sentence, which blends Julie's writing with Frank Feather's quotation, does not make sense. There are three ways to correct this:

See Appendix A,
Contract #4: The
Semi-colon and Colon.

a. Make a complete general statement, which the quotation will then illustrate. Use a colon (:) to introduce the quotation. Frank Feather emphasizes the impact of technology: "the information sector is not just spawning an information economy, it is helping to modernize all other sectors of the economy."

b. Blend your introductory phrase into the quotation: Frank Feather discusses how "the information sector is not just spawning an information economy, it is helping to modernize all other sectors of the economy."

c. Finally, you can change the words of the quote *but not its meaning* in order to make it fit into your text. You must, however, indicate to your reader any changes you make in one of the following manners:

   i. If you leave out certain words, indicate this with ellipsis, or " ... ".

   ii. If you add or change words, indicate this in square brackets "[ ]". Thus, the rewritten sentence could also appear as follows: Frank Feather notes how "the information sector is ... spawning an information economy [and] helping to modernize all other sectors of the economy."

d. Indent and offset quotations of four or more lines in the MLA method or APA method (see Appendix B).

✳ MISUSING SOURCES

Be extremely careful to represent your sources accurately, not only in terms of their actual words, but in their intentions (insofar as you can determine them). It is deceptively easy to quote only part of a statement and thereby distort the author's intention. It is similarly possible to misuse the ellipsis and square brackets to alter an author's original meaning. Notice how the ellipsis in the example above indicates omission of the words "not just," and how the square brackets indicate that the word "and" has been substituted for "it is." Notice also that despite these alterations, the meaning of Feather's original statement remains intact.

Step 6: Editing

The final stage of your research essay process is editing your paper for grammatical and punctuation errors. In a research essay, this carries with it the additional step of ensuring that all formatting is correct, including page layout and documentation format. In general, your instructor will have specific instructions about page layout; otherwise, your MLA or APA handbooks precisely indicate appropriate page arrangement.

DOCUMENTATION: EXACTLY WHAT DO YOU NEED TO DOCUMENT?

Documentation is used to acknowledge material drawn from external sources. While you may put together ideas drawn from various sources in unique ways, you still need to identify where the original ideas were drawn from. Using ideas, information, or actual language from external sources without acknowledging it is tantamount to stealing. As you know, in the educational world, this is known as plagiarism; there is no excuse whatsoever for plagiarism.

REFERENCES

References are like witnesses in a court case; they help to establish the truth of what you are saying. Without them, you are dealing with "hearsay," which is inadmissible, or, in the case of plagiarism, "contempt of court," since you show a disregard for the truth.

See Appendix B. While this section will highlight the main aspects of each of these styles, you should acquaint yourself with the full handbooks and use them when doubts or questions arise.

MLA and APA Style

Each academic discipline uses a form of documentation in its papers. The most common ones are the Modern Language Association (MLA) style, used for documentation in languages and literature, and the American Psychological Association (APA) style, used in the liberal arts. Each of these requires you to document your sources within the text of your essay, and to acknowledge them in full at the end of your essay. Some other disciplines (such as science, engineering, or medicine) have other documentation styles, but MLA and APA are the most common for most students. Handbooks for each of these styles are available through your college or university library, and should be consulted as necessary.

WHAT NOT TO DOCUMENT

While you must document your sources, you do not need to document things that you would expect any general reader to know. In Julie Chau's sample essay, she refers to NAFTA (the North American Free Trade Agreement) without documentation; she can assume that, since it has been in the news since 1993, most people will be familiar with it. You can safely assume that common knowledge and general information need not be documented. You can also safely use facts that are widely used in newspapers, television and radio, and textbooks.

BETTER SAFE THAN SORRY

If you are in doubt about what constitutes "common knowledge," always err on the side of caution. You are always safer to document your source than to make an incorrect assumption, omit it, and find yourself accused of plagiarism.

This is the essay that Julie submitted: it is a good, but not a "perfect" essay; indeed, if you read carefully and analytically, you will notice what appear to be obvious errors. Make note of these; the questions at the end will ask you to correct them.

Sample Research Essay—Final

JOBS OF THE FUTURE IN FASHION

BY JULIE CHAU

The economy of this country has shifted dramatically in recent years. In the past, a student could graduate from college, take a job with a company, and expect to retire from that company forty years later. As we look at the career market in the 1990s and the next century, this is no longer true: people now expect to change their careers many times. This holds for the fashion industry as well as for any other. The question every fashion student of the 1990s must ask is, "What factors must I consider in attempting to chart my educational and professional career of the future?" By considering the influence of the global and Canadian economies and the influence of demographics in light of the impact of information technology over the next ten years, it is possible to chart a personal route for success in the fashion industry. (1)

We are moving away from local or even national economies to more global approaches to business. Agreements such as NAFTA (the North American Free Trade Agreement) and the rapid expansion of Pacific Rim trade makes this a reality. This is causing a shift in the way we think about jobs. Further, with the shift away from manual labour, there is an increased concern with leisure time. (2)

There are two sectors in the economy: service-producing and goods-producing. North America, and Canada in particular, is in the process of switching from a goods-producing to a service economy. It is anticipated both that " ... the service producing sector ... will create four out of five of all new jobs by 2000 ... " (Kleiman 43), and in Canada, 80 percent of Canadians are expected to work in the service economy of the future (Feather 9). While manufacturing is expected to expand and employ 18 million new people in the U.S., Canadian manufacturing is expected to decrease as jobs shift to low-wage areas such as Mexico (Feather 9). Canadian industry will thus focus on customer service. So, as a result, marketing skills will be important to employees of the future. (3)

There is also a new stress on high technology and a heavy demand for computer-literate individuals (Kleiman 48). Information technology will take an increasing level of importance in the economy of the future. It is changing the structure of business and, according to Colin Campbell, in *Where the Jobs Are*, the greatest increase in jobs will happen in companies that are using high technology (35). As Frank Feather states,

> ... the information sector is not just spawning an information economy, it is helping to modernize all other sectors of the economy. Computerized information is essential to modern economic activity ... (10). (4)

Feather continues this argument by suggesting that by the late 1990s, Canadians in the leisure economy will spend increasing amounts of time at home with their personal computers and home entertainment centres,

" ... enjoying all that the leisure and entertainment sector of the economy has to offer" (19). (5)

Demographics, the study of population trends, is also expected to shift as we move into the next century. After World War II, we saw the baby boom. These individuals are now aging and a new potential market, the empty-nester baby-boomer—fifty-plus-year-old baby-boom people whose children are now grown up and have left home—are expected to represent a tidal wave of potential buyers. According to Campbell, these are individuals who, now at their peak of earning power, are relatively debt-free. They will be computer-literate, will likely own personal computers, and with access to internet services (Internet), will spend money on convenience services so long as those services are of value. For fashion students, Campbell suggests

> If you are interested in pursuing a career in this field, your safest bet is to stick with the demographic-oriented markets (177).

Further,

> Less expensive designer lines aimed at the affluent baby-boomers have done well. Similarly, the mini baby boom will lead to more designing for the upscale children's market and the maternity outfit market. Greater emphasis will be placed on meeting the clothing demands of emptynesters and the growing number of retirees. (176–177)

This alone gives a clear indication of how a fashion student should position themselves for the future. Students must focus on this expanding population of relatively debt-free, leisure-oriented, and technically literate people. (6)

By 2005, we will see home-based electronic money transfers and most major purchases made from home (Campbell 6). Through information technology in the home, people will expect to be able to speak to salespeople, order products, and be either automatically billed or have their bank accounts automatically debited. Home shopping, direct selling by television or Internet, is expected to be a $100 billion industry in North America by the year 2000 (Campbell xvii). (7)

Small business and home-based businesses are growth areas for the future. Twenty-five percent of Canadians now work from home, and this figure is expected to rise. By 2000, 50 percent of small and home businesses will be owned by women (Campbell 113), and one-third of all business will be home-based. Carol Kleiman, however, cautions that knowledge of the selected industry for the home business is essential. Eighty percent of owners with prior knowledge of the product or service will remain in business (Kleiman 112). (8)

These arguments suggest some basic requirements for the person seeking a future in fashion. Beyond the obvious idea that people need more than a high-school education, given the emphasis on the service and computer-literate markets, we will need "workers who have specialized skills, are computer literate, intelligent and good communicators" (Kleiman xv). We should thus be developing our computer skills, and honing our interpersonal communication skills. While focusing upon our selected fields, we should also be mixing in arts subjects in order to become well-rounded workers. Our success and salary will be based upon skills, education, and experience. (9)

As we move from this background into our first jobs, we should recognize our need for experience in our field and the opportunity to explore alternatives. We should remember that the goal of a first job is no longer to establish a life-long career, but to establish a work history, and to explore options and opportunities. And, just as an aside, to provide an income while we do these things. (10)

In the fashion industry, there are weak and strong areas to explore. While footware is expected to be a slow area, Campbell says "... an emphasis on the part of consumers to purchase casual clothes" (176). Even major corporations these days are allowing workers to wear casual clothes if they are not meeting with clients. Campbell notes that suit sales were down 25 percent between 1990 and 1991 (177). While custom-tailored fashions are expected to boom and create a need for designers and merchandisers (Feather 76), the Canadian manufacturing side is, as mentioned above, expected to shift to low-wage areas. (11)

Further, there is a shake-out taking place as consumers move from large department stores to smaller, specialized boutiques. In these boutiques, there is a need for management-level individuals who have both training and experience in finance and personnel management, on both local and worldwide bases. (12)

Before concluding with recommendations for current and future fashion students, the impact of the Internet should again be highlighted. Internet, particularly through the World Wide Web, provides an opportunity for the future. Since the college has given each of us accounts on Internet, we have had the opportunity to explore the web. Here we find not only information, but marketing potential for small, home-based businesses. I recently found a Home-Page for a sportswear manufacturer who did custom tailoring based upon orders logged by consumers who supplied their own measurements and credit card numbers. As I investigated this business through private e-mail, I found that it was an individual in Battleford, Saskatchewan, who made clothes to order. Her main clients were the older, health-oriented baby-boomers who accessed her catalogues through the web. This is another opportunity. (13)

The direction of the future becomes obvious based upon this research. A fashion student should focus on the service economy and do the following:

1. Upon completion of their college diploma, they should seek to join small, specialized chain retailers with global possibilities. Through this first, sales-oriented position, they should establish a work history, seek contacts, and learn the business.

2. Simultaneously, if possible, they should open an Internet-based company that caters to the empty-nester baby-boomer and focuses on casual clothes. Demographically, this is the biggest growth area, and in terms of starting a business, it is the least expensive since produc-

tion will be based upon sales. If this grows into a full-fledged, small business, that will be great. If it does not, it may offer not only additional income to the founder, but possibly income to peers in similar programs at the college. This can begin immediately, and through it, we can gain experience that will help in our studies.

3. They should always consider the need for continuing education. Finance, small-business management, and personnel management are essential skills that must be learned, developed, and refined. (14)

As Estelle Hamburger says,

> You will need a clear view of the realities of life, because now as never before the lives and attitudes of people interact with the fashion business. Contemporary clothes are no longer symbols of rank, power, or wealth but an expression of life stripped of its pretensions" (300). (15)

This is the reality that we must face in this industry. People must clothe themselves. For fashion students like me, can we take this reality and turn it into a future? I think we can. (16)

Works Cited

Campbell, Colin. *Where the Jobs Are: Career Survival for Canadians in the New Global Economy.* Toronto: Macfarlane Walter & Ross, 1994.

Feather, Frank. *Canada's Best Career Guide.* 3rd ed. Toronto: Warwick, 1994.

Hamburger, Estelle. *Fashion Business: It's All Yours.* San Francisco: Canfield Press, 1976.

"Internet." *Prime Time News.* Narr. Wendy Mesley. CBC. CBLT, Toronto. 18 June 1995.

Kleiman, Carol. *The 100 Best Jobs for the 1990s & Beyond.* Chicago: Dearborn Financial Publishing, 1992.

Questions

1. Identify the thesis statement. Does it fulfil all of the requirements of a thesis statement? Does it read smoothly and easily? Would you recommend any changes?

2. Identify the *different* rhetorical modes at work in

   a. the second half of paragraph 3;

   b. paragraph 8;

   c. paragraph 11;

   d. paragraph 14;

   e. paragraph 15.

Remember: "research essay" is not a rhetorical mode.

3. What dominant rhetorical mode are the rhetorical modes identified in question 2 being made to serve?

4. Give at least four specific examples of how Julie clearly addresses not only her professor, but the needs of the specific wider audience for which she is writing her research essay.

5. Spot and correct the following:

See Appendix A, Contract #7: Subject/Verb Agreement.

  a. the subject/verb agreement error in paragraph 2;

See Appendix A, Contract #8: Parallelism.

  b. the parallelism errors in paragraphs 3 and 9;

  c. the pronoun reference error in the first part of paragraph 6;

See Appendix A, Contract, #6: Pronoun Reference and Agreement.

  d. the pronoun/antecedent agreement errors in the last part of paragraph 6 and at the start of paragraph 14;

  e. the sentence fragment in paragraph 10;

See Appendix A, Contract #2: Sentence Fragments.

  f. the quotation integration problem in paragraph 11;

  g. the dangling modifier in paragraph 13;

See Appendix A, Contract #9: Misplaced and Dangling Modifiers.

  h. any areas where Julie's essay could benefit from improved transitional phrasing;

  i. any other errors or awkwardness.

6. Evaluate Julie's conclusion: does it flow logically out of the substance of her argument? Are her conclusions adequately supported by her research?

7. Examine Julie's reference list: evaluate the quality of her references and her use of them in supporting her argument. Are you satisfied with her thoroughness in researching the topic? Are any of these sources of questionable merit, in your view? Does she depend too heavily/too little on any of them?

8. What method of documentation did Julie use? Did she use it correctly and completely?

9. Evaluate the voice and tone of Julie's essay. Are they consistent and appropriate for a formal research essay?

Julie was a little annoyed; she told us privately she felt the professor was "stingy."

10. Julie got a B on her paper. What factors justify/do not justify this grade?

SUMMARY

The research essay is not a separate rhetorical mode; it is an essay written in another rhetorical mode (usually analysis or persuasion) that uses research materials to solve a problem or advance an argument. You are being asked to discover what others have thought and said about your subject, and to present these findings in your essay. During research, you should not neglect other sources discussed in Module 2, such as a dictionary of quotations, newspapers, magazines, people, and the Internet (World Wide Web pages and their hypermedia links). For many research topics, however, your most important source of information will be the library. Certain cues in the wording of writing tasks suggest that a research essay is appropriate, but more often the nature of the topic will dictate that research is necessary.

The research essay involves a complex but methodical process based upon scanning and filtering information, and reading only material that you have determined is directly useful. If you follow this process meticulously, you will save time. If you attempt too many shortcuts or skip too many steps, you risk one of several possible fates, such as inadequate or irrelevant research, a lack of focus, or a paper that is a mass of unfocused commentary by other writers. You must demonstrate control of your sources—that you are using them to serve a larger purpose or thesis of your own (whether evaluative, persuasive, or informative). Your "voice" must dominate, and your sources should be quoted and referenced accurately and correctly in order to serve your needs.

CHECKLIST

- Does your essay support a clear, specific, focused thesis statement?
- Does the thesis make clear the essay's dominant rhetorical mode?
- Does your introduction adequately explain the background to and rationale for your research?
- Is your logical reasoning sound and easy to follow?
- Have you acknowledged all sources of specific phrases, as well as paraphrased examples, evidence, and testimony?
- Are all your sources current and applicable to your subject?
- Do your references clearly and adequately support your points?
- Are the arguments clearly organized in order of importance or in another logical sequence?
- Have you used sufficient appropriate transitional phrasing to signal clearly the linkages among points and arguments?
- Does your conclusion both summarize the conclusions arrived at in your essay and explore the implications of the argument, so that the question of the thesis is redirected to a larger framework (such as what the reader should do or has learned)?
- Are your quotations accurate and integrated correctly with your sentence structure?
- Are your in-text citation and final documentation formatted correctly?

Grammar as Contract

As is discussed in the Preface, every writer needs a set of basic writing tools, including a good handbook of English with detailed grammar explanations. Thus, this brief grammar section is meant to *supplement,* not replace, such a text. If you need a quick, easy-to-understand grammar lesson on how to solve your recurring sentence fragment problem, for example, this appendix should be able to help you. If you make major grammatical errors that fall into multiple categories and affect almost every sentence, you will need more help than this appendix can provide.

Your instructor may choose to cover one or two specific "contracts" per module covered in class. Likewise, your instructor may refer you to this appendix for individual work based on your own particular most common errors. Or, lastly, you may choose to work through contracts that you realize will alleviate difficulties for you. Always remember, however, that this is not a complete grammar text; supplemental explanations (from a handbook or instructor) will be required from time to time. In keeping with the contents of previous modules, you should consider this appendix a list of the Top Ten Student Grammar Errors (with Explanations and Exercises). Within that context, it is intended to be as clear, jargon-free, and user-friendly as possible.

WRITING IS HARD WORK; SPEAKING IS EASY

A common complaint made about writing is that it is hard work. As you know from Module 1, we agree with this assessment. Why is it such hard work? For many people, the answer is a second complaint—"There are too many rules." Many of the rules in question fall into the dreaded category of grammar. Having to take grammar lessons can feel like being audited by Revenue Canada—it seems like you have to account for every little detail.

By contrast, speaking seems a lot easier than writing. When you speak, you do not have to think so much about the perfect word, the correct spelling, or the right punctuation. You can "get away with a lot more."

In reality, when you speak, words are only one small component of your overall communication. You can communicate with the tone of your voice, with its pace (how fast, how slow, when you pause), with your body language (gestures), and with your facial expressions and eye contact. You do not have any of these things when you write. You are not always there to watch your readers and realize from their body language, "Oh—you don't understand; I'd better find another way to explain that." Because your essay needs to stand on its own, when you write, you need to be sure you get it right.

GRAMMAR IS A CONTRACT BETWEEN YOU AND THE READER

When you write, all you have is your words. Once your essay passes into the hands of a reader, it is beyond your control. This means that you have to be reasonably certain that it says everything you want it to say, in a way that *every* reader can understand. This is where grammar comes in. Grammar is the set of rules that tells you how to write so others can understand you, and tells you how to read so you can understand others' writing. Grammar is a contract, an agreement between readers and writers about how words can be organized so that they will make sense. Yes, there are many rules, but these rules exist to protect you and your reader.

If you follow the rules of grammar—if you live up to the contract — your message stands a very good chance of being clearly understood. If you ignore some or all of the rules of grammar—that is, if you break the contract—your message may be misunderstood or, worse, ignored. Worst of all, break the grammar contract repeatedly and your reader will stop trusting that you are a reliable source of information.

In the following series of lessons, you will be introduced (or, more likely, reintroduced) to some of the most frequently breached contracts of grammar. Each lesson will have four components:

1. **The contract:** This is an easy-to-understand introduction to the particular contract.

2. **Terms of the contract:** This is everything you need to understand in order to interpret the contract.

3. **Fine print:** This is a brief explanation of those "details" or exceptions that may drive you crazy, but that you need to know.

4. **Authenticating the contract:** This is the most valuable section of all, a series of Study Tips designed to give you strategies for detecting and solving errors or breaches of contract. By using these, you will be able to evaluate your own writing to ensure that you have lived up to the contract in question.

Contract #1: The Sentence

THE CONTRACT

When you write an essay, you are agreeing to a grammatical contract that calls for you to write in complete thoughts. If you write down only half a thought, your reader will not understand you. Further, as you know, the reader does not have the luxury of reading your mind or asking you to explain what you mean. Since a sentence must express a complete thought, if you understand how to identify a sentence, you can be certain of living up to the contract.

THE TERMS OF THE CONTRACT: ACTORS AND ACTIONS/ SUBJECTS AND VERBS

A sentence is a group of words that expresses a complete thought, and therefore can stand alone and make sense. To create a complete thought in English, every sentence must contain two fundamental elements. One is an **actor** (human or inanimate) that does an **action**, which is the other required element. In grammatical terms, these are called the **subject** and the **verb** of the sentence. These are identified for you in the following sentence:

> actor action
>
> <u>Jim</u> <u>enrolled</u> in an architecture program.

When you remove the actor and action from the sentence and examine them on their own, you have the core of the complete thought, which can stand on its own: "Jim enrolled." Notice how the action (verb) includes an idea of when the action occurred (we know that Jim enrolled at some time in the past).

THE FINE PRINT

1. The action can sometimes be a linking verb like "to be" or "to seem," as in "I (actor) *am* (action) cold," or "She *seems* nice."

2. The action can be more than one word. For instance, "She will have told him by noon." You might initially assume that the actor and action are "She told." But "She told" alters the time of the action: it sounds like the action already took place. The complete action is "will have told." "She will have told" provides the actor and the complete action and time.

AUTHENTICATING THE CONTRACT

To find the actor, ask yourself, "Who or what is the star of this sentence?" "Who or what is the sentence about?" Then, to find the action, ask yourself, "What is the actor doing?"

Exercise 1

In the following sentences, circle the actor (subject) and underline the action (verb).

1. The three electricians inspected the wiring system.

2. All the students found the class unusually difficult.

3. You will need a good dictionary.

4. Human resources professionals must have some knowledge of psychology.

5. There are three methods to solve this equation.

Keep in mind that not all sentences are as straightforward as the ones above. In fact, sentences can be twisting and twisted groups of words. Sometimes a sentence will have more than one actor or action, or will have groups of words that make it difficult to figure out exactly who or what does the action. The secret to finding the real subject and verb is to eliminate any extra words or word groups. Try finding the subject(s) and verb(s) in these sentences.

1. Most of my classmates in the Ethics class agreed that the right thing to do is to report the case of fraud at once.

2. Accountants often have the reputation of being uninteresting people, but, as we all know, it is important to take people on an individual basis.

3. Are you sure that the exam is going to be multiple choice?

4. I am sure that he is the guy who snubbed me at the party last week.

5. On the whole, Professor Singh is pretty easygoing until you bring up the topic of late assignments.

Contract #2: Sentence Fragments

THE CONTRACT

Contract #1 stipulates that you have to write in complete thoughts, which means complete sentences. This means that you are not permitted to write in sentence fragments, which are partial thoughts. This is only logical: if your reader is left trying to figure out how to finish your thoughts, how will you be sure that she or he is finishing them correctly?

THE TERMS OF THE CONTRACT: THE THREE KINDS OF FRAGMENTS

Since a sentence has to have an actor and an action, if it is missing one of these it is automatically incomplete, and therefore a fragment. These are the first two types of fragments:

> Went to the dock. (NO ACTOR. Who "went to the dock"?)

> Steve and the rest of the students in his class. (NO ACTION. What did "Steve and the rest of the students in his class" do?)

In the third type of fragment, the sentences appear to have actors and actions, and therefore to meet all contract requirements. More often than not these sentences are fragments because they start with a word that makes the reader expect something more in order to make the sentence whole. These are the third kind of fragment— the *incomplete thought*. When you read an incomplete thought, it will not make sense, and you may find yourself asking "So?" The following are examples of this.

> Although everyone has pitched in with the effort to rebuild the laboratory.

> Which is a point that is often overlooked when choosing where to pursue a postsecondary education.

In order to make incomplete thoughts correct, you must add another group of words that is by itself a complete thought:

> Although everyone has pitched in with the effort to rebuild the laboratory, it will still not be completed until September.
>
> A college's commitment to upgrading its technological facilities constantly is more important than ever, which is a point that is often overlooked when choosing where to pursue a postsecondary education.

The key to solving sentence fragment errors is recognizing what is missing from the sentence, and then adding it, so the sentence lives up to the grammatical contract and makes sense.

THE FINE PRINT

In type 2, sentences may have no action, or they may have an incomplete action. For instance, an action ending in *-ing* cannot stand by itself; it is automatically incomplete. For example, "Kara *saving* her essay on her hard drive." To correct an incomplete action, you must expand the action: "Kara *is saving* her essay on her hard drive."

AUTHENTICATING THE CONTRACT

1. To identify a fragment, pretend someone has just walked up to you on the street and said the sentence out loud. If it does not make sense, ask yourself if it is a fragment. If so, try to identify which kind it is.

2. To find fragments in your own writing, read every sentence in your essay individually, *starting with the last one, and then the second-last one, and so on.* This way, you will evaluate each sentence individually to see if it fulfils the contract. If you look for fragments from start to finish, you may accidentally miss some of type 3 (incomplete thoughts) because they seem to fit in with the flow of your writing.

3. Generally, when you find an incomplete thought (type 3) in your own writing, what you need to do is connect it to a complete thought that precedes or follows it.

Exercise 2

In these sentences, identify which ones live up to the sentence contract and which do not. In the latter case, identify the type of fragment: 1 = no actor, 2 = no action, 3 = incomplete thought. Then correct the problem.

1. Left out in the cold if you cannot use a word processor by the end of your college career.

2. One of the most overwhelming situations facing the new student.

3. For example, broad-based knowledge as a key element of a well-rounded education.

4. Having been given the assignment sheet at the beginning of the class.

5. The incredible growth in Internet use in the last two years alone.

6. In Alberta, things are done a little differently.

7. Because in polls so many Canadians express a similar view regarding capital punishment.

8. Once all the decisions have been made and the plan put into operation.

9. Helga upgrading her skills.

10. After the storm, getting to work was difficult.

Contract #3: Run-on Sentences

THE CONTRACT

Contract #1 stipulates that you have to write in complete thoughts, which are sentences. Very often, however, a sentence contains more than one complete thought. Indeed, it is important to join thoughts together in order to create variety in your sentence structure and to show readers how different ideas are related. If you do not join them correctly, however, you may breach the grammar contract and create problems for your reader.

THE TERMS OF THE CONTRACT: FUSED SENTENCES AND COMMA SPLICES

1. Your reader relies on you to indicate clearly the separations between different thoughts in the same sentence. Without this kind of separation, your reader cannot determine where one thought ends and the next begins. Imagine how difficult it would be for someone to understand your spoken words if you never varied your tone or pace, and never paused. Similarly, the reader who does not know where to pause cannot understand you. If you join two complete thoughts together without putting anything between them, you create a **fused sentence**. Two examples follow: can you identify where the split between the two ideas should take place?

   A new journal of demographics started publication this year many students are trying to get a copy for their marketing assignment.

   The committee has deferred its decision until the meeting next month this almost guarantees the new courses will not be implemented for another two years.

2. A comma is a weak piece of punctuation: it is not strong enough by itself to split two complete thoughts. When you try to use just a comma to join two different thoughts, you again breach the contract. This time, you create a **comma splice**.

   Her parents accused her of not caring about her grades, this was an unfair charge because she was constantly working on her assignments.

   The CD-ROM I want to do my research on is booked for the day, I will reserve a time slot for early tomorrow.

There are five main ways of solving this type of error. It is essential to understand all of them, and it is sensible to learn them in the order listed here, which is designed to minimize the amount of memorization necessary. You need to know all of them so you have a variety of ways to avoid this problem and keep your sentence structure interesting.

Period

Use a period to separate the two complete thoughts into two separate sentences.

> Her parents accused her of not caring about her grades. This was an unfair charge because she was constantly working on her assignments.

> A new journal of demographics started publication this year. Many students are trying to get a copy for their marketing assignment.

THE FINE PRINT

See Module 3: The Essay: How to Say It, Coherence, p. 59, and Contract #10: The Paragraph.

This is an excellent strategy, but you cannot use it all the time, or your writing will never flow together, but will instead consist only of short, choppy sentences.

FANBOYS

Use a comma followed by one of the FANBOYS to join the two sentences. The FANBOYS are **for, and, nor, but, or, yet, so**—all two- or three-letter joining words (conjunctions) that you use to connect two complete thoughts. Just remember the word FANBOYS, memorize the words it stands for, and remember to use a comma before them whenever they are joining two complete thoughts.

> The CD-ROM I want to do my research on is booked for the day, **so** I will reserve a time slot for early tomorrow.

> The committee has deferred its decision until the meeting next month, **and** this almost guarantees the new courses will not be implemented for another two years.

THE FINE PRINT

A very common error is the placement of a comma *after* one of the FANBOYS, for instance,

> I would prefer to take this class by computer conferencing but, it is only offered in the regular classroom format.

This is incorrect. A comma virtually never goes after one of the FANBOYS because the FANBOYS are part of the second complete thought in the sentence, not the first. Reread the example above: *but* does not makes sense as part of the first thought. The comma must be placed *before* the *but* to show it is part of the second thought. If you use a comma immediately after one of the FANBOYS, you are likely breaching the contract.

Semi-Colon

Unlike the comma, a semi-colon by itself is strong enough to connect two complete thoughts. As a rule, you can put a semi-colon where you would put a period, and vice versa.

> Her parents accused her of not caring about her grades; this was an unfair charge because she was constantly working on her assignments.

> A new journal of demographics started publication this year; many students are trying to get a copy for their marketing assignment.

THE FINE PRINT

If you connect two complete thoughts with only a semi-colon, the sentences must have a clear and strong relationship. Thus, the following is not acceptable:

> Of course, Ramon attended the stockholders' meeting; he went on vacation to Guatemala last year.

This revised version is acceptable because the two complete parts are logically connected:

> Of course, Ramon attended the stockholders' meeting; he fought vigorously against the planned phase-out of the pension plan.

Transitional Phrase (conjunctive adverb)

You can use a transitional phrase that shows the relationship between the two parts of the sentence. When you use one of these, you place a semi-colon before it and a comma after it. The most common transitional phrases are the following:

> as a result, by contrast, consequently, furthermore, however, in addition, more-over, nevertheless, subsequently, then, therefore, thus

Two examples of transitional phrases in action are as follows:

> Her parents accused her of not caring about her grades; **nevertheless,** this was an unfair charge because she was constantly working on her assignments.

> The committee has deferred its decision until the meeting next month; **conse-quently,** this almost guarantees the new courses will not be implemented for another two years.

Subs

The final method of fixing a fused sentence or comma splice is with the aid of a **sub (subordinating conjunction)**. Some of the most common subs include the following:

> after, although, as, because, before, even though, if, since, though, unless, until, when, where, whether, while

THE FINE PRINT

This is by no means a complete list of subs; there are more subordinating conjunctions than there are FANBOYS and transitional phrases combined. Thus, if you memorize your FANBOYS and your transitional phrases, along with the punctuation that is appropriate for each, you can expect that virtually every other connector will be a sub.

When you use a sub, you create one idea that cannot stand on its own. These are the "incomplete thoughts" that were the third type of fragment in Contract #2: Sentence Fragments. For instance,

When Heidi entered the journalism program.

The solution to the incomplete thought/sentence fragment was to join the incomplete thought to another complete thought as follows:

incomplete thought   complete thought
When Heidi entered the broadcast journalism program, she was nineteen years old.

incomplete thought   complete thought
Because the municipal government increased taxes, several industries left the city.

The trick here, however, is that the punctuation changes according to where you place the incomplete thought (which begins with the sub). If the incomplete thought comes first, as in the examples above, it is followed by a comma and then the complete thought. If the complete thought comes first, no punctuation is needed. You can see this in the following examples, which turn the order around:

complete thought   incomplete thought
Heidi was nineteen years old **when** she entered the broadcast journalism program.

complete thought   incomplete thought
Several businesses left the city **because** the government increased taxes.

AUTHENTICATING THE CONTRACT

1. To identify a fused sentence or comma splice, try reading your sentence quickly while ignoring commas. Do not pause unless you reach a piece of punctuation stronger than a comma. If the sentence does not make sense when you do this, take a close look. Try to pick out the different complete or incomplete thoughts, and whether you have joined them in a correct fashion.

2. Remember, your five solutions are

   a. Complete thought. Complete thought.

   b. Complete thought, **FANBOYS** complete thought.

   c. Complete thought; complete thought.

   d. Complete thought; **transitional phrase**, complete thought.

   e. **Sub** incomplete thought, complete thought.

     Complete thought **sub** incomplete thought.

3. As a quick way to verify that you are using a semi-colon correctly, try this trick when you use it: cover up everything you have written after the semi-colon. Is everything in front of the semi-colon a complete thought that can stand on its own? If so, now cover up everything in front of the semi-colon: is everything after the semi-colon a complete thought that can stand on its own? If the answer to both questions is "yes," then you have used the semi-colon correctly to join two thoughts. Notice that this works for semi-colons with transitional phrases as well. For example, try the test on the following sentence:

> **Coffee prices are fluctuating because of crop damage; as a result, it is tempting to charge our customers more.**

If, however, the material on one side of the semi-colon turns out to be an incomplete thought, you will need to adjust your punctuation. Correct the following example:

> **After he completed the summary module; Ali was convinced the rest of the modules would be simple.**

Exercise 3

1. Examine the sentences below for their sentence structure and punctuation.

2. Identify any problems, such as a) fused sentence, b) comma splice, c) misuse of punctuation.

3. Correct the problems in at least two different ways; try to practise using all five different methods of joining thoughts.

A. Mrs. Tandon took the plane to Vancouver the flight lasted four hours.

B. William's placement was in a child-abuse treatment centre, there was a lot of sadness there.

C. Students applying for the fashion program must show great creativity and independence, only one in five is accepted.

D. I finished grade 12 last June now I'm in my first year of college.

E. Tourism is Canada's second-largest employment sector, and it provides a wide range of potential careers.

F. Some students are provided with opportunities to work for three terms as paid employees in their field however; only the most academically qualified are taken.

G. Lena had a difficult time deciding she finally enrolled in the Law and Security program.

H. Marketing is not just sales or advertising, it is the system that brings a company to life.

I. Controlling accounts receivable is essential for a successful business a computer-based accounting package will help us track our receivables, ultimately someone has to collect.

J. Svend is really tired, he will be leaving work early today.

Contract #4: The Semi-colon and Colon

THE CONTRACT

When you write a sentence, you agree to assign the common values to the various forms of punctuation. This is essential because your use of punctuation is a road map of your sentence structure, and a guide to how the various components of the sentence fit together. Your readers are depending on your map; if you give them the wrong directions, you cannot expect them to arrive at an understanding of your meaning. As you learned in Contract #3, the comma is a relatively weak form of punctuation. The semi-colon and colon are stronger forms: when readers see them, they are expecting very specific things.

THE TERMS OF THE CONTRACT: THE SEMI-COLON

As you learned in Contract #3, a semi-colon can be used in the following ways:

1. To show connection between two complete thoughts.

   Patricia believes her grammar is correct; I do not share her view.

2. With a transitional phrase between two complete thoughts.

   Nurses traditionally work in a hospital; however, with the support of community resources, they also care for patients in their homes.

3. The third use of a semi-colon is in a group of words in a list, when one or more of the items already contains a comma. For example, examine the following sentences:

   We received shipments from Kamloops, British Columbia, Red Deer, Alberta, Truro, Nova Scotia, and Timmins, Ontario.

   The invoices were dated July 26, 1994, November 30, 1995, and August 24, 1996.

Right now, the first sentence sounds as if shipments were received from eight different places. The second sentence sounds as if the invoices had six different dates. This is misleading and confusing for the reader. The writer of these sentences needs to specify more carefully the different divisions between the categories. This can be done with a semi-colon, as follows:

> We received shipments from Kamloops, British Columbia; Red Deer, Alberta; Truro, Nova Scotia; and Timmins, Ontario.

> The invoices were dated July 26, 1994; November 30, 1995; and August 24, 1996.

THE TERMS OF THE CONTRACT: THE COLON

The colon is an even stronger piece of punctuation than the semi-colon. It has three main functions, which are related.

1. The colon can introduce a list of items after a complete thought. In this case, the colon is like an equals sign (=).

> In the first semester of my Office Administration program, I must take the following courses: English, Business Preparation Skills, Microcomputers 1, Introduction to Word Processing, and Transcription Techniques.

2. The colon can also be used after a complete thought to introduce a second complete thought that explains or clarifies the first. Be careful, however: it must be introducing a complete thought that can stand on its own. In this situation, what it effectively means is, "What I mean is that ... ".

> Alicia is a wonderful manager: **(what I mean is that)** she was very understanding when my daughter was ill, and I had to miss three days of work.

> Life is like a box of chocolates: **(what I mean is that)** you never know what you're going to get.

See Module 12: The Research Essay, Quotation Integration, p. 254.

3. The colon can be used after a complete thought to introduce a quotation that is also a complete thought.

> The *MLA Handbook* reminds us of the importance of all stages of the research process: "Because research has the power to affect opinions and actions, responsible writers compose their work with great care."
> [From Joseph Gibaldi. *The MLA Handbook for Writers of Research Papers*. 4th ed. New York: Modern Language Association of America, 1995, xiii–xiv.]

> Julie Chau underlines the significance of students starting low-cost Internet-based businesses: "This can begin immediately, and through it, we can gain experience that will help in our studies."

See Subs, p. 270.

Both the opening unit and the quotation itself must be complete thoughts; if one of the two is an incomplete thought, simply follow normal rules for linking incomplete and complete thoughts.

THE FINE PRINT

1. *Never* use a colon after *such as. Such as* and the colon serve identical functions: you need to use one or the other, not both.

> Many travellers are deciding to buy time-share condominiums in American destinations, such as Florida, Hawaii, or Arizona.

In this case *such as* already means "What I mean to say is"; using the colon after *such as* would be redundant.

2. The colon can only be used after a complete thought; therefore, it cannot normally be used after the verb *to be*. Once again, the verb *to be* is serving the same function as the colon: you need to use one or the other, not both. For example, it is not correct to say

> **The admission requirements were: satisfactory grades in mathematics, physics, and English; successful completion of mathematics and English assessments; and attendance at a program information session.**

Instead, the colon should be omitted: "The admission requirements were satisfactory grades in mathematics, physics, and English; successful ... ". A second alternative would be to add the phrase *as follows*: "The admission requirements were as follows: satisfactory grades in mathematics, physics, and English; successful ... ".

Exercise 4

Identify which of these sentences live up to the semi-colon and colon contracts, which do not, and which need semi-colons or colons added. Correct any omitted or incorrectly used punctuation.

1. Stefan has a good point, it is crucial to get student assistance applications in on time.

2. Upper Canada makes very good beer, therefore you will likely enjoy their Wheat beer.

3. Important dates to remember this term are October 1, the last day to drop classes and receive a partial refund of fees, November 15, the last day to drop a class without academic penalty, and December 17, the date by which all term work must be submitted.

4. The following skills are very important, analytical skills, communications, technological literacy, mathematics, and interpersonal skills.

5. You should see how well they treat that cat, she even has her own teddy bear.

6. There are three kinds of professors, those who are barely competent, but think they know it all, those who are extremely competent, and know they know it all, and those who are truly competent, and are modest enough not to tell us.

7. What is a turtle an amphibian or a chocolate?

8. Working with the elderly can be extremely rewarding: as a result I strongly recommend gerontology as a career choice.

9. School is a simple equation; if you study hard, then you succeed, if you do not work, you fail.

10. Her words were clear and defiant, "I will not pay the rent increase until the heat and electrical system are functioning normally."

Contract #5: The Comma

THE CONTRACT

When you speak, you include natural, brief pauses. Much of this is automatic and based (at least partially) upon where you take your breaths. In writing, these brief pauses, indicated with a comma (,) are more formal. Like the semi-colons and colons discussed in Contract #4, commas are an important part of the road map through your writing. They direct your readers to the ways to understand word groups within your sentences. If your road map is wrong, a driver may end up in Mississippi rather than Manitoba. If your commas are misused, your reader may misinterpret or simply not understand your meaning.

THE TERMS OF THE CONTRACT

The comma is the most important and common piece of punctuation after the period. While the period indicates a full stop and the completion of a thought, the comma indicates a short pause. The sound of your sentences will often help you to identify where commas should be placed, but you should not always rely on this. Being familiar with the terms of the comma contract will ensure that you give your readers the directions they need and expect. Each of these will be discussed briefly.

Joining Complete Thoughts with FANBOYS

As you learned in Contract #3, you use a comma followed by one of the FANBOYS to join two complete thoughts. The FANBOYS are *for, and, nor, but, or, yet, so*—all two- or three-letter joining words (conjunctions). Just remember the word FAN-BOYS, memorize the words it stands for, and remember to use a comma before these words whenever they join two complete thoughts.

> Parara went to the test centre, **for** she needed to write her make-up examination.

> Parara studied very hard for the make-up examination, **but** she failed because she did not understand the basic concepts.

In each of these examples, two complete thoughts have been joined. The comma has been used before the FANBOYS that connect them.

After Introductory Word Groups

Commas in this category indicate material that could be left out without affecting the main complete thought of the sentence. Introductory words and phrases lead to the main idea of the sentence, but if they are completely eliminated, the main idea will still stand alone.

> **Quietly,** Shu-Fen completed her work.

> **By rushing to the library,** I found the book before anyone else could sign it out.

> **Because I arrived first,** I waited in the library.

See Contract #1: The Sentence.

In each of these instances, the complete thought that is the core of the sentence follows the comma. The word, phrase, or incomplete thought before the comma is simply introducing this thought. In this category, the third example above is an

See Contract #3: Run-on Sentences, Subs.

incomplete thought of the kind discussed in Contract #2: Sentence Fragments, and also in Contract #3: Run-on Sentences, Subs.

A Series or List

When your sentence presents words or word-groups in a series, they must be separated. The basic rule here is that any items that serve the same function in the sentence and are presented in a series should be separated by commas. Notice the parallel structure as discussed in Contract #8: Parallelism.

> She studied mathematics, English, and environmental science in her first semester. (words in a series)
>
> Going to class, studying at the library, and braving the cafeteria are part of student life. (parallel phrases in a series)
>
> After class, Hanna helped her son with his homework, she completed her own assignments, and finally she tidied up before going to bed. (complete thoughts in a series)

When the series is made up of descriptive words, commas are also used.

> When I considered my future, I wanted a career that would be interesting, fun, and lucrative.
>
> Kui-Lam wrote quickly, quietly, and intensely.

In the first example, commas separate adjectives, all of which describe *career*. In the second example, commas separate the adverbs that modify the action (verb) *wrote*.

THE FINE PRINT

1. When you use commas in a list, use the word *and* before the last listed item. This sentence is: "My brother has the new albums by Moist, Pearl Jam, TLC, Sarah McLachlan." We need an *and* before the last unit to signal to the reader that the series is at an end: "My brother has the new albums by Moist, Pearl Jam, TLC, and Sarah McLachlan."

2. The comma before the final *and* is optional: you can leave it out as long as there is no chance the reader will misunderstand. However, it is useful to get into the habit of including it since this can never be wrong.

Interrupted Thoughts

Meaning is all-important in your writing, and meaning is based upon the smooth presentation of your thoughts. But what do you do when you wish, intentionally, to interrupt that flow in order to enhance your meaning? You need to indicate the interruption to the reader, and you do this with a comma. The following are some situations in which you will use the comma to indicate a deliberate interruption.

Words and Phrases. When a word or phrase interrupts the flow of meaning, use commas.

> It is wise, **is it not,** to revise before handing in your work for grading?
>
> Your assignment is due today, but, **if it makes your life easier,** 9:00 a.m. tomorrow morning is also acceptable.

I do not, **however,** disagree with all of your ideas.

We must, **on the other hand,** discuss the alternatives.

Listen, **Sri,** we must determine the correct way to do this.

Read the following two sentences: can you spot interrupting phrases or words that should be surrounded by commas in order to help the reader follow the sentences' flow?

I should remind you that you always of course have the right to pursue this with the authorities.

I think if you want to know my opinion that another course of action would be better.

In these instances, if you remove the material bounded by the commas, the sentence's main meaning remains the same. The material within the commas adds an extra element of emphasis to the sentence.

Afterthoughts. Just as you need a comma after introductory word groups, you also need a comma before a word or word group joined as an afterthought to your sentences.

You have not closed the bookstore yet, **have you**?

Let us consider the alternatives, **please**.

I would like to discuss my grade, **if you do not mind**.

As with introductory word groups, removing the afterthought completely proves the need for the comma. The core meaning of the sentence remains without this material.

Nonessential Information. Look at the following pair of sentences. The only difference in each sentence is the commas, but these commas entirely change the meaning of the sentence.

1. Melido's brother, who lives in Gander, is a terrific painter.
2. Melido's brother who lives in Gander is a terrific painter.

According to sentence 1, how many brothers does Melido have? Reread it carefully. Because of the commas, in sentence 1 Melido has only one brother. The commas mean that the information about where Melido's brother lives is nonessential. If you left it out entirely, the reader would still have enough information to know which person you are talking about. If "Melido's brother" is enough information, Melido can only have one brother. "Who lives in Gander" is not necessary for the reader; rather, it is a piece of additional information.

Now, according to sentence 2, how many brothers does Melido have? Reread it carefully. In the second sentence, which does not have commas, the additional material about where the brother lives is essential for the reader to understand who Melido's brother is. Melido, therefore, must have more than one brother: perhaps he has a second brother who lives in Moose Jaw. Thus, the writer specifies "who lives in Gander" and does not place it between commas.

Now read this pair of sentences. According to each, how many novels has Douglas Coupland written?

1. Douglas Coupland's novel, *Generation X*, has been very influential.
2. Douglas Coupland's novel *Generation X* has been very influential.

According to sentence 1, Douglas Coupland has written only one novel. According to sentence 2, Douglas Coupland has clearly written more than one novel; that is why the writer specifies *Generation X* (the novel's title) without commas. Unless this title is specified, the reader will have no idea which novel is being discussed. The use of commas thus signals the relative importance of material, and can completely alter meaning.

> Ms. Hassanein, the vice-president for the past three years, congratulated me for my work.
>
> When I went to the Orkneys, which are an archipelago off the north coast of Scotland, I stayed in a bed-and-breakfast.
>
> Yuk Man, MD, diagnosed my allergies.

In the first and third of these examples, the initial proper names (Ms. Hassanein, Yuk Man) give the reader a specific identification of who is being discussed. Thus, the additional material in the commas, however interesting, is nonessential: we already know exactly whom we are talking about. In the second sentence, the phrase in the commas clarifies what the Orkneys are, but is again unnecessary: there is only one set of Orkneys in the world.

 AUTHENTICATING THE CONTRACT

1. Additional material after a specific person's name (Ms. Kowalski) or a place name (Trois Rivières) or any other proper name can usually be considered nonessential and placed in commas: the reader should already understand whom or what you are talking about. Otherwise, simply evaluate on a case-by-case basis whether the material is essential or not: most times this will depend upon the context of your writing.

2. In Contract #4: The Semi-colon and Colon, you learned the cover-up technique to test whether or not your use of a semi-colon was correct. If you are unsure about whether you have an interrupting thought that should be set off with commas, use a removal technique. If you completely remove the word or phrase, will the meaning remain clear? If so, this is an interrupter of some kind and must be set off with commas. This will be especially useful, moreover, when you use transitional phrases within sentences that are *not* made up of two joined complete thoughts.

See Contract #3: Run-on Sentences, Transitional Phrase; also, look at the use of the word "moreover" in this sentence as an example.

Dates and Place Names. Commas are used before the year in a date:

May 12, 1957

July 13, 1966

Commas are used to separate each different part of a place name:

Oshawa, Ontario, Canada

Murrieta, California, U.S.A.

Direct Speech in Quotations. If, in your writing, you use direct speech or thought in quotation marks, signal your reader by using commas both before and after the words in an interrupted speech. This may become particularly useful in narration.

See Module 5: Description and Narration.

"Can you meet me," she asked, "before we go to the school dance?"

He wondered to himself, "Why would she want to meet me before the dance? Maybe she likes me."

"If he will meet me before we go," she thought, "I'll have a chance to get to know him better."

AUTHENTICATING THE CONTRACT

While the main tests for comma usage will be reviewed here, the best rule is still common sense: use commas to help clarify the meaning of your writing; never sprinkle them throughout as the mood strikes you. These are four essential facts that you must always remember about the comma:

1. It is a weaker mark in comparison with colons, semi-colons, and periods.

2. It is only used within sentences.

3. Its main purposes are

   a. to separate elements that could be misinterpreted;

   b. to set off elements that interrupt the flow of meaning and are not essential to the main complete thought;

   c. to set off introductory materials and afterthoughts.

4. A comma is never used to separate the bare subject (actor) from its verb (action). For example, you would never use a comma in this way: "The blue-green lake, rippled slowly in the breeze." This is like driving a wedge through the marriage between the actor and the action. The actor by itself or the action by itself is meaningless.

Above all, use the comma to increase clarity. If being as clear as possible is your primary concern, whether you have used the comma correctly or not should be obvious.

Exercise 5

Add commas and any other punctuation needed to the following sentences. Examine carefully the existing punctuation, and correct it where necessary. Each time you add, change, or remove a comma, be certain you can explain why you are doing it.

1. Mr. Newhi the sales manager said that on December 15 1997 this division the potentially largest in the company should reach its goals.

2. As part of my advanced coaching techniques diploma I have to take a series of difficult but stimulating subjects, including Sport Psychology Sport Physiology and Sport Nutrition.

3. The train stopped at Montreal Quebec Toronto Ontario Winnipeg Manitoba Regina Saskatchewan and Vancouver British Columbia.

4. Before I, handed in my business plan which I had worked on for many long weeks I proofread it for comma errors.

5. During my two semesters in the Palliative Care certificate program I studied with Ilsa Reibin, RN the demanding professional practitioner who supervised Fieldwork I Fieldwork II and Fieldwork III and who gave me a final grade.

6. While I may disagree with your findings I do nevertheless see that your procedures, were correct.

7. Public employment positions may include jobs in municipal building departments New Home Warranty programs conservation authorities and housing authorities. Graduates may also find employment with private companies such as developers general contractors architectural offices engineering offices testing agencies bond and insurance companies and banks.

8. Library technicians are hired to work in public libraries schools, postsecondary institutions and libraries in organizations as diverse as banks hospitals law firms museums government departments churches, social, and academic, research areas and nonprofit organizations.

9. Yumin who is running for College Administrative Council, heard that while there is some truth to the rumour about deep painful budget cuts there is still some discretionary funding available for initiatives that although costly to start promise to generate real ongoing revenues in the future.

10. This exercise is quite challenging and if you want my opinion, I think that it forces me to know exactly where and why each comma, is being used.

Contract #6: Pronoun Reference and Agreement

THE CONTRACT

When a store is out of an advertised sale item, it very often offers a similar item as a substitute. Consumers are willing to take the substituted item if it is close enough in quality and value to replace fairly the original item. A pronoun is a word like *he, she, it, they* that literally stands in for a noun (hence the name "pro-noun"), which is a person, place, or thing. Like the store owner substituting for the similar item in the store, however, the pronoun user has to be certain to make a fair substitution. When you use a pronoun, you must be certain that your pronoun agrees with the noun it is replacing (its antecedent) in number, person, and gender.

THE TERMS OF THE CONTRACT: PRONOUN REFERENCE

The contract governing pronoun use means that you can use a pronoun only if it is clear from your sentence or paragraph exactly what it is replacing. This is logical because a pronoun has no value by itself; it has real meaning only in direct relation to whatever it is replacing. For example, look at the following statements. In each case, the pronoun is in bold, and the word it is replacing (the antecedent) is underlined.

> Hanifa, Janet, and Miguel are monitoring <u>the experiment</u> right now, and **it** seems to be working smoothly.

> <u>The Member of Parliament</u>'s outspoken views have gotten **her** into trouble several times with the Speaker of the House.

> <u>Several witnesses</u> claim **they** saw a <u>middle-aged man</u> limping away from the scene. **They** cannot, however, agree on how tall or heavy **he** was because **he** was wearing a bulky coat.

No confusion exists in these sentences because each pronoun clearly refers directly to the word it replaces, thereby living up to the contract. Four major pronoun problems can occur, however, when certain breaches of the contract take place.

Pronoun Does Not Replace Anything

Take a look at these statements:

> You know what **they** say: a penny saved is a penny earned.

> In the book **it** says that writing is hard work.

In the case of the first statement and other statements like it, have you ever wondered who "they" are? If so, your confusion is natural. In this situation, "they" are nobody because "they" does not replace another word. This does not live up to the pronoun contract, and it simply does not make sense. In the second sentence, what is "it?" "It" cannot be the book, because "it" (whatever "it" is), according to the sentence, is "*in* the book." These pronoun reference errors can be corrected by eliminating unclear pronouns, for example in the following fashion:

> As the saying goes, "a penny saved is a penny earned."

> The book says that writing is hard work.

Remember that you can use a pronoun only to replace something specific that you have already mentioned. Otherwise, no pronoun should be used.

Pronoun Reference is Uncertain

A similar problem can occur when your pronoun could refer to more than one possible item in a sentence. Examine the following sentences and their corrections.

Unclear: As the electricians found, the changes took time for **them** to complete as **they** were quite complicated.

Problem: Who are "them?" Who are "they?"—the changes or "the electricians"?

Clear: It took the electricians time to complete the changes as they were quite complicated.

Unclear: Jeremy talked to Sal about their group project, and now **he** is angry about how much work **he** has to do.

Problem: Who is angry, Jeremy or Sal?

Clear: Jeremy talked to Sal about their group project, and now **Jeremy** is angry about how much work **he** has to do.

Unclear: When Teresa dropped her beaker into the terrarium, **it** shattered.

Problem: Did the beaker shatter, or did the terrarium?

Clear: When Teresa dropped her beaker into the terrarium, the beaker shattered.

As a rule, your reader will assume that your pronoun refers to the closest previous noun that agrees with it in person, number, and gender. If this is not what it should refer to, you will need to eliminate your pronoun and instead repeat your noun as in the second and third examples above.

Sexist Pronoun Reference

Be very careful not to use just the pronoun *he* or just the pronoun *she* to replace a noun that could be masculine or feminine. This is a sexist, inaccurate, and misleading replacement.

Each student is responsible for revising and editing **his** own work.

After a worker punches out, **she** generally goes home.

Unless the student referred to in the first sentence attends a boy's school, and unless the workforce discussed in the second sentence consists entirely of women, this is sexist language. To correct sexist language, you should use variations on *he or she.*

Each student is responsible for revising and editing **his or her** own work.

After a worker punches out, **she or he** generally goes home.

If you find using *he or she* and its variations to be too awkward, try rephrasing these sentences in the plural:

All **students** are responsible for revising and editing **their** own work.

After **workers** punch out, **they** generally go home.

See Contract #7: Subject/Verb Agreement.

Indefinite Pronouns

The pronoun contract requires the same treatment with pronouns created with *any-, some-, every-,* or *no-* (for instance, *anybody, no one, everybody, someone,* and so on). These are always singular and always male or female because of their indefinite meaning: *anybody* literally means "any *one* body"; *someone* means "some *one* person."

Somebody lost **his or her** umbrella.

THE FINE PRINT

1. Usage of the plural pronoun *they* or *their* with singular nouns is very common; however, it is also very confusing and incorrect because it violates the grammar contract. Two examples follow:

   Somebody lost their umbrella.

   Each student is responsible for revising and editing their own work.

   The reader's natural question on reading these sentences should be "Who are *they*?"—a question with no answer, because as you can see, there is no noun anywhere in each sentence that could be replaced by the plural *they*. If you get into the habit of using *they* for singular nouns, this also forces you into several other problems. For example, look at the following sentence:

   A rock star who would kill themselves is an idiot.

   With *themselves,* it now sounds like the single rock star has more than one self! If you try the singular *themself,* you are creating a word that does not exist. Living up to the pronoun contract by making sure your pronoun and noun always agree in number solves all of these problems:

   A rock star who would kill him- or herself is an idiot.

2. Being consistent in the use of pronouns, especially when using *one* is essential. *One* is a pronoun of its own and cannot be mixed interchangeably with *he, she,* or *they.* Thus, this sentence is incorrect:

   One sometimes discovers while reading secondary material that his thoughts are overwhelmed by other writers' ideas.

   To keep the pronoun consistent, this sentence should read as follows:

   One sometimes discovers while reading secondary material that one's thoughts are overwhelmed by other writers' ideas.

   Once you start using *one,* (or *he, they,* and so on) continue to do so.

3. Avoid the redundant pronoun.

   The professor in my information technology class, she said my assignments are improving.

   My parents, who still are not quite used to Canadian customs, they grew up overseas.

   In these sentences, the pronouns *she* and *they* serve no purpose and should be removed.

4. Avoid the sudden shift to *you.*

   The reader of *Reading Writing* can only marvel at the variety of writings you find there.

Like any pronoun, *you* must clearly refer to someone already mentioned. Thus, it cannot be used here, but should be replaced by *he or she,* which refers to "the reader." You will notice that most of this textbook is written directed to "you"; this is acceptable because it is a book designed to instruct and help you, and also because this pronoun is consistently used.

AUTHENTICATING THE CONTRACT

When you use a pronoun, be sure it is needed to replace a noun (a person, place, or thing). Check that the closest previous noun that corresponds in terms of number, person, and gender is the one you intend to replace. It has to be absolutely clear what your pronoun is replacing, and you must be certain to use the appropriate pronoun.

Exercise 6

In the following sentences, verify the pronoun contract. Make certain that the pronouns agree in number, person, and gender with the items that they are replacing (antecedents). Eliminate unnecessary pronouns, and correct any incorrect, unclear, or sexist pronoun usage.

1. Since no one seems terribly interested in the experiments, the first employee to volunteer for it will have their Christmas bonus increased.

2. After workers become accustomed to shift work, he or she quickly learns the importance of keeping a regular schedule, and you also make sure to get a good night's sleep before work.

3. After Stan struck Sebastian, he started crying, and saying he was sorry.

4. On the sign it said, "No playing on the grass."

5. While one of the policewomen walked through the door, their co-workers played a trick on them by dropping a bucket of water.

6. At Lollapalooza, they said that the band did not have any more backstage passes, so you would have to wait outside with everybody else.

7. Anybody with a little intelligence knows his multiplication tables better than Pietro.

8. When a student graduates and needs to get a job, you soon realize that shabby running shoes, torn jeans, and oversized flannel shirts, they are no longer an appropriate wardrobe.

9. One of the first *Superman* comic books, it was stolen from his owner yesterday.

10. My daughter Ilyana, she threw her porcelain doll at the glass clock and broke it.

Contract #7: Subject/Verb Agreement

THE CONTRACT

As Contract #1 specified, a sentence by definition must have an actor and an action—also known as a subject and a verb. In fact, sentences often have more than one subject and more than one verb. When you write a sentence, you are agreeing to give all subjects the appropriate form of the verb; this is the only way your reader can match each subject with each verb, and therefore understand your thoughts. In order to stay in the bounds of the grammar "law," it is always necessary for the verb to agree in number with the subject. In other words, a singular subject takes a singular verb, but a plural subject takes a plural verb. If you do not live up to this contract, your reader becomes confused about what actor (subject) is doing what action (verb).

Look at the following sentences. In each sentence, there is at least one fundamental breach of the rule of subject/verb agreement—that binds the actor (subject) to the action (verb). Circle all subjects and underline their complete verbs. Correct the verbs so they agree with the subjects.

1. The Ethics class were cancelled yesterday.

2. More and more students has been required to take part-time jobs to help pay for tuition.

3. The CGA designation are highly sought after by many students.

4. Technological advances has influenced many people so much that they now gets retraining within their fields.

5. Toula, Arthur, and Leslie is all graduating from the electronics program this June.

THE TERMS OF THE CONTRACT

As in the examples above, subject/verb agreement is mostly self-evident. In some cases, however, finding the subject of the verb can be a little tricky. Here are a few difficult situations you can run into when determining whether a subject is singular or plural.

1. Sometimes words come between the subject and the verb. Examine the following three sentences:

   A briefcase filled with her notes were thrown onto the desk.

   The spelling errors on his covering letter shows his lack of professionalism.

   Each of the girls were a model child.

   In these three cases, the rule of subject/verb agreement has been broken. The simple way to discover this is to specify precisely what subject goes with what verb. In the first sentence, exactly what was thrown? Were "her notes" thrown, or was "a briefcase" thrown? It was a briefcase (which happened to be filled with her notes) that was thrown. In the second sentence, is it "his covering letter" that shows a lack of professionalism, or is it "the spelling errors on his covering letter"? It is the latter. In the third sentence, is it the girls who "were a model child"? This does not make sense; instead, it is "*each* (one) of the girls" who was a model child. Thus, to live up to the subject/verb agreement contract, the verb forms should be rewritten in the following ways to agree with the actual subjects:

A **briefcase** filled with her notes **was thrown** onto the desk.

The **spelling errors** on his covering letter **show** his lack of professionalism.

Each of the girls **was** a model child.

2. A similar breach of the subject/verb contract occurs in the following situations:

Being visa students create many disadvantages for us.

To learn new programming languages are extremely difficult.

According to the first sentence, it is not the visa students who create many disadvantages; it is "*being* visa students" that creates disadvantages. Similarly, it is not the new programming languages that are extremely difficult; "*to learn*" these languages is difficult. Whenever you have an *-ing* verb or a *to* verb (gerund or infinitive) as a subject, these always take a singular verb. This is logical because "being visa students" and "to learn programming languages" are actions that happen only once. Thus, to live up to the subject/verb agreement contract, the sentences should be rewritten as follows:

Being visa students **creates** many disadvantages for us.

To learn new programming languages **is** extremely difficult.

3. It is important to make sure that you have identified the complete subject. Remember that subjects that are connected by *and* or subjects that come in a list with commas between the various items are plural.

The professor and student **are collaborating** on the government-sponsored study.

The administration, the student association, and the faculty alike **approve** of the decision to invest more in computers and modem access to the college.

4. As discussed in Contract #6: Pronoun Reference and Agreement, pronouns are words that replace nouns. The words *who, which,* and *that* are pronouns that can be singular or plural, and that take the place of other words. Whenever the subject of your verb is one of the pronouns *who, which,* or *that,* you must discover what other word it is replacing in the sentence. Then make the verb after the *who, which,* or *that* agree with the original word being replaced. Never simply assume that *who, which,* or *that* is singular.

Student loans, which **are** difficult to obtain, must be spent wisely.

Which is plural because it replaces "student loans"; therefore, the verb is plural, too.

The sexual harassment charges that **were** discussed will be on the agenda for tomorrow's meeting.

I prefer an instructor who **encourages** groupwork in the classroom.

5. When using pronouns created with *any-*, *some-*, *every-*, or *no-*, the verb is always singular.

> **Everyone** in the three groups **is puzzled** by the sudden outbreak of yawning.
>
> **Nobody** in the office **remembers** seeing anything unusual the afternoon the photocopier disappeared.

THE FINE PRINT

1. Whenever you write some variation of *there is* or *there are,* remember that *there* is not the subject. What comes *after* the verb *to be* is the subject; thus, the verb must agree with this subject. Take the following sentence:

> There are thirty different diploma programs offered at the college.

If you turn the sentence around, you can see how this works:

>   subject   verb
>
> <u>Thirty different diploma programs</u> <u>are offered</u> there at the college.

Thus, in the following sentences, the verbs agree not with *there,* but with the subjects that follow them:

> There **is** an outstanding Thai restaurant down the street.
>
> There **is** a lack of accepted young fashion designers in Canada.
>
> In all, there **are** more than 100 children at that day care.
>
> There **are** six influential studies of the impact of aquaculture programs.

LAZY LANGUAGE

Using *there is* or any of its variations is a form of lazy language. When good writers edit their writing, they remove most of these phrases and substitute more active and direct verbs. For example, consider the sentence "There are two squirrels in the park." It sounds here as if the squirrels are simply lying immobile in the park. When the lazy language is replaced, the idea becomes much more active and effective: "Two squirrels are racing through the park."

2. Be careful of words that look plural but, in fact, are singular. Some of these simply end in *-s,* such as *news* and *measles*; others are disciplines like physics, economics, and mathematics; others are units—kilograms, metres, seconds, dollars—that measure mass, length, time, and money.

> Economics **is** often accused of being less a science than an educated guessing game.
>
> In a recent survey, health sciences students discovered that 3.6 km/week **is** what the average person walks.

AUTHENTICATING THE CONTRACT

1. The general rule to remember with subject/verb agreement is to find the bare subject, or the *specific* actor, doing the action. In order to do this, first locate the verb (action) in your sentence; this is generally not a problem. Now find the specific subject or actor. Do not be distracted by the extra words or phrases: ask yourself who or what is the star of the sentence, and make sure that your verb agrees with this subject.

2. When you have found the subject and made sure the verb agrees, look at just these two by themselves: do they correspond with the main idea of the sentence, or have you been distracted by something that is not the subject?

3. Subjects and verbs most often cannot both have -*s* endings. Most plural nouns end in -*s* while many singular verbs end in -*s*. Thus,

   Peaches taste good.

   Jaime tastes the peach.

   If your subject and verb both end in -*s*, double-check them; chances are good that you have made a mistake.

4. If subject/verb agreement is a common error for you, keep track of which specific kinds of subject/verb agreement errors you make, and be sure to check during editing for these specific types.

Exercise 7

Check the following sentences for subject/verb agreement by circling the bare subjects and their verbs. Correct any errors in agreement, and double-check to make certain you have correctly identified the bare subject. Note: many sentences have more than one subject and verb; be sure to check all verbs in each sentence.

1. Students sometimes complains that mathematics require too much concentration and memorization.

2. In order to receive a diploma, a program of eight core courses and four options have to be completed.

3. The old saying "No news is good news" do not always hold true.

4. Surprisingly, the mock investigations in the law enforcement class has uncovered a real case of fraud; to bring this to the attention of the college administrators present a difficulty, however.

5. Is there people here who knows CPR?

6. My father remembers when $300 were enough to cover car insurance for a year; however, now that cover only one or two months in most cases.

7. Each of the four friends takes a turn in making up sample quiz questions that is used in the exam review; whenever there is several correct answers, some students, such as Shiraz, is very good at discovering them all.

8. The survey shows that at least half of the student population work out at least once a week.

9. Many factors, including lack of sleep, has been known to have a negative effect on test results.

10. Naturally, everyone at the film studios are rather upset by the study's suggestion that going frequently to the movies have a negative impact on children's socialization.

Contract #8: Parallelism

THE CONTRACT

You coordinate your clothes: you make sure that you are wearing the same colour of socks or shoes, for example. You also make sure that the colour of your pants or skirt complements the colour of your shirt or blouse. Similarly, in a sentence, parallel items should be coordinated. Items that are *parallel* are items that serve the same purpose in the sentence and therefore should be constructed in the same way. If you use different structures for items that are serving the same function—that is, if you use faulty parallelism—it is like wearing socks of two different colours. To your reader, you seem confused, clumsy, and careless.

THE TERMS OF THE CONTRACT

See Contract #5: The Comma, A Series or List, p. 276.

Parallel lines are lines that run in the same direction the same distance apart from each other. In general, like parallel lines, units of your sentence that are equal in function should be structured in the same way: your reader should see how they run parallel to one another. This holds true for listed items, or items presented in a series. For example, the following sentence is not structured in a parallel fashion:

The office was spacious, sleek, and had a modern sensibility.

To be parallel, the three items describing the office should be structured in the same way. Here are two different corrections; notice how each now contains three units that are equal in function and structured so that they sound alike. The first uses single words (adjectives); the second uses several words (verb-adjective-noun).

The office was 1) <u>spacious</u>, 2) <u>sleek</u>, and 3) <u>modern</u>.

The office 1) <u>provided</u> ample space, 2) <u>used</u> sleek decoration, and 3) <u>had</u> a modern sensibility.

The basic principle here is that units equal in value should be equal in structure (and therefore similar in sound) as well.

Here are some more sentences that exhibit good parallelism. In each case, number and underline each unit that is parallel in the same way as the examples above.

Indicate the exact limits of each parallel item, ensuring that the two or more parallel items you identify look and sound reasonably alike.

1. Lori studies at college, goes to the gym, and works part time.

2. Immigration officials generally want to know where you have come from, why you have come, and how long you will be staying.

3. Leaving home for the first time and coming to a strange new school have made this a very scary time.

4. Lori is a student, an athlete, and a part-time employee.

5. Obtaining your pilot's licence may help you to conquer your fear of heights and to demonstrate your self-reliance.

6. Abrahim is anxious, Carrie is cautious, and Shaid is sure.

7. Hiking, canoeing, swimming, and relaxing are my ingredients for a productive summer.

THE FINE PRINT

Certain constructions, which create links between pairs of items, also necessitate careful attention to parallel structure. Whenever you use one of the following constructions, the grammar contract requires that what follows each of the two words be constructed in the same fashion:

> both ... and; not only ... but; (n)either ... (n)or
>
> rather ... than ... ; whether ... or

Two examples of this are as follows:

> **Not only** 1) <u>is this the most effective way to get an internship right now</u>, **but** 2) <u>it is also a way to make contacts for the future</u>.

> You have two choices: we can **either** 1) <u>watch television all evening</u> **or** 2) <u>finish the chores we have been putting off</u>.

Now look at the following sentence:

> He needs to decide whether to attend college or university.

On first glance, it may look acceptable, but does it live up to the parallelism contract? Look at exactly what comes after *whether,* and then look at what comes after *or.* A parallel version of the sentence would instead be "He needs to decide whether 1) to attend college or 2) to go to university." Now both items consist of actions and places.

The same principle is true of comparisons: you can only compare two items that are alike. Thus, you would not say, "To jog is better than swimming." Instead, you would make the two actions parallel in structure: "*Jogging* is better than *swimming.*"

AUTHENTICATING THE CONTRACT

1. To verify parallelism, split up any listed items and compare them. If you like, you can do this by numbering them. Do they all look and sound alike? Do the *Sesame Street* test: often "One of these things doesn't belong," and the key is to number the units and/or say the sentence out loud so you can see and hear which one does not belong. When you find the item that does not fit, adjust it so that it looks and sounds like the others.

2. As you learned in Contract #5: The Comma, commas are used to split up items in a list. These listed items should always be parallel in structure; thus, when you write a list or edit one, check to see whether the unit before each comma is structured in the same fashion or not.

3. If you are making a comparison, or if you are using one of the pairs of words listed in The Fine Print, match up the two; for example, make sure that what follows the words *not only* corresponds to what follows the word *but*.

Exercise 8

Examine the following sentences carefully. In each case, number and underline each unit that should be parallel. In cases where the items are not parallel in structure, rewrite them to correct this problem. Be careful to indicate the exact limits of each item so that you can ensure exact parallelism.

1. We not only missed the refund date but also the "withdrawal without academic penalty" date.

2. The recipe suggests both adjusting the amount of curry powder and fresh chili peppers according to your taste.

3. Karel's family, his friends, and colleagues all saluted him at his retirement party.

4. The Research Essay module requires patience, familiarity with your college library, and you need to have some idea what you are looking for.

5. Your responsibilities as the coordinator are administrative paperwork as needed, to train new employees, checking invoices for goods received, and to complete all daily banking.

6. It's obvious that getting welfare benefits is much easier than unemployment insurance.

7. I will either take my vacation in March or July.

8. We have a fundamental choice to make: whether to tear down the entire structure or renovating.

9. Henry Fielding was a judge, a devoutly religious man, and wrote famous novels.

10. Three representatives of the business community, five politicians, and six faculty members formed a committee for studying the impact of funding cuts on graduates' skills and to suggest any improvements.

Contract #9: Misplaced and Dangling Modifiers

THE CONTRACT

A recipe often calls for you to follow a series of steps in a specific order. If you alter the order of the steps, you end up with a different dish and a different taste sensation. Sentence construction also consists of adding various elements together in a variety of ways: just like in a recipe, however, the order of the elements is extremely important in determining the product that is created. *Modify* means to change. The meaning of specific words, or even of complete ideas or sentences, will change depending on where you place modifiers, which are the words or groups of words that directly refer to (or modify) specific actors or actions. As such, you must be careful to place your modifiers so that they will clearly describe what you intend. Consider the following two sentences:

> He told **only** Nadia what he wanted.
> He told Nadia **only** what he wanted.

Clearly, the meanings of these two sentences are different although exactly the same words have been used. The placement of the modifier *only* changes not only the meaning but also the tone of the two sentences.

THE TERMS OF THE CONTRACT

As a rule of thumb, modifiers should be placed as close as possible to the words to which they refer. As you revise your writing, you should focus on the modifiers that you use and make certain that they do refer to the appropriate words or thoughts. Three types of modifiers should be considered in order to fulfil this contract.

Misplaced Modifiers

Misplaced modifiers are words or word groups that are placed so far away from the word they refer to that the reader may become confused. Examine the following sentence:

> The junior clerk was told that he was laid off by his supervisor.

The question that this sentence does not answer is, "Who made the decision to lay off the clerk?" The sentence suggests that the supervisor made the decision. But is this correct? Consider the alternative:

> The supervisor told the junior clerk that he was laid off.

In the first sentence, the reader is left with a question; in this new version, where the supervisor is linked to the action "told," the meaning is clear—the supervisor did the telling only, but someone else made the decision. When you write a sentence, you know what you want to say: creating questions about your meaning in the minds of your readers violates the grammatical contract (and limits your success in transmitting your meaning).

Dangling Modifers

The most frequent component of a dangling modifier is an *-ing* verb. When such a modifier dangles, it does not clearly refer to some specific word in the sentence, or it seems to refer to a word that does not make sense. While they can occur anywhere in a sentence, the most common place for a dangling modifier is at the beginning of a sentence.

> **Standing on the platform,** the train entered the station.

> **Cashing her cheque at the bank,** the toddler watched her mother.

Whenever you see an *-ing* modifier, the obvious question is "Who or what is doing this action?" The answer—the actor—should be the closest noun (person, place, or thing). The question in the first sentence is "Who is standing on the platform?" According to the sentence, the train is, which is both illogical and impossible. Clearly a person is standing on the platform, and this person needs to be specified. The question in the second sentence is "Who is cashing her cheque?" According to the sentence, the toddler is, which makes little sense since most toddlers do not draw a paycheque. The solution is to make certain that every *-ing* modifier is next to the actor (subject) who is doing this action.

> Standing on the platform, **I** saw the train enter the station.

> The toddler watched her mother **cashing her cheque at the bank.**

Squinting Modifers

Squinting modifiers look two ways: to the word or idea before and to the word or idea after. As such, they are another source of confusion in the sentence recipe.

> **The person who shares my rent currently is out of work.**

Look at the word *currently*. As the sentence is written, the word refers either to the person who shares the rent right now, or to the fact that this person is out of work at the present time. This sentence needs revision in order to clarify which meaning is the correct one.

> **The person who currently shares my rent is out of work.**

or

> **The person who shares my rent is currently out of work.**

In each of these two revised examples, it is clear what the modifier refers to.

AUTHENTICATING THE CONTRACT

As you edit your writing, listen to what you have said. Do your modifiers sound right to you? Ask yourself the following questions:

1. To whom or what does the modifier refer?
2. Does it do so clearly and logically?
3. Is it close enough so my reader will understand?
4. Is there any way that my reader could misinterpret?
5. Can I reduce the possibility for misunderstanding by moving the modifier or adding some clarification?

Exercise 9

Rewrite the following sentences to correct or clarify any misplaced, dangling, or squinting modifiers.

1. Because of serious illness, the garage has lost almost half of its staff.
2. Lying on the floor, Charity found her diskette.
3. I do not enjoy dinner parties where the hostess serves her guests on napkins rather than china plates.
4. At the age of 10, Jamal's father remarried.
5. I negotiated a loan from the bank that I need to pay for my car.
6. Sai Woo whom I visited recently went to Calgary.
7. Struggling with the questions, Tina's last examination was finally finished.
8. The instructor picked up the essay that José had written with a sigh.
9. Having finished the dishes, the movie was watched.
10. A person who shows off frequently may be insecure.

Contract #10: The Paragraph

THE CONTRACT

Contracts #1 through #9 help you to write clear, complete, and effective sentences. They help you to identify and correct common problems in the grammar contract in order to enhance the clarity of your writing. When you combine several sentences into a paragraph, you are simply entering into a higher-level contract with your reader. When your readers start reading a paragraph, they expect a coherent unit of thought—a series of sentences that develop a single idea in depth.

THE TERMS OF THE CONTRACT

A paragraph is a group of sentences that explain, explore, or develop a single topic. In the paragraph, you put forward an idea and explain it fully so your reader can understand it in detail and draw some kind of conclusion. Length can vary, but generally, you will need at least three sentences to form a complete paragraph.

Two main elements make up a paragraph. These are the **topic sentence**, which states the main idea, and two or more sentences in the body, which support the main idea with particular facts, arguments, or examples.

The Topic Sentence

See Module 2: What to Say, The Outline, p. 36, and Module 3: How to Say It, Coherence, p. 59

The topic sentence states the main idea of the paragraph, and therefore defines the paragraph as a whole and the relationship among sentences. Since it states the major point that subsequent sentences will support, the topic sentence tends to be more general than the other sentences in the paragraph. Most often, your topic sentence is the first sentence of the paragraph, although in some cases it can be located elsewhere. Collectively, the topic sentences of the paragraphs of your essay act as a skeleton showing how the overall line of the essay's thought develops. In general, use your topic sentence to get to the point quickly and narrow it clearly. Be direct, clear, and specific.

Look at one of the essays that you have written, and isolate the topic sentences of your body paragraphs. Do they, collectively, outline the overall argument that you are attempting to make? Are there any discrepancies between your topic sentences and your overall train of thought?

Every good topic sentence should meet the following criteria:

1. It should tell the reader the main idea of the paragraph.

2. It should make a point about this main idea.

3. It should make a statement that is neither too broad nor too narrow to be covered in a single paragraph.

Here is a series of topic sentences for paragraphs. By testing them out against the three criteria for topic sentences listed above, decide why each sentence is or is not a good topic sentence.

1. In this paragraph, I will talk about structural steel.

2. Without a basic knowledge of word processing, essay writing will be more time-consuming.

3. Focusing your product marketing strategy at a specific market niche will lead to a successful campaign.

4. I love animals.

5. Acting on overdue accounts receivable improves business cash flow.

The Body

See Module 2, Step 2: Content Generation, p. 26.

See Module 2, Step 3: The Outline, p. 36.

The purpose of the body is to explain, support, and elaborate upon the general idea presented in your topic sentence. As such, it is made up of a series of sentences that have a direct and obvious relation to your topic sentence. These sentences contain examples, reasons, facts, and so on. These are identified through your content generation and narrowed through the process of outlining.

While there are many ways to organize a paragraph, the most common are the following:

See Module 3: How to Say It, Organizing Principle, p. 58.

1. **Logical order:** Start at one point and move logically to the next. You would use this when one point must be explained before the next point can be understood.

2. **Chronological order:** This is organizing by time, or moving from the beginning to the end. You might use this to describe something that happens, like an event or a process.

3. **Spatial order:** This is organizing by space. For instance, you might describe a room from left to right, a country from east to west, a building from top to bottom, and so on.

4. **General to particular:** Starting from your general statement, you move to particular examples. For instance, a paragraph on petty theft might begin by defining it generally, and then provide a series of specific examples.

5. **From particular to general:** Here, the opposite is true. Starting from a series of particular examples or facts, you move to a generalization. For instance, you might move from a discussion of specific small thefts and end with a definition of petty theft that encompasses all of your examples. In this case, your topic sentence would likely appear last in your paragraph.

6. **By rhetorical modes:** Toward the end of most of the rhetorical mode modules, a brief section describes other uses of the particular rhetorical mode. In *See Modules 5–11.* these, you will find examples of various rhetorical modes (description, narration, process, comparison/contrast, definition, classification, cause and effect, persuasion, analysis) being used to organize paragraphs or sections of essays written in different rhetorical modes.

Achieving Unity

Every sentence must relate back to one central idea. This is unity in paragraph writing. Focus on developing your topic, because a paragraph that attempts to discuss multiple ideas usually discusses none of them well.

✳ IRRELEVANCIES

Every sentence must bear on the main idea of the paragraph. An irrelevant sentence that digresses from the central focus violates the paragraph contract, distracts and confuses your readers, and, ultimately, leaves them wondering, "What is the point here?" Check the sentences in your body to be certain that each relates directly to your topic sentence.

Coherence

While unity means that sentences must relate back to the topic sentence, coherence means that each sentence must relate directly back to the sentence that came before it. You accomplish this by both relating ideas and using mechanical devices. Some useful ways to achieve coherence are as follows:

1. **Synonyms:** Rather than repeating the same word in each sentence, can you find another word with a similar meaning? Look in your thesaurus, and then look up the alternative word in your dictionary to be certain you are using it correctly.

See Contract #6: Pronoun Reference and Agreement.

2. **Pronouns:** Instead of repeating a name, you can use a pronoun instead. This gives a sense of variety and avoids monotony.

3. **Repetition:** Sometimes, you just cannot avoid repeating the same word pattern; nevertheless, avoid repetition wherever possible. Try to use it only for emphasis.

See Contract #3 for punctuation with connecting words.

4. **Transitional words:** Connecting words—words such as *consequently, hence, however, therefore*—will help to link your ideas and enhance both unity and coherence.

THE FINE PRINT

Contrary to the way many newspaper articles are written, paragraphs should not consist of only one or two sentences. Do not allow one or two sentences to stand as a paragraph unless you have a very good reason (such as emphasis). Underdeveloped paragraphs suggest poor organization, and a lack of real thought and effort in developing a subject. Such paragraphs, moreover, clearly do not live up to what the topic sentence promises.

AUTHENTICATING THE CONTRACT

Because every paragraph by definition presents a very obvious contract, verifying paragraph integrity should be a simple matter. When you reread a paragraph, simply compare your topic sentence's promises to what the body of the paragraph actually delivers. So long as the two correspond, you have written a good paragraph. More specific questions to ask are the following:

1. What is your topic sentence? Does it explain the main idea of the paragraph and make a point about that idea?

2. Does your body develop the idea sufficiently through examples, facts, and reasons?

3. Is there a clear, sensible reason why the body sentences are organized in this order?

4. Is each idea in the body a clear fulfilment of the topic sentence's promise?

5. Does each sentence flow logically out of the previous one?

Exercise 10

Carefully examine the paragraphs that follow and improve them. In many cases, you will need to alter the order of the sentences significantly. Reorganize, rewrite, and, where necessary, eliminate or expand ideas so that each paragraph:

1. begins with a clear, appropriate topic sentence;
2. presents a body that delivers what the topic sentence promises, and that is organized in a specific, useful pattern;
3. is completely coherent (i.e., no excessive repetition of words or ideas, and clear connections between sentences);
4. consists of material entirely relevant to the topic sentence.

A. We have decided to reduce kitchen expenses, kitchen furnishings, and discretionary honoraria by $800 over the fall and spring terms. These cuts have been itemized as a gesture of good faith to show the Board of Directors that the Division's efforts to reduce its financial problems are legitimate and ongoing. An ad-hoc committee of North Division members met during the last two weeks in order to make specific budget cutbacks designed to help the division reduce shortfalls in revenue due to vacancies. We are reducing $1000 from house expenses in each of the fall and spring terms. These are only the first cuts: more will likely be made over the course of the year (certainly the committee will hold further meetings on the subject). We are reducing the entire fall and spring social budgets (total $1500) to zero.

B. Recently, the issue of assisted suicide has been in the news. Dr. Death is a very controversial figure. In the 1950s he supported "judicial euthanasia." American prisoners who were condemned to death would be placed under anaesthetic. Medical research would be conducted on their bodies until they were dead. He has been very controversial because he has recently favoured allowing condemned prisoners to die under anaesthetic and to donate their organs for desperately needed transplants. Many doctors oppose this controversial idea because it makes doctors who have sworn to preserve life into executioners. The very controversial Dr. Death feels it allows these criminals a chance to contribute something good to society.

C. Some politicians deliberately lie and manipulate us to win votes, and this deserves a rebuke. We punish politicians who do not do what they promised to do. Are politicians *never* allowed to be inconsistent like us? Are they *never* allowed to discover that something promised in good faith simply cannot be done? Are they *never* allowed in good faith to change their minds and pursue a different policy that is realistic? We crucify politicians every day of the week for not keeping their promises. Jean Chrétien seems like an honest politician. By expecting them to be unwaveringly consistent, are *we* the true hypocrites, since we too act inconsistently every day of the week?

D. Nothing disturbed the still morning splendour of Shawinigan Lake. The canoe lay on the eastern shore of the lake inverted on its gunwales, next to a tent nestled into the bush. On the western shore could be seen a quiet cottage, a thin curl of smoke barely visible rising from the chimney. The day before it had been very hot. Birds sang to the morning sun as it rose into the cloudless eastern sky. In the centre of the grey lake a tiny tribe of Canada geese, a mother and six youngsters in her wake, swam slowly west.

Documentation Styles

The purpose of documentation is to enable readers to trace all ideas or quotations back to their original sources. This appendix highlights two major styles of documentation for essays. These are the Modern Language Association (MLA) and the American Psychological Association (APA) styles. Each of these associations publishes full reference books on how to document sources. These will be readily available in most libraries. Your instructor will usually specify which to use for an assignment. Note: as this section is of primary use in conjunction with research essay assignments, many of the examples in this appendix are drawn from Module 12: The Research Essay.

MLA STYLE

The MLA style of documentation uses a combination of in-text citation and a detailed list of Works Cited at the essay's end.

Citing in the Text of the Essay

The purpose of in-text citation is to identify readily the sources of specific information that you have used in your essay. Your in-text citation should lead your readers directly to the list of Works Cited at the essay's end for your source's publication information. You therefore need to provide readers with sufficient information so that, when they refer to your list of Works Cited, they can easily and with certainty determine the source of a specific idea. A typical in-text citation is made up of the author's last name and the page from which you drew the source:

> 80 percent of Canadians are expected to work in the service economy of the future (Feather 9).

If you use more than one source by the same author, you will need to distinguish which title you are referring to by adding an abbreviated italicized or underlined title:

> 80 percent of Canadians are expected to work in the service economy of the future (Feather, *Best Careers* 9).

> Demographics are shifting to aging baby boomers (Feather, *Future Consumer* 88).

If you state the author's name within the statement, you need only give a page reference:

> Campbell notes that suit sales were down 25 percent between 1990 and 1991 (177).

PROVIDE THE MINIMUM NECESSARY INFORMATION

MLA in-text citation is based upon the idea that you want to give readers the absolute minimum amount of information that they will need to be able to trace the source from your Works Cited list: if the minimum is a page number, provide that; if the minimum is an author name and a page number, provide that; and so on.

RUNNING IT IN OR SETTING IT OFF?

When you use a short quotation, you should run it into your text. A good rule of thumb is that if the quote is four lines or less, it should be run directly into the text. If the quote is over four lines, it should be isolated. Note that, in the case of a short quote, the end punctuation comes after the citation:

> It is anticipated that " ... the service producing sector ... will create four out of five of all new jobs by 2000 ... " (Kleiman 43).

In the case of longer quotes set off and isolated from the rest of the text, the parenthetical documentation appears after the quotation and its end punctuation. Again, if the name of the author has appeared in the text, you do not need to include it in the parenthetical documentation:

> Colin Campbell suggests that

> > Less expensive designer lines aimed at the affluent baby-boomers have done well. Similarly, the mini baby boom will lead to more designing for the upscale children's market and the maternity outfit market. Greater emphasis will be placed on meeting the clothing demands of empty-nesters and the growing number of retirees.... [Thus,] if you are interested in pursuing a career in this field, your safest bet is to stick with the demographic-oriented markets. (176–177)

See Module 4: Summary Skills.

ACKNOWLEDGING A PARAPHRASE OR SUMMARY

When you paraphrase or summarize the statements of an author, you still need to document them. In this case, note that the punctuation still appears after the citation:

> By 2005, we will see home-based electronic money transfers and most major purchases made from home (Campbell 6).

OTHER RULES TO REMEMBER

1. **For works by more than one author:** If there are three or fewer authors, include all the names; for example, (Smith and Jones 46) or (Smith, Jones, and Singh 46). If there are more than three authors, you can use *et al.*, which is Latin for "and others":

    (Smith et al. 46)

2. **For works without a listed author:** If there is no identified author, such as in a general business report, you should use a shortened version of the title:

(*1995 IBM Annual Report* 37)

3. **For indirect sources:** If you want to refer to somebody who has been quoted in an article, use the abbreviation "qtd. in" (quoted in):

(Smith, qtd. in Jones 61).

4. **For an idea found in more than one source:** As you research, you may find that an idea has been used by more than one author. This is compelling evidence of your sound research: be certain to document both—or all—authors:

(Edwards 144; Wakersly 72).

List of Works Cited

Works Consulted vs. Works Cited

Your parenthetical in-text citations refer directly to the list of works that you have cited (called "Works Cited") found at the end of your essay. The list of Works Cited details all books, articles, films, radio and television programs, and even interviews to which you have referred in your essay. Keep in mind that there is a difference between a list of Works Cited and a list of Works Consulted. In the former, you document only those that you mentioned in your essay. In the latter, you document everything that you consulted during the various stages of writing your essay. Instructors generally specify whether they want a list of Works Cited or a list of Works Consulted.

STEPS TO FOLLOW

1. Your Works Cited section should begin on a new page, and the heading should be centred 2.5 cm from the top of the page.

2. Skip two lines and then begin every entry flush with the left-hand margin.

3. The second and subsequent lines of each entry should be indented about five spaces.

4. List works alphabetically according to the last name of the author or the first word of the title (not including *a*, *an*, or *the*) if the author is unknown.

5. Always double-space.

MLA CITATIONS: BOOKS

Here are a few rules for citing books, in the order in which they should be followed:

1. Start with the last name of the author, followed by a comma, followed by the author's first name, followed by a period and two spaces.

2. Italicize or underline the title of the book, followed by a period and two spaces.

3. State the city of the publication, followed by a colon.

4. Give the name of the publisher, followed by a comma.

5. State the year of publication, followed by a period.

CITATION AS SENTENCE

Think about citations as a series of sentences, each of which ends in a period. Each sentence contains specific information: the author sentence, the title sentence, or the publication information sentence.

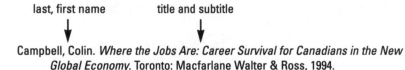

last, first name   title and subtitle

Campbell, Colin. *Where the Jobs Are: Career Survival for Canadians in the New Global Economy.* Toronto: Macfarlane Walter & Ross, 1994.

Publication information

Sample Citations

The following are some of the more common forms of full documentation that you will use in your Works Cited or Works Consulted list:

A book by a single author:

> Hamburger, Estelle. *Fashion Business: It's All Yours.* San Francisco: Canfield Press, 1976.

A book's edition: The edition must be noted (if it is anything other than the first edition):

> Feather, Frank. *Canada's Best Career Guide.* 3rd ed. Toronto: Warwick, 1994.

A book by two or more authors: Only the name of the first author is entered in the reverse order. The names of second and subsequent authors are listed in normal order:

> Sneddon, S., L. Hopperton, and L. Fried. *Writing for Real.* Toronto: Nelson, 1996.

A multiple-volume work:

> McClelland, James L., and David Rumelhart. *Parallel Distributed Processing.* 2 vols. Cambridge: MIT, 1988.

An edited book: You have a question to answer here. Are you referring to an edited reading, or to the comments of the editor or editors? When referring to the text of the book, rather than to the editorial comments, cite the author of the reading:

> Dickens, Charles. *Hard Times.* Ed. David Craig. New York: Penguin, 1977.

If you refer to the commentary provided by the editor, the name of the editor or editors should come first:

> Perry, John, and Michael Bratmen, eds. *Introduction to Philosophy: Classical and Contemporary Readings*. Oxford: OUP, 1993.

An essay in an edited anthology: Cite the essay rather than the collection:

> Nagel, Thomas. "War and Massacre." *Introduction to Philosophy: Classical and Contemporary Readings*. Eds. John Perry and Michael Bratman. Oxford: OUP, 1993.

UNDERLINING/ITALICIZING VS. QUOTATION MARKS IN TITLES

Notice that in the last example, the title is in quotation marks rather than being underlined or italicized. A common error is to underline all titles. Only book titles or periodical titles—that is, the titles that appear on the *outside* of a work—are underlined. Any internal title, including that of an article, poem, or short story title, is placed in quotation marks.

MLA CITATIONS: ARTICLES

As with books, there are a few rules for citing articles:

1. Start with the last name of the author, followed by a comma, followed by the author's first name, followed by a period and two spaces.
2. Instead of underlining or italicizing, enclose the title of the article in quotation marks, followed by a period and two spaces.
3. Underline or italicize the title of the magazine or journal in which the article appears, followed by the volume number.
4. The date of the publication follows, enclosed in parentheses, and followed by a colon.
5. Lastly, include the page numbers in which the article appears, followed by a period.

Sample Citations

The following are some of the more common forms of article documentation that you will use in your Works Cited or Works Consulted list:

An article in a scholarly journal: You will need to include both a volume and an issue number. This example cites volume 22, issue number 1 of the *Canadian Journal of Educational Communication*. Notice that the volume and issue numbers are separated by a period.

> Bazalgette, Cary. "Setting an Agenda for Training." *Canadian Journal of Educational Communication* 22.1 (1993): 27–36.

An article in a magazine: Here you have no volume or issue number, so the year and month become the primary distinguishing features:

> Burns, Rebecca. "San Francisco: Capital of the New Age." *Leisure Ways* Apr. 1993: 66–67.

An unsigned article in a magazine: In magazines, the name of the author of an article is often omitted. In this case, begin with the title:

> "Enduring Classics: Furniture Fashions That Never Go Out of Style." *Century Home* May 1995: 22–24.

An article in a daily or weekly newspaper: Give the title of the newspaper as it appears on the front page, but without the article *the*; hence, *The Vancouver Sun* becomes *Vancouver Sun*. Give the date, the edition if appropriate, and the pages of the article, including the section if appropriate:

> Kirk, Janis Foord. "Creative Job Hunting Takes Time and Hard Work." *Toronto Star* June 24, 1995: K1.

SPECIFIC DATES ARE IMPORTANT

Remember that for readers to be able to locate an article, magazine, or newspaper, they will need to know a year, month, and even day of publication, not just a volume number.

MLA CITATIONS: OTHER SOURCES

All information drawn from external sources must be documented. This includes nonprint sources such as television, radio, and computer databases including the World Wide Web.

Sample Citations

The following are a few examples of forms of documentation for nonprint sources that you will use in your Works Cited or Works Consulted list:

A television or radio program: You must italicize or underline the name of the program, and include the network, local station, city, and date of the program. If you are citing a section of a fuller program, you can treat it as you would an article and put it in quotations:

> "Internet." *Prime Time News*. Narr. Wendy Mesley. CBC. CBLT, Toronto. 18 June 1995.

Material from a computer service: Use the same format as you would for documenting an article, but be sure to include any filing information provided by the computer service:

> Johnson, Cary. "Bidding for Government Contracts." *Harvard Business Review* Sept.–Oct. 1995. Online 196+. DIALOG file 228, item 138716 679134.

Information from the World Wide Web: If the author is known, the name must be specified as with any article or book. Frequently, there will be no author specified: in this case, all you need to do is ensure that your reader can relocate the information. Every Web page has an address specified by its URL (Uniform Resource Locator). If Julie had cited information on marketing clothes from the WWW, this would have to be documented. For example, if she referred to information from Duthie Books, a Vancouver-based bookstore selling across the Web, her documentation would look something like

> "Selling on the Net: The Virtual Bookstore." On-line. Available World Wide Web: http://www.wimsey.com/Duthie/.

An Interview: The format for this depends upon whether you did the interview (first example), or you are citing someone else's interview (second example). Notice that in both cases, the reference appears under the name of the person being interviewed:

> Hicken, Dr. David. Personal interview. 30 October 1996.

> Layton, Irving. "Poet as Prophet." *In Their Words: Interviews with Fourteen Canadian Writers.* By Bruce Meyer and Brian O'Riordan. Toronto: House of Anansi Press, 1984. 10–24.

MLA Documentation: Endnotes

Endnotes are explanatory notes that you need to include for clarity or additional explanation, but that would interfere with the flow of your essay. They are indicated by a raised number in the text that corresponds to one on the Endnotes page. There are two main times when these will be used:

1. **When multiple authors make the same point:** Rather than having an extended string of names and page numbers in parentheses in your text, create an endnote. Separate author names and pages with semi-colons.

2. **For explanation:** In this instance, the note is used to provide comments or explanations, or to clarify a point made in the essay. This is strongly discouraged, however.

AVOID ENDNOTES OR FOOTNOTES

Do not use endnotes or footnotes in MLA style unless absolutely necessary. As a disruption of the normal simplicity of the reference style, they should be used sparingly, if at all.

APA STYLE

Citing in the Text of the Essay

As with MLA style, in-text citations using APA are intended to refer clearly to a list, titled "References," placed at the end of your paper. With in-text documentation, you want to provide your readers with sufficient information so that, through your list of References, they can trace the idea back to its source. A typical reference is made up of the author's last name and the year of publication from which you drew the source. Page references are used only with direct quotations:

> 80 percent of Canadians are expected to work in the service economy of the future (Feather, 1994).

APA style generally allows you to differentiate multiple works by the same author simply by using the date:

> **80 percent of Canadians are expected to work in the service economy of the future (Feather, 1994).**
>
> **Demographics are shifting to aging baby boomers (Feather, 1992).**

If you state the author's name within the body of your essay, you need only give a date in parentheses:

> **Decker (1992) used the experimental design with randomly selected subjects for relaxation therapy to demonstrate that relaxation training improved several psychological parameters associated with the quality of life in patients undergoing radiation therapy.**

RUNNING IT IN OR SETTING IT OFF?

When you use a short quotation, you should run it into your text. A good rule of thumb is that if the quote is three lines or less, it should be run directly into the text. If the quote is over three lines, it should be isolated. Note that, in the case of a short quote, the end punctuation comes after the citation:

> **It is anticipated that " ... the service producing sector ... will create four out of five of all new jobs by 2000 ... " (Kleiman, 1992, p. 43).**

In the case of longer quotes, set off and isolated from the rest of the text, the parenthetical documentation appears after the quotation and its final punctuation. Again, if the name of the author has appeared in the text, you do not need to include it in the parenthetical documentation:

> **Colin Campbell (1994) suggests that**
>
> **Less expensive designer lines aimed at the affluent baby-boomers have done well. Similarly, the mini baby boom will lead to more designing for the upscale children's market and the maternity outfit market. Greater emphasis will be placed on meeting the clothing demands of emptynesters and the growing number of retirees.... [Thus,] if you are interested in pursuing a career in this field, your safest bet is to stick with the demographic-oriented markets. (176–177)**

ACKNOWLEDGING A PARAPHRASE OR SUMMARY

See Module 4: Summary Skills.

When you have paraphrased or summarized the statements of an author, you still need to document this. In this case, note that the punctuation appears after the citation:

> **By 2005, we will see home-based electronic money transfers and most major purchases made from home (Campbell, 1994).**

OTHER RULES TO REMEMBER

1. **For works by more than one author:** If there are two to five authors, include all names; for example, (Smith & Jones, 1996) or (Smith, Jones, & Singh, 1995). If there are more than five authors, you can use *et al.*, which is Latin for "and others":

> **(Smith, et al., 46)**

2. **For works without a listed author:** If there is no identified author, such as in a general business report, you should use a shortened version of the title:

   (*IBM Annual Report,* 1995)

3. **For indirect sources:** If you want to refer to somebody who has been quoted in an article, mention the author of the quote in the body of your text, and the author of the article or book with the date of publication in parentheses.

4. **For an idea found in more than one source:** As you research, you may find that an idea has been used by more than one author. This is evidence of your good research, but you need to document both—or all—authors:

   (Edwards, 1994; Wakersly, 1995).

APA—References

As with MLA style, your parenthetical notations refer directly to the list of works that you have cited (called References) found at the end of your essay.

STEPS TO FOLLOW

1. Your References section begins on a new page, and the heading should be flush left, 2.5 cm from the top of the page.

2. Skip two lines, and then begin every entry's first line flush with the left-hand margin.

3. The second and subsequent lines of each entry should be indented about five spaces.

4. Works are listed alphabetically according to the last name of the author or, when the author is unknown, the first word of the title.

5. Always double-space.

APA CITATIONS: BOOKS

Here are a few rules for citing books, in the order in which they should be followed:

1. Start with the last name of the author, followed by a comma, followed by the author's initials, followed by the date of publication in parentheses. Use only initials for first names, never the full names.

2. Underline or italicize the title of the book, followed by a period and two spaces. Only the first word of the title and subtitle, and any proper names, are capitalized.

3. State the city of publication, followed by a colon.

4. Give the name of the publisher, followed by a period.

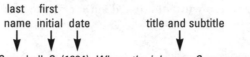

Campbell, C. (1994). *Where the jobs are: Career survival for Canadians in the new global economy.* Toronto: Macfarlane Walter & Ross.

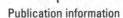

Publication information

Sample Citations

The following are some of the more common forms of full documentation that you will use in your References list. Notice that only the first word of titles and subtitles is capitalized:

A book by a single author:

> Hamburger, E. (1976). *Fashion business: It's all yours.* San Francisco: Canfield Press.

A book's edition: If the book is a second or subsequent edition, this too must be noted:

> Feather, F. (1994). *Canada's best career guide* (3rd ed.). Toronto: Warwick.

A book by two or more authors: Unlike the MLA method, all author's names are entered in the reverse order. Use commas between each name and an ampersand (&) before the last name listed:

> Sneddon, S., Hopperton, L., & Fried, L. (1996). *Writing for real.* Toronto: Nelson.

A multiple-volume work:

> McClelland, J.L., & Rumelhart, D. (1988). *Parallel distributed processing.* (Vol. 2). Cambridge: MIT.

An edited book: You have a question to answer here. Are you referring to an edited reading, or to the comments of the editor or editors? When referring to the text of the book, rather than the editorial comments, cite the author of the reading:

> Dickens, C. (1977). *Hard times.* (D. Craig, Ed.). New York: Penguin.

If you refer to the commentary provided by the editor, the name of the editor or editors should come first:

> Perry, J., & Bratmen, M. (Eds.). (1993). *Introduction to philosophy: Classical and contemporary readings.* Oxford: OUP.

If you are referring to an essay that appears in an edited anthology, cite the essay rather than the collection. Note that you do *not* put quotation marks around the essay title:

> Nagel, T. (1993). War and massacre. In J. Perry & M. Bratman (Eds.), *Introduction to philosophy: Classical and contemporary readings.* Oxford: OUP.

APA CITATIONS: ARTICLES

As with books, there are a few rules for citing articles:

1. Start with the last name of the author, followed by a comma, followed by the author's initials, followed by the year of publication in parentheses, followed by a period and two spaces.

2. Do not underline the title of the article or use quotation marks. The article title is followed by a period and two spaces.

3. Underline or italicize *all* of the following: the title of the magazine or journal in which the article appears, followed by a comma, followed by the volume number. This is followed by a second comma. Capitalize the words in the magazine or journal title in the same way they appear on the journal or magazine itself.

4. If there is an issue number, place it in parentheses beside the volume number; do not underline or italicize it.

5. Lastly, include the page numbers. If there is no volume number, use the abbreviation *p.* for a single page, or *pp.* for multiple pages.

Sample Citations

The following are some of the more common forms of article documentation that you will use in your References list:

An article in a scholarly journal: Notice the use of capitalization in the journal's title:

> Bazalgette, C. (1993). Setting an agenda for training. *Canadian Journal of Educational Communication, 22*(1), 27–36.

An article in a magazine:

> Burns, R. (1993, April). San Francisco: Capital of the new age. *Leisure Ways,* pp. 66–67.

An unsigned article in a magazine: In magazines, the name of the author of an article is often omitted. In this case, begin with the title:

> Enduring classics: Furniture fashions that never go out of style. (1995, May). *Century Home,* pp. 22–24.

An article in a daily or weekly newspaper: Give the title of the newspaper as it appears on the front page, including the article *the*. Give the date, the edition if appropriate, and the pages of the article, including the section if appropriate. Precede the page numbers for newspaper articles with *p.* (for one page) or *pp.* (for multiple pages).

> Kirk, J. (1995, June 24). Creative job hunting takes time and hard work. *The Toronto Star,* p. K1.

APA CITATIONS: OTHER SOURCES

A television or radio program: Begin with the name of the key person behind the broadcast, his or her title, and the date of the broadcast in separate parentheses.

Include the title of the segment and follow this by the name of the program in which it appears, if applicable, and the network location:

> Mesley, W. (Narrator). (1995, June 18). Internet. In J. Smith (Producer), *Prime Time News.* Toronto: CBC.

Online information: Citing online information is similar to citing other materials, except that you must specify that the material is electronic and indicate where the material can be found:

> Johnson, C. (1995). Bidding for government contracts. [On-line] Available +196 DIALOG file 228, Item: 138716 67134.

If the material is available through anonymous file transfer protocol (FTP) or through return electronic mail, specify this command at the end of your citation.

An interview: If you are citing someone else's published interview, the reference appears under the name of the person being interviewed:

> Layton, I. (1984). Poet as prophet. [Interview with B. Meyer and B. O'Riordan.] *In their words: Interviews with fourteen Canadian writers.* (pp. 10–24). Toronto: House of Anansi Press.

If you have done a personal interview, this falls under the category of "personal communications" because the data is not recoverable. Cite personal communications only in your text, not in your list of references, in the following fashion:

> (Dr. D. Hicken personal communication, October 30, 1996)

APA DOCUMENTATION: ENDNOTES

Endnotes and footnotes are rare in essays written using APA style. Since multiple authors and sources are listed within the body of the text, the only times that you will need an endnote are on the very rare occasions when you want to amplify or clarify a point in the text.

Copyright Acknowledgments

Permission to reprint copyright material is gratefully acknowledged. Information that will enable the publisher to rectify any error or omission will be welcomed.

All definitions from the *Gage Canadian Dictionary* © Gage Educational Publishing Company, Scarborough, Ontario. Reprinted by permission.

Ann Trick, "Can Stress Be Managed?" *OOHNA Journal* 14.1 (Spring 1995):10. Reprinted by permission.

Neil Bissoondath, "Campfires, Idealism and Pieces of Sky," *The Globe and Mail* (27 May 1995):D2. Originally published as "Pieces of Sky" in *If You Love This Country: Fifteen Voices for a Unified Canada*. Toronto: Penguin Books Canada, 1995. Copyright © Penguin Books Canada Limited, 1995. Reprinted by permission of Penguin Books Canada Limited.

Tomson Highway, "What a Certain Visionary Once Said," in "A Portrait of Canada" in *Bank of Montreal Annual Report*. Reprinted by permission of the author.

Upper Canada Brewing Company advertisement reprinted by permission of The Upper Canada Brewing Company.

Carlyn Zwarenstein, "Teens Not the Problem and Tired of Being Told They Are," *Toronto Star* (12 December 1994): A17. Reprinted by permission of the author.

Alyssa Diamond, "Greasing the Wheels of Commerce," *The Gardner Report* (Spring 1995). Reprinted by permission.

Allyson Jeffs, "Disturbing Discoveries About What Children Recall," *The Calgary Herald,* reprinted in the Toronto Star (4 December 1994):D4. Reprinted by permission of The Calgary Herald.

Judy Margolis, "Learning Where to Find Financing," *Canadian Banker* (September/October 1994):12-13. Reprinted by permission of the author and Canadian Banker.

Anna Nike Mineyko, "Hard Part of Language Is Learning What You May Say," *Toronto Star* (21 March 1995). Reprinted by permission of the author.

Ruth Morris, "A Practical Path to Transformative Justice." Reprinted by permission of the author.

Michael Schulhof, "Why Business Needs Scientists," *Scientific American* (November 1992). Reprinted by permission. Copyright © 1992 by Scientific American, Inc. All rights reserved.

Student essays reprinted by permission of the respective authors.

Index